The BEST Book of
RUGBY
FACTS
&STATS Ever!

THIS IS A CARLTON BOOK

This edition published in 1999

10 9 8 7 6 5 4 3 2 1

Copyright © Carlton Books Limited 1999

A CIP catalogue record for this book is available from the British Library

ISBN 1 85868 755 1

Project Editor: Martin Corteel
Production: Sarah Schuman

Printed in Great Britain

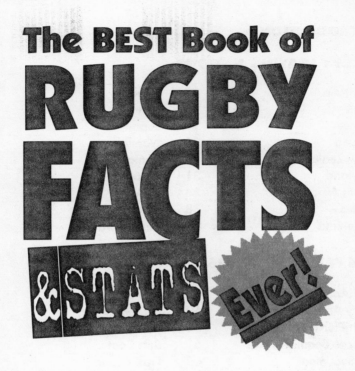

The BEST Book of
RUGBY
FACTS
&STATS
Ever!

RICHARD BATH

CARLTON

CONTENTS

THE FAMOUS COACHES

TEST GREAT RUGBY CLUBS

THE GREAT INTERNATIONAL COMPETITION 249

THE GREAT MATCHES 285

THE GREAT STADIUMS 309

Introduction

Comparisons across the ages are invidious. Each generation is bigger than the last, and if quantifiable sports such as athletics are any guide, our sportsmen get quicker, stronger and fitter with each decade. This was brought home to me all too powerfully when I was researching the chapter of Great Players for *The Ultimate Encyclopedia of Rugby*, the book's big brother.

I came across a 1992 photo of two Springboks, the great 1960s second row Frik du Preez and the up-and-coming 1990s scrum-half Robert du Preez. The second row was marginally the shorter of the two and only slightly stockier. Would he, could he, survive today when he would have to concede half a foot and five stone to the average international second row? I suspect not, yet size is not important in itself for the purposes of inclusion here: the only thing that matters is how a player or match or stadium matches up to its contemporaries. Even so, there has been a marked emphasis on the exploits of players in living memory.

The importance of a yardstick by which to judge players and events is also a prerequisite to a balanced appraisal of their historical performance, and this led to a problem peculiar to rugby union – how to gauge the impact of players who have played very few games against the best in the world. For that reason, Hugo Porta is the only player profiled outside the Big Eight nations (England, Scotland, Ireland, Wales, France, South Africa, New Zealand, Australia).

Other than the exclusion of players from what was until recently the second tier of rugby nations, I have tried to stick to the principle of giving equal billing to each of the Big Eight. In many cases, such a distortion was unavoidable – the Great Players chapter would have been nothing but a procession of Springboks and All Blacks unless I had adhered to this principle.

This has inevitably led to many players who you might think should demand inclusion to being left out, and it is certainly an anomaly that names such as Springbok "Boy" Louw or All Black Ken Gray have been overlooked.

Wherever I have been unable to choose between two players, I have chosen the player who I have seen play the most often. The choices I have made are completely subjective and are mine alone.

This is not the case with the Great Matches. Although I have erred on the side of recent matches, some contests are of such renown that it would be impossible to disregard them. I have therefore had to rely on written recollections rather than film or video footage of the games in question. Once again, there has been a conscious effort to reflect the spread of top-class Test rugby around the world, so all Big Eight nations are featured at least once.

Of the more factual chapters, such as the Chronology, there has been little or no effort to be comprehensive. Rather, by highlighting examples of change, I have tried to explore the trends in the game. I have also tried not to be completely dominated by rugby's abiding principle for over a century – amateurism. It has not been possible to dwell at sufficient length on the effect that this concept had on some of the game's institutions and competitions, and here I refer most particularly to the Great Competitions.

This book could not have been compiled without the help and sense of perspective provided by many of the game's elder statesmen. In every country there was at least one veteran rugby man willing to take the time to sift through files and ancient magazines to find nuggets of information that have remained buried for years. I am indebted to the following, who contributed either their time, wisdom or words to this book: John Reason, Terry O'Connor, Mark Reason and the staff at the RFU library (England); Sean Diffley and Peter McMullan (Ireland); Peter Thorburn, Norman Mair and Alasdair Reid (Scotland); Howard Evans (Wales); Ron Palenski (New Zealand); Barry Glasspool (South Africa); John Blondin (Australia); and Chris Thau (France, Romania and the rest of the world!).

The unsung heroes of this book also deserve a mention. Foremost among these is my wife, Bea, who had to read a quarter of a million words before the *Ultimate Encyclopedia* was published two years ago, only to find herself forced to re-read it all again. My apologies to children Ollie and Ailsa for being absent without leave during much of the revision necessary to produce this concise edition.

Any errors you spot – and despite the best efforts of myself and the copy editors at Carlton Books, there will be some – are my responsibility. But I trust that they are minor enough not to detract from your enjoyment of a work of reference which was, for me, a labour of love.

RICHARD BATH
Dumfriesshire, May 1999

Rugby Playing Nations

Initially confined to a small part of the English upper-class, rugby is now played in nearly 100 countries throughout the world, and boasts a World Cup that is the most watched sporting event after the Olympic Games and soccer's World Cup.

In the 176 years or so since William Webb-Ellis first picked up the ball and ran with it at Rugby School, the game has undergone a dramatic transformation.

With China joining the rugby community in earnest in 1997, the game has at last become truly international with virtually every corner of the globe now boasting a club-house and a band of rugby enthusiasts. Played from Argentina to Japan, from Canada to New Zealand; rugby has put down deep roots in all four corners of the world.

After the first international between England and Scotland in 1871, the game quickly spread throughout the British Empire, crossing the Channel and becoming an established part of life in the large ex-pat communities in the Far East, North America and Argentina before gaining widespread popularity amongst the wider population.

By the beginning of this century, the game was a firm fixture in the original "Big Eight" – the original International Rugby Board (IRB) members, England, Ireland, Wales, Scotland, France, New Zealand, South Africa and Australia – and had established a firm foothold in countries as diverse as Argentina, Japan, Canada, Romania and Fiji. And now, with the game going openly professional and the number of rugby playing countries expanding remorselessly, the future looks rosy for the world's fastest growing team sport.

These are the main rugby-playing nations, although lack of space means there are notable exceptions which appear only in the unabridged version, such as Fiji and Korea.

Australia

Year founded:
1949
Colours:
Gold shirts with olive green trim,
olive green shorts, olive green socks
with gold trim
No. of clubs:
413
No. of players:
33,950

In rugby terms, Australia, as a nation, is a little misleading, for the game has never been widely played across the country. Indeed, for long periods, New South Wales – or, more precisely, the metropolitan area around the state capital Sydney – was the only area to fly the Rugby Union flag in the face of intense competition from the competing codes of Australian Rules Football and Rugby League.

That Rugby Union has had a precarious existence in Australia is all the more strange considering that it was the first country outside Britain to adopt the game. The Wallaroo Football Club was formed in 1870, followed in the same year by Sydney University and The King's School, and the game was first played on an organised basis in 1875.

Although the explosion in clubs in Sydney – from three in 1870 to 13 two years later – makes it look as if the code quickly established itself in Sydney, the truth is a good deal less simple.

In its early days, rugby football was competing with "Victorian" football (later to become Australian Rules) and soccer. Although the Southern Rugby Football Union (SRFU) was formed in 1874, virtually all of the member clubs played all three codes or a hybrid mixture of the three. Matters came to a head in 1877 at the SRFU annual general meeting, when J.H. Carruthers, a representative of the University Club, introduced a motion to: "abolish scrimmages and running with the ball", a proposal which the Wallaroo club, for one, denounced as: "in reality a hidden attack upon the most vital aspects of the Rugby game."

The proposal was roundly defeated and, although advocates of the Victorian code, and those who wanted a hybrid game, continued to press their case, the SRFU went from strength to strength, climbing from 17 member clubs in 1878 to 41 in 1880. Crowds of 5-6,000 were not uncommon in Sydney by 1880, but it was not until 1882 that the game was successfully transplanted to Queensland.

The progress of the game in Queensland – again, essentially the metropolitan area surrounding the state capital, Brisbane – was far less smooth than in New South Wales where, by 1880, it had established itself as the premier code. In Queensland, the game struggled to put down deep roots, although the state did go through something of a golden period in the decade leading up to 1900, when its side beat New South Wales a total of 11 times in the original "State of Origin" games. New South Wales were not the only casualties, as Queensland stunned an unofficial British team led by the Reverend Matthew Mullineaux – the first British side to visit Australia since the ill-fated 1887 British touring party, whose captain, R.L. Seddon, drowned in the Hunter River.

In 1903, Queensland and New South Wales combined to meet New Zealand in Sydney, losing that initial encounter 22–3. It was a result that the Wallabies – as the Australian national side became known – were to get used to. All Black great Dave Gallaher returned two years later with his Originals, winning 14–3 on their way to whitewashing the British Isles.

Until Australia became a force in the 1970s, wins over their closest rivals were agonisingly hard to come by, the Wallabies managing just 14 in the first 67 games of what became the Bledisloe Cup series (after a donation by Lord Bledisloe, Governor-General of New Zealand, in 1931).

The first full Wallaby touring side, however, did not leave Australia's shores until 1908, when Dr Paddy Moran's party came, saw and conquered by beating England 9–3 at Blackheath. The players were in England at the same time as the Olympic Games were held in London, and they returned home triumphant having also won a stack of Olympic gold medals in the process.

Seen at the time as the start of Australia's pre-eminence, that tour in fact marked a dramatic downturn in the fortunes of Australian Rugby Union as the touring party converted almost en masse to Rugby League.

It was a body-blow from which the 15-man code in Australia has long struggled to recover. If the effect on the Sydney competition was dramatic, it was as nothing compared to Queensland, where the game ceased to exist for a decade following the First World War before eventually being re-established in 1929.

The story of Australian Rugby Union from the 1908 tour is one of a code fighting for survival against Rugby League.

League quickly established itself as the top game in Queensland and NSW, where union remained the preserve of the middle-class elite from a handful of private schools. There were also clubs scattered throughout parts of Western Australia, Victoria, Tasmania and South Australia, but they were based around schools and the expatriate community, and it seemed little effort was made to spread the gospel.

In the face of League's challenge, tentative steps were taken to make the Union code more appealing. The clearest example was the "Australian dispensation", which essentially said that players could not kick directly to touch from outside their own 25-yard line (22-metre line). Union, though, remained very much the poor relation in terms of playing numbers, crowds and profile.

Far from being allowed to plough their own furrow, Australia's Union followers have always had to cope with League raiding parties arriving at top clubs, such as Gordon, Manly and Randwick, chequebook in hand, to whisk away the brightest young talent. For every player who reached the top level, two would have taken the League dollar. It was amazing that Australia still turned out a string of outstanding backs, men such as Trevor Allan, Cyril Towers, Ken Catchpole and Cyril Burke.

In fact the problem wasn't a lack of pace and power behind the pack, but in it. Despite fielding teak-hard men such as Steve Finane and Graham Cooke, the Wallabies were vulnerable up front, a shortcoming which the New Zealanders profited from in Bledisloe Cup battles.

Australia's elevation to the elite of the modern game began in 1973, after Tonga had humiliated them, winning 16-11 in Brisbane.

Spurred into action, the Australians enlisted the help of the best coach in the world at that time, Welsh visionary Carwyn James. With his help, they began to graft some forward grit and purpose onto their good back play. and by 1984, when Alan Jones brought a young Wallaby side to Britain, the Australians had developed 15-man "total rugby" to a fine art.

This was the Grand Slam tour in which Mark Ella marshalled a flat backline that bewitched British defences as the Wallabies easily won all four Tests.

Australia continued to make steady progress throughout the eighties, winning the Bledisloe Cup series against the All Blacks, and reaching the semi-final of the 1987 World Cup where they lost a thrilling match 30-24 to the French.

Four years later they went one better and reached the final, beating England at Twickenham. Undoubtedly the secret of the Wallabies' success during this era was the astute captaincy of scrum-half Nick-Farr-Jones and the tactical nous of coach Bob Dwyer.

Although disappointingly beaten by England in the 1995 World Cup, Australia's consistently impressive performances in the Tri-Nations Cup – against New Zealand and South Africa – have proved that the Wallabies are at the pinnacle of the world game.

England

Year founded:
1871
Colours:
All white except black socks (with white trim)
No. of clubs:
2,049
No. of players:
160,000

Although William Webb-Ellis is said to have picked up the ball and run with it in 1823, it was not until 1863 that the game of rugby really existed in England in the sense that we would now understand it. Although Rugby School continued to play its own code, it was not until the historic meeting of 1863, when schools and clubs from the "kicking code" (soccer) and the "carrying code" (rugby) finally reconciled their differences to form one code, that rugby was really born.

Eight years later, on 26 January 1871, the Rugby Football Union was born when 20 clubs met under the chairmanship of Edwin Ash at the Pall Mall Restaurant in London. Of those clubs, less than half still exist (Blackheath, Richmond, Guy's Hospital, St Paul's School, Civil Service, Wellington College, Harlequins and King's College),

with the remaining clubs now defunct (Law, West Kent, Belsize Park, Mohicans, Gipsies, Addison, Lausanne, Clapham Rovers, Flamingoes, Wimbledon Hornets, Marlborough Nomads and Queens House). It was under the auspices of the RFU, less than a year after its formation, that a 20-strong England team led by Blackheath's Fred Stokes met and lost to Scotland, led by F.J. Moncrieff of Edinburgh Academicals, the famous club formed in 1859.

The game soon found enormous popularity in England, particularly in the north. Indeed, until the great schism of 1895, when 20 of the north's most prestigious clubs withdrew from the RFU to form the Rugby League, the north was a Union hotbed , producing some of the finest players ever to have played either code. With the split, men such as R.L. Seddon of Broughton Rovers, who captained England on their tour to Australia in 1887 (and tragically drowned in the Hunter River in NSW), were lost to the Union code.

Rugby Union in the north has never recovered the supremacy it enjoyed in the 1880s and early 1890s. After 1895, the direction of the game was dictated by the leading London clubs and the Oxbridge brigade. This, plus the fact that an unusually high percentage of administrators came from the top rugby-playing public schools, meant that English rugby has generally retained the conservative and Corinthian values that were so evident at the debate of the broken-time issue in 1893. Indeed, was England was steadfast in its refusal to contemplate a Rugby World Cup, and was one of the stiffest opponents of professionalism.

As the inventor of Rugby Union, England remains the spiritual homeland of the game, although the ascendancy of the southern hemisphere nations has gradually eroded that status over the past century. The most populous of all the world's rugby nations with 2,200 clubs and 200,000 players, England has conspicuously failed to make this weight of numbers count at international level, oscillating between the European supremacy of the mid-1920s and the early 1990s, and the dismal Five Nations form of the late 1970s. England have rarely been able to live with the southern hemisphere triumvirate, winning only 15 of the 50 Tests it has played against South Africa, New Zealand and Australia.

At international level, England has yet to develop a set style of play, with the adventurous pre-Second World War running game of men such as Adrian Stoop, Wavell Wakefield and Alexander Obolensky eventually giving way to the more muscular mauling game typified by forwards in the mould of Billy Beaumont and Dean Richards. Many of the prob-

lems in the English game can be traced to a century-long structural malaise: without a Currie Cup, Ranfurly Shield or Bouclier de Brennus to bring talent to the surface and help it develop in a genuinely competitive atmosphere, many of England's finest players played out their days in endless friendlies at unfashionable clubs.

Until the 1970s, when the knock-out competition was first played, the County Championship and cross-Border clashes with Welsh clubs provided the only real benchmark of performance. The County Championship, the pinnacle of the English game since it was first contested in 1889, has been dominated by seven counties, in essence players from the 15 or so top clubs. Unlike Wales, Ireland and Scotland, which all had five or six main clubs, the huge pool of players and clubs England was able to draw on was, paradoxically, its main weakness. Not until the Mallaby Committee recommended that an annual cup be started was there any attempt to overhaul the structure of English rugby. The commencement in 1970 of what was to become the Pilkington Cup revolutionised domestic rugby by bringing in the Merit Table which, a decade later, led to the of a full league structure in the 1987–88 season.

The introduction of leagues in 1987 changed English rugby forever. Famous old clubs such as Moseley, Coventry and

Bedford slipped down the ladder while a whole batch of aggressive and less well established clubs such as Bath, Orrell, West Hartlepool and Saracens finally had an objective benchmark by which to judge themselves, and prospered accordingly. The traditional giants of the game had to look at their priorities and adjust. Harlequins and Leicester did so without breaking sweat. Others, such as Richmond and Northampton, took longer to get into gear.

The club game soon became the dominant force in domestic rugby, with the County Championship fading to the point where, from 1996, only players from the lower leagues were allowed to play.

An attempt to implant a Divisional Championship in the early eighties finally ran out of steam around the same time.

Between 1987 and '96 the League was dominated by Bath and Leicester, with only Wasps able to break the two-club duopoly. With club rugby the domestic be-all and end-all, the entry of the top four club sides into the European Cup has taken rugby in England towards a Super 12-style set-up.

Bolstered by a strengthened domestic game, England have prospered since the mid 1980s. With a new management team in coach Geoff Cooke and captain Will Carling, England started a new era

in 1988 when a 28–19 defeat of Nick Farr-Jones' Australians launched a run of success unprecedented since Wavell Wakefield's side won back-to-back Grand Slams in 1923 and '24, two of six Grand Slams won from 1913 to '28.

Whereas post-1988 England were a muscular crew who bludgeoned their way to success, this had not always been the case with English international teams.

While strong up front, the early England sides were renowned for their innovative and adventurous back play. Men such as W.J.A. Davies, Wavell Wakefield, Cherry Pillman, Harry Vassall and Alan Rotherham delighted fans with audacious running, and they were by no means alone. Theirs was a legacy passed down to the post-war generation, as the conveyor belt of superb backs turned out world-class players in the shape of Bev Risman, Richard Sharp, Dickie Jeeps, Peter Jackson and Jeff Butterfield.

The decline in back play and the emergence of the more predictable forward-based game of today has its roots in the weakness of the England forwards in the 1960s and 1970s.

Despite men of the calibre of Peter Wheeler, Fran Cotton, Roger Uttley, Chris Ralston and a host of exceptional forwards, England were regularly outgunned up front during this period. Some of the blame lay in poor and inconsistent selection policies, and some in the failure to define a tactical framework for England players to fit into. Yet the end result was a scarcity of ball for backs such as David Duckham and Keith Fielding, and an obsession with out-muscling sides up front.

Although Carling's men looked as if they were about to break the mould with some sparkling performances between 1988 and '90, defeat by Scotland in the 1990 Murrayfield Grand Slam decider saw England retrench and adopt a leaden (if effective) approach that remains the closest England have to a national style.

Yet if England have found that a conservative game plan is often enough to overwhelm their Home Union rivals, it is certainly an attitude that has failed miserably against the three southern hemisphere sides.

Tours to England before 1960 were generally attempts to halt the progress of outstanding sides such as New Zealander Dave Gallaher's "Originals" in 1905, or of the famous 1932 Springboks, or of Cyril Burke's all-conquering Wallaby side of 1948.

England did not venture on a major southern hemisphere tour until the Australasian tour of 1963, in which they were whitewashed. Apart from the odd, brief, respite, England have never been able to dominate outside Europe as they have within it.

In three World Cups, England have only once won a game against southern hemisphere opposition when they beat Australia in the quarter-finals in 1995.

Then, they were completely steamrollered by Jonah Lomu and company in the semi-final. In 1987, England lost to Australia before being put out by Wales in the quarter-finals, and in 1991, after losing to New Zealand at the group stage, England lost to Australia in the Final.

In the period leading up to the fourth World Cup, to be held in Europe in Autumn 1999, England have brought in a new coaching team but have struggled to break out of their tactical straight-jacket.

Coach Clive Woodward has found that the high numbers of non-English players plying their trade in the Allied Dunbar premiership has meant that, in the short term at least, there are not enough good young English players breaking through.

This has had several effects, not least the fact that when an English second-string toured the southern hemisphere in the summer of 1998, it was beaten 76-0 by Australia.

Problems in personnel meant that France claimed back-to-back Grand Slams in 1997 and '98, but under the leadership of Lawrence Dallaglio, England have done enough to prove that on their own patch they can beat any of the southern hemisphere giants.

FRANCE

Year founded:
1905
Colours:
Blue shirts and socks (with white
trim) and white shorts
No. of clubs:
1,720
No. of players:
93,670

The successful establishment of rugby in
France has long provided a puzzle for
sporting historians. At the end of the 19th
Century when the game first took root,
France was recovering from its crushing
defeat at the hands of the Prussians and
education was far higher up the agenda
than sport for the gallic elite. Indeed,
sport was barely on the agenda at all.

Nevertheless, he first recorded game
of rugby on French soil occurred in 1872
between the English wine merchants of
Le Havre, who organised a game at a
ground somewhere between Rue Francis
1st and Rue Augustin Normand. Not surprisingly, to this day the colours of the
first rugby club in France, Havre Athletic
Club, are the dark blue of Oxford and the
light blue of Cambridge.

For the next twenty years, rugby in
France remained the preserve of the English abroad and the next club to emerge
was in 1877 when English textile merchants in Paris formed the cunningly
named English Tailors Club. At this
stage, though, the game was gradually
being taken up by small numbers of
Frenchman and in 1879 the Paris Football Club was formed.

In 1885 the Parisians toured England, but returned with a record of played
four, lost four. Shattered, the club folded
the following year. Despite this setback,
Parisian rugby was improving steadily
and the Racing Club de France, formed
in 1882, was acting as a powerful missionary force for the game in the north of
the country.

Yet as the clubs led the way, one of
the most important developments in
French rugby was happening at schools
level. Baron Pierre de Coubertin, who
was to enjoy greater fame for his
Olympic vision, became a convert to
rugby after visiting Thomas Arnold at
Rugby School in the early 1870s, when
the game was in expansionist mood.

De Coubertin was instrumental in
laying the foundations for rugby's successful germination into France's sporting psyche. An educationalist, he took an
active role in promoting the game in
schools and rugby at that level took off.
In 1890 the first Schools Championship,
featuring the three Lycées of Lakanal,
L'Ecole Monge and L'Ecole Alsacienne,

was launched by the enterprising Baron.

The final of the first French Championship (as opposed to the Schools Championship) was contested by Racing Club and their arch-rivals Stade Française, the only two entrants, but it was a tremendous success. Baron de Coubertin, its organiser and referee, presented the winners with a superb wooden trophy, described by an eye-witness as "a magnificent trophy of breathtaking beauty and nobility".

This trophy, which is called the Bouclier de Brennus, went on to become French rugby's equivalent of the Ranfurly Shield or Currie Cup.

The tournament was such a success that the number of entries for the second Championship went up to five, with all the clubs hailing from the Ile de France in Paris. In 1896, however, the emphasis shifted from Paris, when the Toulouse club challenged its Bordeaux counterpart to a game of rugby. That game, eagerly awaited and raucously attended, acted as a catalyst and, within months, rugby was taking the country by storm.

In 1900, when the second Olympic Games were held in Paris, France selected its first national team to compete in the new tournament and emerged triumphant, winning the gold medal by beating Frankfurt Fusball Club 27–17 in the first game and Moseley Wanderers 27–8 in a surprisingly one-sided final.

At this time rugby was sweeping through France, moving from village to village, symbolising regional and local rivalries, although quite how the game made its dramatic transition from a middle-class game enthusiastically adopted by the students of the north to become the favourite pastime of the farmers and labourers of the rural south is a moot point.

Explanations have varied from a theory that the game followed in the footsteps of the medieval game of Soule, to the thought that it was the anti-clerical south's reaction to the priests of the north for whom soccer was the game of choice. Whatever the origins, however, "Le Jeu Anglais" soon came to represent to the south of France its own unique identity which, in turn, explains why the sport's progress faltered in the north.

The growth of the game was also helped by the addition of some high profile players from Britain. In particular, Percy Bush, of Cardiff, Wales and the Lions, joined the British Consulate in Nantes as his playing career drew to a close and gave rugby in France a real boost.

By 1905–06 the French Federation felt strong enough to throw down the gauntlet to the perfidious Albion and took on England in Paris. Any optimism proved to be sorely misplaced, however, as the English steamrollered the home side to win by a massive 35–8. Further setbacks followed against Wales (36–4 in Cardiff in 1908), Ireland (19–8 in Dublin in 1909) and Scotland (27–0 at Inverleith in 1910). The diet of defeats continued relentlessly, until the tide finally turned in the spring of 1920 when the Irish succumbed by 15–7 in Dublin.

However, while the French were becoming increasingly competitive, it brought problems off the field. A culture apart, the amateur ethic which the British held so dear to their hearts was not quite as well entrenched in either French rugby or the French psyche. With domestic rivalries so great, and the incentive to poach players more intense than in Britain – except in Wales, where rugby was the game of the people rather than the professional classes – the result was petty professionalism and extreme violence.

It was not a situation which found favour with the amateur die-hards, but when, in March 1931, 12 of France's top clubs overtly started to pay players, the conflict came into the open and France's international development was abruptly curtailed.

The Home Unions sent a communiqué to CF Rutherford, the secretary of the FFR, saying: "Owing to the unsatisfactory state of the game in France ... neither our Unions or clubs will be able to arrange fixtures with France or French clubs ... until we are satisfied that the conduct of the game has been placed on a satisfactory basis."

It was not until after the war that France was allowed to re-enter the community of rugby playing nations, and the four Home Unions soon found out that post-war France was a unrecognisable from the pre-isolation team. In the 1920s, France had produced outstanding flair players, such as Jarreguy, Ribere, Gallia, Cassayet-Armagnac and Mauriat, yet the side lacked the cohesiveness and grit to succeed at international level.

The 1946 version, with magnificent Lourdes forward Jean Prat leading from the front and Basquet, Dufau, Pomathios and Alvarez following, was a different proposition.

That transformation was completed with a gritty 3–0 win over the touring 1956 All Blacks at the Stade Colombes and France soon became a real force in the Five Nations, which they first topped in 1954 when they shared top spot with England and Wales, although they had to wait until 1968 for the first of their six Grand Slams (others followed in 1977, 1981, 1987, 1997 and 1998).

The impact of France has been more than simple statistics or even that the game has flourished. Above all, France provides top-flight world rugby, with a bit of colour, but offers a completely different cultural experience. Domestically, the ferocity on the pitch is matched only by the internecine warfare at committee and management level.

As a touring destination, France offers a remarkable change, while as a rugby nation, the savagery of domestic competition has produced, on one hand, uncompromising, teak hard forwards – men like Gerard Cholley and Olivier Merle – while on the other, sublime three-quarters such as Jo Maso, the Boniface brothers, Jean Trillo, Claude Dourthe and Philippe Sella.

It is this potent mixture which threatens the Anglo-Saxon hegemony. At the first World Cup in 1987, France stole the show with a last-minute 30–24 win over hosts Australia in one of the best matches of all time. Only they ever seemed likely to resist the all-conquering All Blacks before finally falling 29–9 in the Final.

Although they were less successful in 1991 – losing to England in the quarter-finals – France soon proved their mettle in a remarkable 18 months that started in 1993. After a drawn series against Australia, they recorded an unprecedented away series victory in South Africa, and whitewashed the All Blacks 2–0 in the one of the most thrilling series ever in New Zealand.

The 1995 World Cup turned out to be something of a damp squib for the French. They had improved with every match and reached the semi-final, where hosts South Africa were the opponents.

Unfortunately a deluge left the pitch at Durban's King's Park flooded and, after a delay of 90 minutes, the game – more water polo than rugby – went ahead, but South Africa scraped though by 19–15, courtesy of some very dubious refereeing from Wales's Derek Bevan.

Professionalism had always been a reality in France, helped by crowds of 20,000 at the top clubs and the fact that municipal support from local councils is the norm. So when the game went pro after the 1995 World Cup, it scarcely affected the day-to-day running of French rugby.

The top players tend to play for their local town club, with many retaining part-time jobs which meant they could train in the morning and evening and work during the day. Several top players departed for England, and some foreign players – such as Scotland's Gregor Townsend – arrived in France, but by and large French rugby avoided the upheavals that beset the game across the Channel.

Back-to-back Grand Slams in 1997 and 1998 seemed to confirm France as Europe's top nation, until the 1999 Five Nations, when they finished bottom of the table. Only a last-minute penalty against Ireland saving them from the indignity of a first post-war whitewash.

Ireland

Year founded:

1874

Colours:

Green shirts and socks (with white trim) and white shorts

No. of clubs:

205

No. of players:

16,000

Barry McGann, the Irish outside half of the late 1960s and early 1970s tells a story that perfectly sums up what the Irish mean to rugby. "Towards the end of my international career, Syd Millar was the coach and I had the reputation of being a very laid-back player. Because of work I was late to a training session, and it was in full swing when I got there. I went over to Syd and apologised for being late and asked him what he wanted me to do. I had a strong feeling he didn't believe I had made much of an effort to be there but he told me to warm up. Instinctively, I rubbed my hands together and blew on them and said: 'Okay, coach, I'm ready.' He just looked at me."

Yet if the Irish have long been the flag-bearers for the off-field bonhomie that distinguishes Rugby Union from other sports, once on the field they play with a passion and commitment other countries find hard to match.

It is no coincidence that "the Garry-owen" – where the fly-half kicks the ball high and deep into the opposition half, giving his team time to charge up and flatten the catcher – is named after one of Ireland's greatest clubs. As England's veteran back-rower Mike Teague once said: "No pack of forwards in the world is more frightening than the Irish in full cry – it's just a good job they all drink so much Guinness that they can only keep it up for 20 minutes. A full game of that would be murder!"

Given Ireland's small player base of around 16,000 players in 200 clubs (greater London has seven times more players than Ireland), the Irish have until recently managed to remain remarkably competitive in international terms. A nation with such little strength in depth will always be prone to peaks and troughs, but as well as producing out-standing players such as Willie-John McBride, Jackie Kyle and Mike Gibson, Ireland have also managed to claim the Triple Crown six times, while also win-ning the Grand Slam in 1948.

There is a story that Ireland is the real home of rugby union, and that William Webb-Ellis actually learnt the game during the period when his father, James, was stationed in Tipperary whilst serving with the 18th Royal Irish Regiment. There, it is said, the young Webb-Ellis came into contact with a thousand-year-old Irish game called "Cad", which was the traditional game played in rural areas, particularly in Munster. A game in which crowds of youths battled to gain possession of the Cad – an inflated bull's scrotum – it was a game in which the emphasis was in running with the ball. Hence the theory.

It is more likely, however, that rugby was introduced into Ireland from 1850 onwards by former pupils of Rugby School and Cheltenham College, who began to play the game on an organised basis at Trinity College – the spiritual home of Irish rugby – as early as 1853. Perhaps it was because the game was so closely related to Cad that "football" made rapid progress throughout Ireland, with NIFC (North of Ireland Football Club) being established in Belfast in 1859 as the number of clubs mushroomed. But as in Australia, where the code of rugby had to compete for space and players with Association Football and Victorian Football, so too did Irish rugby have to compete with Gaelic football and Association Football, while hurling was also a popular pastime.

The difference, according to Jacques McCarthy, that famous chronicler of Irish rugby's early days, was as follows: "Football in Ireland may be said to consist of three parts, Rugbeian, Associationist and Gaelic. The rule of play in these organisations has been defined as follows – in rugby you kick the ball; in Association you kick the man if you cannot kick the ball; in Gaelic you kick the ball if you cannot kick the man!"

In 1868 two Trinity students, Charles Barrington and Robert Wall, laid down the ground rules for rugby in Ireland. About this time several football clubs (such as the famous Laune Rangers in Kerry) opted for Gaelic football, yet the number of rugby clubs continued to increase rapidly and in 1879 the Irish Football Union was formed ... precisely four years after Ireland's first international against England at The Oval. The delay, which was caused by a spat between the Dublin and Belfast factions, was resolved just in time for a 20-strong united Irish side to register its first win, over Scotland, in 1881. Matters remained chaotic, however, down to the point where during the 1882 match against Wales, two Irish players were so appaled at the violence that they simply walked off the pitch never to be seen again, while two years later against Wales, Ireland turned up two players short and had to borrow two Welshmen.

The early years of international rugby were trying ones for the Irish. Naturally relaxed characters, the thought of training did not even occur to the earliest Irish sides, with the consequence that the team beaten by England at The Oval in 1875 was described in one newspaper report as: "immaculately innocent of training ... one player looked like Falstaff – a mountain of tummy." With a write-up like that, it is hardly surprising that it took until 1881 for Ireland to register its first international win, beating Scotland by one drop-goal and one try to nothing in Belfast. Another six years passed before Ireland claimed another scalp, England being beaten at the thirteenth time of asking with Wales succumbing the next year. That victory heralded one of Ireland's purple patches and in 1894 and 1899, Ireland completed a clean sweep to claim a brace of Triple Crowns. However, it took until 1948 before Ireland won their first and, to date, only Grand Slam.

In 1964 prop Ray McLoughlin was appointed captain, a decision that proved a watershed for Irish rugby. A meticulous planner, McLoughlin frowned upon the: "it'll be all right on the night" approach, preferring instead to hold long training sessions and lengthy team talks, striving all the while to develop an "Irish" style of play. He did not last as captain for more than two seasons, but McLoughlin's influence has stayed ever since.

No matter how successful (or otherwise) Irish rugby is, however, the game in the Emerald Isle is maintained by the wealth of characters who have graced its rugby fields. There have been many eccentrics, such as D.B. Walkington of NIFC who wore a monocle throughout games, taking it off only to tackle and replacing it as soon as the man was downed. Then there was Basil Maclear of Cork County and Monkstown, who used to wear snow-white evening gloves throughout each game. It is larger than life characters – and clashes between them – which do so much to endear the Irish to the rugby world. And, with the Irish famously loving a heated debate, one of the most famous rows in Irish rugby history occurred in the late 1970s and early 1980s when the whole of Irish rugby raged with debate on which Dubliner should play fly-half for Ireland: the free-running Tony Ward or the metronomic kicker Ollie Campbell. The debate came to a head in 1979 when Ireland sent a party to Australia and Campbell famously kicked the tourists to victory while Ward kicked his heels. In many ways, the depth of division and the passions raised said as much about rugby in Ireland as the debate itself.

Campbell helped Ireland win Triple Crowns in 1982 and 1985, but since then Ireland has struggled to maintain its traditional position in the world pecking order, a position that has been challenged in the 1990s as never before, and recent home defeats against emerging nations

Western Samoa and Italy have under-lined the decline in standard of Irish rugby over the last few years.

An intensely conservative rugby country, change does not come easily to the IRFU, although change is now being foisted upon it by force of circumstances. At a domestic level, the Union has responded and competition is increasing on a year by year basis. The All-Ireland League started in 1990 (Ireland were the last major nation to inaugurate such a tournament) and participation in the European Cup from 1995 has raised stan-dards to the point where Ulster won the 1999 European Cup.

Ireland have also managed to per-suade virtually all of its current interna-tional squad to stop plying their highly-paid trade with top English clubs and return to Ireland, but whether Ireland will be able to compete long-term still remains to be seen.

The All-Ireland League has been implanted alongside the existing struc-ture, the pinnacle of which is the Inter-provincial series between the four provinces, Ulster, Leinster, Munster and Connacht. This has long been a regular feature of Irish rugby, while Leinster started its own Cup competition in 1882, Ulster in 1885, Munster in 1886 and Connacht in 1896. The nature of the game in each of the provinces varied wildly, however. In Leinster and Ulster,

the game is predominantly a game of the professional classes, while in Munster – or certainly in the City of Limerick – it is stoically and proudly a game that crosses all social boundaries. Connacht, the smallest and most rural of the four provinces, has a relatively small playing population and no major clubs save for Galwegians. Schools rugby is very strong throughout Ireland.

Strangely, given the initial fall-out between Belfast and Dublin, the IRFU remains the only major sporting body to encompass both sides of the divide in Ireland.

Although sectarian politics have inevitably intruded on the game at times – it is generally perceived by the nationalist community in Ulster as a Protestant game – there has always been a concerted effort not to involve politics in rugby, and nei-ther the British nor Irish national anthems are played before games.

As Garryowen bruiser Tom Reid replied in 1955 when asked what he thought of the political situation in South Africa at a reception for the Lions: "As a southern Irishman with me own political problems, I keep me views to meself." Virtually the only way that politics have become involved in Irish rugby life is through the fact that two of Ireland's most famous statesmen – Eamonn de Valera and Dick Spring – were devoted players of the game.

New Zealand

Year founded:
1892

Colours:
Black shirts, shorts and socks (with white trim)

No. of clubs:
600

No. of players:
33,973

Historically the strongest of rugby countries and home of the famous All Blacks, New Zealand sides are some-times feared but always respected and not beaten anywhere near as often as other countries would like.

In a sentence that has been echoed by countless players before and since, Gareth Edwards, the great British Lions and Wales scrum-half, said, after first playing against New Zealand in 1967: "There is something about the All Black jersey that sends a shudder through your heart."

The All Blacks have habitually founded their game on a strong pack of forwards – believing that possession is everything – though it has seldom been at the expense of effective, and some-times brilliant, back play. The All Blacks echo the domestic New Zealand game with a methodical, no-nonsense approach and the long-held belief that it is winning that matters, not the taking part.

New Zealand rugby is based on a playing structure that has been the envy of other rugby-playing countries. The All Blacks, the national team, membership of which represents an entree to New Zealand's most exclusive club, forms the apex of the playing triangle. Below them are the 27 provincial unions which have a tradition of home and away "friendly" fixtures and – since 1976 – a national provincial championship in three divisions.

Since the introduction of profession-alism, a new tier has appeared, fitting between the provinces and the national side: the Super 12 teams, which are regional groups of provinces, play Australian states and South African provinces in an early-season competition from March until May.

Provincial teams also contest, the Ranfurly Shield, a challenge trophy named after the Earl of Ranfurly, Gover-nor of New Zealand early this century. Challenges are usually at the holder's home stadium and though smaller unions have previously held the shield, it is now almost exclusively first division property – in particular Auckland's, who held it for a record 61 challenges between 1985 and 1993. Auckland have also won the National Provincial Championship first division 11 times since 1976.

The base of the New Zealand playing triangle is the clubs, who play in competitions organised by the provincial unions. Since professionalism, the top 140 or so players have been contracted to, and paid by, the New Zealand union. Some provinces separately contract other players and there is commercial movement of players at club level as well, but it is not widespread. However, such has been the level of international, Super 12 and provincial commitment in recent years, that it has become increasingly rare for the top players to also play for club sides.

Rugby was introduced to New Zealand in 1870 by Charles John Monro, son of the Speaker of the New Zealand Parliament at the time. He had been sent to England for his education and attended Christ's College in Finchley. At CCF he learned to play rugby (where another devotee was Percy Capmael, founder of the Barbarians) and on his return to his native Nelson in 1870, Monro persuaded the boys of his old school, Nelson College, and a town club to play the game.

Using a steamer provided through his father, Monro took the Nelson College team to Wellington and arranged games

there and formed New Zealand's oldest continuous rugby club, the Wellington Football Club. As boys left school and went to work around the country, they took rugby with them establishing it in a remarkably short time.

New Zealanders took to rugby not only because of the influence of the well-educated (and therefore wealthy), but also because it was a game that suited the rugged individualism of early New Zealand, anxious to retain its British roots but just as anxious to prove itself an independent force.

Rugby's appeal to its indigenous people, the Maori, was another great benefit. Unlike in some other countries, there were no social or legal impediment to their playing alongside the Europeans ("the Pakehas").

Maori have always had a profound influence on rugby, not least by organising the pioneering tour of Britain and Australia in 1888 by the New Zealand Native team, a tour that allowed New Zealanders to compare their standard and style of play with what they saw in Britain.

A British team also toured New Zealand in 1888, but Tom Ellison, a Maori and one of the seminal men of early New Zealand rugby, remarked rather archly in his book, The Art of Rugby Football, that they learned little from the British team.

Ellison, who had toured Britain with the Native team, was instrumental in the development of two unique features of the New Zealand game, the evolution of the five-eighth positions (as opposed to inside-outside centres) and the introduction of the wing-forward, a position that was abolished in 1931.

But Ellison's most enduring claim to rugby fame came at the New Zealand Rugby Football Union's first annual meeting in 1893, when he suggested that the New Zealand team uniform consist of a black jersey with a silver fernleaf motif. He also proposed white shorts although this was later changed to black in 1901.

After the playing success of the 1888 Natives, the New Zealand Union yearned and planned for nearly a decade a tour of Britain by a full New Zealand team; and they achieved their aim in the season of 1905–06 when the Originals, led by wing-forward Dave Gallaher, made a pioneering and historic tour.

When the New Zealanders beat Devon 55–4 in their first match, one London newspaper sub-editor was so sceptical of the result he reversed the scoreline.

It wasn't long before the team, sweeping all before them, became known as the All Blacks. The name evolved from the colour of their uniform rather than the apocryphal tale that another sub-editor changed the phrase "all backs" (because of the forwards' speed) to All Blacks.

Their one defeat in the 32-match tour was to Wales, 3–0, a try to nothing. The match has grown in rugby folklore because Bob Deans was said to have scored what would have been an equalising try, but had been dragged back over the line before the referee, in street clothes, could catch up with play. The All Blacks avenged that defeat in 1924, when "The Invincibles" – as the party became known – made their first unbeaten tour of the British Isles, although sadly that tour did not include a game against Scotland, who were then at one of their peaks.

New Zealand also developed enduring and, at times, troubling relations with South Africa, who they regard as the most consistently difficult opponents. Indeed, it took until 1996 for the All Blacks to win a series in South Africa.

The relationship with South Africa was made difficult for more than purely playing reasons. Under apartheid and before, South Africa had refused to host New Zealand teams containing Maori, and as the anti-apartheid movement increased internationally, New Zealand was seen to be at fault for bowing to the South African wishes.

Contact between the two countries was completely severed after the 1981 tour of New Zealand was marred by widespread protests which at one stage became so severe that "the barbed wire tour" looked capable of fomenting civil war among New Zealand's deeply divided population – a planned 1985 tour to South Africa was later stopped by legal action – and the rivalry was renewed with all its old intensity only when the abolition of apartheid began in 1992.

New Zealand's other enduring international relationship is with her closest neighbour, Australia. Regular test series between the two countries are for the Bledisloe Cup, although the All Blacks had almost permanent possession until the late Seventies.

New Zealand rugby used to regard Australian rugby in much the same way as Australian cricket regards New Zealand cricket, but there is now intense and unpredictable competition between the two with the Bledisloe Cup matches guaranteed sell-outs.

New Zealand has contributed many of rugby's greatest players, from full-back Billy Wallace and captain Gallaher of the first British tour and the full-back in every game of that tour, George Nepia, to John Kirwan and Michael Jones of the 1987 World Cup winning side.

Bob Scott of the post-World War II era was another of the standout full-backs, but it has been for hard, uncom-

promising forwards that New Zealand rugby has best been known.

Players such as the legendary Colin Meads – who most New Zealanders would regard as the best player ever to have pulled on a black jersey – or the captains in Britain in 1963.

Other greats include Wilson Whineray, 1967, Brian Lochore, the flanker, Graham Mourie, who led the first All Black side to achieve a Grand Slam in 1978, and the remarkably durable hooker, Sean Fitzpatrick, who played in New Zealand's World Cup-winning team in 1987, and led the All Blacks to their first series win in South Africa in 1996.

In fact, most New Zealanders failed to realise quite how important Fitzpatrick was to the All Blacks. When the veteran hooker was forced to retire in 1998, it marked the beginning of the most trying period in All Black rugby history.

Fitzpatrick's retirement coincided with that of two of the team's other unsung heroes, long-term No.8 Zinzan Brooke and ageless centre Frank Bunce. The effect on the team was immediate and disastrous. Although the country's Super 12 teams are still formidably competitive, both Australia and South Africa routinely beat New Zealand throughout 1998-9, leading to coach John Hart's team posting the worst record of all time during that season.

Scotland

Year founded:
1873
Colours:
Navy blue shirts and socks (with
white trim) and white shorts
No. of clubs:
276
No. of players:
10,707

Although the game of rugby union was famously first played in England in 1823 at Rugby School, it is Scotland which boasts the oldest club not based in a school or university. Edinburgh Academicals, the Raeburn Place club, was founded in 1858, four years before Blackheath – or "The Club" as the London outfit styles itself.

Indeed, Raeburn Place was the venue for the first ever international match, held in 1871, when England were beaten by one try and one goal to one try by Scotland in front of a crowd of several thousand in a forerunner of the Calcutta Cup.

Edinburgh Academicals, the old boys club for Edinburgh Academy, represents a distinct brand of rugby in Scotland, that of the Old Boys clubs, upon which much of domestic Scottish

rugby has always been based. Edinburgh Academicals may have been the first, but it was not long before they were vying for supremacy with a host of other old boys sides, such as Heriot's FP (former pupils), Watsonians, Stewart's Melville FP, Dundee HSFP and Glasgow Academicals.

Throughout the mid to late 1870s, another almost parallel world of club rugby grew up in the sparsely-populated and rural Borders area. This brand of rugby, imported from Yorkshire through the burgeoning woollen industry, was a world away from the refined old boys circuit of the major cities.

The sparsely-populated Borders region remains the only area in Scotland – outside the predominantly middle class atmosphere of the Edinburgh elite – where rugby has really managed to take root. In small towns where there was little or no association football, clubs such as Gala, Hawick, Selkirk, Kelso, Jed Forest and Melrose soon became the sporting focus for the hardy farming communities living nearby.

As well as being geographically and culturally divorced from their city counterparts, the Borders clubs soon developed a competition of their own, the Borders League, which is still contested and remains the oldest organised league competition in world rugby. Although the population of the Borders is only 100,000, its unique cauldron of local rivalries has produced many of the best players to come out of Britain, and tradition has it that the best Scotland sides are those which contain a majority of Borderers.

It says much for the area that the three most enduring club sides in Scotland – Hawick, Gala (Galashiels) and Melrose – have populations of 10,000, 5,000 and 2,500 respectively.

The Borders was also the birthplace of the abbreviated code of Sevens, somewhat ironic given the fact that Borders rugby is traditionally founded on forward muscle rather than fluent back play. The code was invented in 1883, when Melrose butcher and fly-half Ned Haig suggested a shortened version of the game as a means of raising money at a local fair.

The idea was a roaring success, with Melrose beating Gala in extra time to win the competition, and soon most towns in the Borders staged their own annual sevens tournaments in April and May.

So seriously do the Borderers take the game that when in 1983 the victorious French donated their Melrose Sevens winners' medals to local lasses as tokens of affection, there was uproar in the town – all Borderers see a Melrose Sevens winner's medal as the next best thing to a Scottish cap.

As with the rest of the European nations, the power in Scotland has always rested with clubs rather than any province or other grouping, although there has been a concerted but as yet unsuccessful attempt to create a divisional aspect to Scottish domestic rugby of late, with an Inter-District competition featuring five sides (the North & Midlands, the South, Glasgow, Edinburgh and the Exiles).

In the new professional era, this first became a four-district structure, and then through financial necessity later became a two-Superteam structure, with the best players in the country contracted to either the Glasgow Caledonians or the Edinburgh Reivers. There have been some profound problems with the structure – especially in terms of finding enough worthy opposition outside of the European Cup – but it is now the favoured option of the Scottish Rugby Union.

With a small playing population of just around 25,000 and almost 250 clubs, it has been a marvel that Scotland has managed to remain consistently competitive at international level. Much of the credit for that goes to a well defined national style of play at Test level which is based squarely on a fierce rucking game. It echoes the domestic club game, a no-frills approach owing much to fitness, speed of movement away from the breakdown and speed of thought, rather than sheer forward muscle. If Scottish rugby has traditionally had one great strength, it has been in tenacious back-row players and hard-running half-backs. Without front fives physically strong enough to impose themselves, Scotland have long looked to move the ball away from set-piece and tight loose play by adopting an all-action, fast rucking game designed to unsettle heavier opposition and create space for the fit Scots.

A small playing base means that Scotland have often struggled at the top level. Indeed, only against Ireland of the major rugby-playing nations, do Scotland still have a positive record, while in the early 1950s they suffered 17 consecutive defeats.

Nevertheless, they have by far the most well defined style of play among European nations, especially since coaches such as Ian McGeechan and Jim Telfer made a conscious effort to ensure that every potential international player understood how the national side played. This, plus a wide-ranging search for Scottish grandparents, has allowed Scotland to play beyond their resources, allowing players struggling at international level to take the step up more easily than they could in England or Wales.

Although Scotland have yet to beat New Zealand, they have recorded wins over South Africa and Australia, and have completed the Five Nations Grand

Slam three times: in 1925, 1984 and 1990. Of those, the 1990 win will always be best remembered, not least because it was won during a highly-charged Grand Slam play-off decider at Murrayfield against the Auld Enemy, England.

Scotland had won their first three games relatively comfortably, but had done little to suggest that they could beat an England side which had played some of the finest rugby ever seen in Britain and which clearly saw itself as ready to claim only its third Grand Slam since 1928. However, Scotland captain David Sole gained a vital psychological edge when he calmly walked his men onto the pitch before wreaking havoc on the English for the most famous 80 minutes in Scottish rugby history.

Although Scotland came close to repeating the feat, when they met England at Twickenham in a 1995 Grand Slam decider, they were totally overwhelmed, and the achievements of Sole's men stand as Scotland's finest hour.

Jim Telfer's side did come close to emulating that feat by winning the 1999 Five Nations trophy, however. Playing by far the most expansive, adventurous rugby of all the nations, Scotland won three of their four games and were beaten at Twickenham solely because their place-kicking let them down, only for Wales to beat England through an injury-time try in tournament's last game.

South Africa

Year founded:
1889

Colours:
Olive green shirts and socks (both with gold trim) and white shirts

No. of clubs:
1,116

No. of players: 60,000

When Cecil Rhodes, then governor of the Cape Colony, invited Scottish rugby missionary Bill MacLagan to put together a British side to visit South Africa in 1891, he could never have guessed the scale of the sporting love affair he had set in train.

This relationship was consummated 104 years later as the South African Springboks claimed the game's greatest prize, lifting the World Cup in front of 80,000 screaming fans at Ellis Park in Johannesburg.

The most uncompromising and physically demanding of opponents, the South African Springboks are rivalled only by the New Zealand All Blacks in their capacity for recognising that it is the winning, not the taking part, that matters to them. Because the Springboks are

so rarely bettered, claiming the Springbok head – awarded to the first team to beat the touring Springboks – or winning a Test on South African soil is the pinnacle of achievement for touring players and national sides alike.

As New Zealand legend Colin Meads said: "This is what it has all been about. This is South Africa and these are the players you most want to beat. If you're ever going to play good rugby, you'll play it in South Africa. The atmosphere demands it of you – to beat South Africa in South Africa, what a dream!"

As with New Zealand and Australia, the basis of South African domestic rugby is the provincial system which has the Currie Cup as its pinnacle. First presented by Sir Donald Currie, the founder of the Currie shipping line, in 1891 to the side which performed the most creditably against MacLagan's tourists (which turned out to be Griqualand West, who lost 1–0), the golden cup is now played for by South Africa's top provinces.

In its early years, Western Province virtually owned the mug, winning it 19 times out of 27 attempts, with Transvaal emerging as the Capetonians' main challengers.

Although there are over 1,000 clubs and 100,000 players in South Africa, virtually all the top talent is concentrated in the six provinces in the Currie Cup top flight: Eastern Province, Natal, Northern Transvaal, Orange Free State, Transvaal and Western Province. Rather than playing for both province and club, the top players now play exclusively for a provincial side.

The Currie Cup was so successful even when the ugly spectre of Apartheid cast its shadow across South African rugby and led to the cessation of international playing contacts for almost a decade, that the competition was able to sustain the standard of South African rugby to the point where the incoming "rebel" tours that did play during this period were all well beaten.

Rugby was introduced into South Africa in the 1860s, but really made strides in 1875 when the British garrison in Cape Town took on a team from the city. Within fifteen years, the game had become established enough for the South African Rugby Board to be formed and MacLagan's invited to tour the country with his scratch team.

Although routed by MacLagan's men, who scored 224 points while conceding only one in twenty games, the South Africans were nothing if not quick learners, and by 1896 they were able to win one of three tests against a strong British touring side led by the legendary Johnny Hammond, MacLagan's vice-captain in 1891.

The Boer War broke up the pattern of incoming tours, but the Brits were back in 1903, when Scotsman Mark Morrison came, saw and went home with a series loss to his credit. Resplendent in green and sporting the Springbok emblem for the first time, this was South Africa's first series win and set a pattern of success against British tourists that was not to change until Willie John McBride's 1974 British Lions memorably whitewashed the amazed Springboks.

Such was the strength of South African rugby that when Paul Roos led the first touring party to Britain in 1906 and won 25 of the 28 matches played, the consensus in Britain was that his side was even better than Dave Gallaher's 1905 All Black "Originals".

This feeling was consolidated in 1912, when Billy Millar's touring Springboks gave several virtuoso demonstrations of back play to overcome the elements and win all five tests on their tour of the British Isles, beating bemused Ireland by the then record score of 38–0.

Success kept coming, even after South Africa had their first contact with New Zealand and Australia after the First World War when Theo Pienaar led a touring party to the Antipodes in 1921. But the manner in which the success was achieved began to change as the century wore on.

Where the early Springboks had been

famous for adventurous and scintillating back play, the later teams became notable only for their belief that Test match-winning teams are the ones which make the fewest mistakes.

This approach was exemplified by Bennie Osler, the fly-half, kicker and captain of the 1931 side. Using huge forwards such as Boy Louw and Chris Koch to gradually wear down opposing packs, Osler would only unleash his backs within hailing distance of the opposition goal-line, preferring to use his own cross field kicks or raking grubbers from scrum-half Danie Craven up to that point.

In a country blessed with strapping Afrikaners, it was never more popular than when Fred Allen's 1949 All Blacks were intimidated and out-muscled into a 4–0 series defeat.

While results justified the approach, the safety-first, stick-it-up-your-jumper policy prevailed, but when the 1955 British Lions arrived and shared the series while playing some very exciting rugby, the momentum for a more interesting approach to the game became virtually unstoppable.

That mood was reinforced by the 1956 tour to Australia and New Zealand when the All Blacks called up former heavyweight boxer Kevin Skinner, who proceeded to pummel one Springbok prop after another into submission as the New Zealanders won the series 3–1. As well as forcing a rethink of attitudes, the 1949 and '56 series created a heated rivalry between the Springboks and All Blacks that remains as keen today as it was then.

Unlike New Zealand, however, Apartheid meant that the indigenous South Africans were unable to play rugby alongside whites, a situation that inevitably provoked problems, particularly as a substantial number of New Zealanders were either Maoris or Polynesians.

A remark attributed to Stellenbosch's all-powerful Dr Danie Craven, effectively the administrator who ran rugby in South Africa – that a black player would play for the Springboks over his dead body – hardly improved matters, even if Craven later point blank denied saying any such thing.

Although the black rugby union, SARU, refused to play touring sides, the SARB did make token efforts at multiracialism such as scheduling tourists to play township sides from 1972 onwards, and picking gifted black fly-half Errol Tobias for his first cap against Ireland in 1981.

By this stage, however, whether or not rugby was getting its house in order was virtually irrelevant, and after the 1981 tour to New Zealand caused serious civil disturbance, isolation beckoned.

After England toured in 1984, South Africa's only taste of international competition came from rebel tours such as that of the Argentine-dominated South American Jaguars or the New Zealand-by-proxy side, the Cavaliers, until reintegration into international sports came about in 1992.

It took a while for the Springboks to recover from the years of isolation, and in the first year there were defeats on home soil by Australia and New Zealand, plus defeats in England and France. Yet with an unrivalled rugby infrastructure, South Africa soon began to string together some favourable results. In a country where touring is particularly hard – especially when the itinerary alternates fixtures between the thin air of the high Veldt and the coastal venues – South Africa quickly managed to regain their form.

The culmination of the Springboks' rehabilitation was when they hosted the 1995 World Cup. Despite New Zealand playing the most dynamic and enthralling rugby of the competition, the South African people and their Springbok side pulled together to beat the All Blacks in thrilling style via a Joel Stransky dropped-goal in overtime.

The enduring memory of post-Apartheid rugby in South Africa will remain captain Francois Pienaar's dedication of the victory to the new "Rainbow Nation" and Nelson Mandela's emotional and public support for a white-dominated Afrikaner sport that once stood for everything he despised.

Since then, the South Africans have been able to keep up the post-Apartheid momentum by participating in the two most competitive competitions in world rugby, the Super 12 and the Tri-Nations Series.

The Super 12 series, which pits the top South African provinces against their Australian and New Zealand counterparts, has allowed the number of players coming through to climb steadily and has ensured that all have been hardened against the southern hemisphere's best players.

Although South African provinces have sometimes struggled to live with the pace of competition, it has provided the Springboks with a steady flow of players ready and willing to take on the best in the world.

The benefits of such competition have already been proved in the Tri-Nations, but they have also been shown in the wider contacts with other Test-playing countries.

For example, when the Bok side captained by Gary Teichmann eventually lost at Twickenham in 1998, it was their first loss in 17 tests and left them having equalled an All Black record widely believed to be unbeatable.

Wales

Year founded:
  1881
Colours:
  Red shirts and socks (with white trim) and white shorts
No. of clubs:
  372
No. of players:
  18,000

Of all the countries in the northern hemisphere, only Wales can claim that rugby is the national sport. So deeply embedded is the game in the Welsh psyche, and so deep is the love for it in Wales, that rugby is almost a national barometer charting the state of the nation.

Success on the rugby field is, for many Welshmen, one of the main props of their national identity and self-esteem, and the Welsh have long acted as rugby missionaries. Where else, for instance, could a comedian/entertainer like Max Boyce become a spokesman for the people?

Rugby in Britain has always been a middle-class game, save for fanatical pockets like the West Country, the Scottish Borders and the Irish city of Limerick. Yet as the sport of all men, the game in Wales is markedly different, one where doctors and lawyers have traditionally rubbed shoulders with miners and dockers on a Saturday afternoon.

Indeed, as with New Zealand, much of the immense strength of Welsh rugby has been in the fact that, despite being a relatively small country, virtually all sports-inclined youngsters were exposed to the sport and few athletes were left uncovered or their talents unused. As Gareth Edwards once said: "Growing up in Wales meant two things to me: rugby on Saturday and chapel on Sunday. The thought of doing anything else just never crossed our minds as youngsters."

Although the game is sewn into the fabric of the whole of Welsh society, it was in the industrial south, rather than the rural north, where the game took root. The wide belt of steelworks and coal mining areas stretching from English-speaking Newport in the East, through the Valleys of the Rhondda and across to Welsh-speaking Llanelli in the West, have provided some of the greatest players the game has ever seen. Yet while the industrial base conjures up images of iron-hard hulking forwards, the defining trait of Welsh rugby has long been its outstanding backs.

While Welsh rugby can boast some of the hardest forwards ever to lace up a pair of boots, men such as Clem Thomas, Rhys Williams, Delme Thomas and Graham Price – who were never renowned for their gentle temperaments once the red mist descended – and Welsh club rugby has long been recognised as among the most physically testing in the world, if you ask any Welshman what sets the pulses racing, the answer is not a foot-slogger, but a twinkle-toed, dancing brave at fly-half.

So powerful is the legend of Wales as a fly-half factory, that if there was to be a Welsh Rugby Hall of Fame, then it is easy to imagine which would be the first names pencilled in: famous No.10s Barry John, Cliff Morgan and Phil Bennett would undoubtedly hog centre stage.

But if Welsh rugby is all about the forward fury Welsh-speakers call "hwyl" and three-quarter panache, it has also been enlivened by a fanaticism of support that can only exist in a country where rugby is the sporting be-all and end-all, and where singing is revered. But while the legions of followers of the game in the Principality have been united behind the national side since it first took on the English at Blackheath in 1881, the regional and club rivalries that were once the lifeblood of domestic rugby have now conspired to hold back the development of Welsh rugby.

With occasional interruptions since the mid-1870s, club rugby west of the Severn river has been dominated by a small coterie of City clubs. Swansea, Newport and Cardiff (the club which in 1885–86 introduced the three-quarters formation we have today and which is the self-styled "Greatest Club in the World"), were the original "Big Three" and have dominated ever since, while Llanelli, Pontypool, Neath and Bridgend have also enjoyed spells of pre-eminence.

The fierce rivalries between these clubs – plus a continual diet of shockingly brutal clashes with top English sides, particularly mighty West Country neighbours Bath, Bristol and Gloucester – ensured that Welsh rugby was always very competitive.

Touring sides also gave Welsh rugby some of its greatest moments. Cardiff's wins over South Africa in 1906, Australia in 1947 and, most particularly, New Zealand in 1953 are mentioned in hushed tones, while Pontypool's 1927 double victory (over the Australian Waratahs and the New Zealand Maoris), Swansea's defeat of the All Blacks in 1935 and Newport's lowering of the Springbok standard in 1912 are all discussed in clubhouses as if they occurred just last week.

For all the great deeds of derring-do, however, Welsh rugby suffers from its insularity and has gradually lost ground against the main forces in world rugby in recent times. The incursion of Rugby League, which has claimed almost one in four of all Welsh internationals, has not helped the cause of the 15-man game, and the steady decline of heavy industry has also contributed to a worsening record (where once the majority of top players were miners or steelworkers, now it is possible to count the number on one hand).

More than anything else, however, Welsh rugby has had to fight against the sheer weight of numbers of players in the super-powers: England, France, South Africa, Australia and New Zealand have all had access to at least three times as many players as Wales, and with just 372 clubs and 18,000 players, the lack of numbers has told.

The outstanding generation of players that emerged at the beginning of the 1970s papered over some of the structural problems that have subsequently appeared in Welsh rugby. Throughout the 1970s, a procession of gloriously talented players, including Barry John, Gareth Edwards, J.P.R. Williams, Mervyn Davies, John Taylor, Phil Bennett, J.J. Williams and the Pontypool front-row of Price, Faulkner and Windsor, held sway over Britain and the world.

As the core of the victorious British Lions tour of 1971 to New Zealand and to South Africa in 1974, that generation of Welshmen represented the finest group of players ever to pull on a Lion's jersey in the history of the game.

As that pool of players dried up, Welsh fortunes began to change. By the mid-eighties, the national side was on the wane, and in the World Cup semi-final against New Zealand in 1987 the chickens came home to roost in spectacular fashion as Wales were humiliated 49–6, a reverse that was to be repeated the following year when Wales lost 52–3 and 54–9 on their tour of New Zealand. Worse was to follow in the 1991 World Cup in their opening game at the National Stadium they lost to the unfancied Western Samoans, a blow from which the national side are only just threatening to recover.

The era from 1985 to 1995 was the most miserable in Welsh rugby history, and despite the temporary fall-out with its two top clubs, Swansea and Cardiff, there is a new realism with structures in place to ensure that national and club sides prosper.

The benefits are beginning to show, while the emergence of the European Cup has enabled the top players to widen their experience. The return of Rugby League players such as Scott Gibbs, Allan Bateman and Scott Quinnell was one of the reasons for the outstanding British Lions series victory in South Africa in 1997, and has given the national side some much needed experience and steel in the lead-up to the 1999 World Cup, which Wales is to host.

Argentina

Year founded:
1899
Year joined IRB:
1987
Colours:
Light Blue/White
No. of clubs:
270-280

Of all the touring venues outside the "Big Eight", none is more testing than Argentina. A land where they breed 'em big, Argentina is one of the great touring venues but is notoriously a country where visitors invariably leave nursing physical and psychological bruises courtesy of some uncompromising local sides.

Of the British sides to visit Argentina, few have found the Pumas (the national side's nickname) a soft touch: indeed, in four Tests from 1981–90, a resurgent England could only win two, while Scotland fared even worse, losing both tests on their 1994 tour.

Argentina is a land of striking paradoxes and contrasts. The game was started by the British community in Buenos Aires as long ago as 1886 and remains a fiercely amateur sport played by the elite of the establishment. Yet travel a few hours up country from the refined grounds of the Rosario Athletic Club or the Buenos Aires Football Club and you reach Tucuman, the land where passions run high on the terraces and the ceremonial burning of the opposition flag is de rigueur. Traditionally it has been this region that has provided Argentina with some of its toughest forwards, men like man-mountain prop-cum-hooker Federico Mendez or second row and national captain German Llanes, both of whom are now playing their rugby in England.

The game was implanted into the Argentine as far back as 1886, when Buenos Aires Football Club and Rosario Athletic Club met in a fixture that was a mix of rugby and football. The flavour of the early game in Argentina becomes clear through a glance down the names that comprised what was then called the River Plate Rugby Union: Elliot, Anderson, Thurn, Baikie, Taylor, Corry-Smith, Jacobs, Leicht, Brodie and Bellamy. Brits to a man.

Although boasting almost 300 clubs and 30,000 players, Argentina have long been out on a rugby limb. Ever isolated, Argentina's first contact with the wider rugby world was in 1910, when an England team led by J. Raphael turned up, won all six matches and left with a record of 213 points scored, 31 conceded.

Further contacts went along much the same lines, with David McMyn's stylish England touring party scoring 295 points while conceding only nine in their 1927 whitewash visit to South America, while the Junior Springboks fared much the same in 1932, as did another British side in 1936.

Eager for wider competition (there is a South American Championship which the Pumas have won each of the 14 times they have contested it since 1958), the Pumas turned their sights overseas after 1945.

The most significant tour, however, was to South Africa in 1965. Despite faring badly, the Argentineans made contact with Izak van Heerden, a coaching genius from Natal who was to accept an invitation to stay in Buenos Aires and who was to revolutionise Argentine play in the late 1960s.

If the Pumas were lucky to discover Van Heerden, they were even luckier to possess in fly-half Hugo Porta (1974–90) an exquisite talent to go with the outstanding packs that were coming off the Pampas production line after 1945.

Porta led the ultra-competitive Argentine sides of the late 1970s, and reached his zenith in South Africa when he was absolutely outstanding for the South American party which controversially toured the republic in defiance of the ban on playing there.

Indeed, the Jaguars' stunning and totally unexpected 21-12 Test victory over the Springboks in April 1982 – regarded as Porta's greatest hour – still ranks as one of the greatest matches of all time.

Although a tricky proposition on their own patch, the Pumas do not generally travel well and have under-performed in all three World Cups. In the 1995 tournament they finished at the bottom of their pool having lost all three matches. However, their most recent international fixture was against England in December 1996 at Twickenham, although they again lost, the margin was only two points, raising hopes for the future.

There is also hope for the future in that so many top Argentine players are now well-travelled. While rugby is still true-blue amateur and very middle class back in Argentina, may Pumas or potential Pumas are now playing professionally abroad.

Several – such as Serafin Dengra and Diego Dominguez – have become Italians, but others such as Mendez, Llanes, Richmond scrum-half Agustin Pichot and flanker Rolando Martin have come on in leaps and bounds through playing in Europe. Only events in the World Cup will show whether the Pumas have now picked up the habit of winning on the road as well as at home.

Canada

Year founded:
1929
Year joined IRB:
1986
Colours:
Red/White
No. of clubs:
175

Canada will always means the land of big hits and even bigger second rows. The country finally broke through into the top-ranked nations in 1991 when a win over the touring Scots was followed by an outstanding showing at the World Cup where hard-fought wins over Romania and Fiji, plus a narrow defeat by France, saw the Canucks reach the quarter-finals.

Once there, they impressed everyone in a second half of sheer guts and determination which saw them outscore and out-All Black the All Blacks. Despite losing in the rain in Lille, it was clear Canada had arrived at last, a fact confirmed by the stunning 26–24 victory over Wales at Cardiff and a defeat of France the following year.

That 1991 vintage was typical of Canadian rugby. Huge forwards such as Norm Hadley, Al Charron, Dan Jackart and Eddie Evans, feisty half-backs Chris Tynan or John Graf, and a fly-half with a howitzer boot, Gareth Rees. That is the Canadian way: tackling hard and giving little or no quarter.

Even great Canadian backs, such as Spence McTavish, Mark Wyatt or Dave Lougheed conform to a pattern that owes much to a British heritage.

The bulk of the Canadian national side, for example, come from the Vancouver Island area of British Columbia, where the style of rugby remains very forward-orientated.

Former Wallaby lock Peter FitzSimons gave a pretty good indication of the way the game is played in BC when he recalled a past tour there: "The local boys are particularly notable for the ferocity of their forward rushes. I personally got in the way of one of them near our tryline and some mornings when the light is right I can still make out the outline of stampeding footprints as they make their way across my body."

Most of the star Canadian players grew out of the competitive Vancouver circuit, which makes the Pacific Coast state of British Columbia Canada's centre of rugby excellence. Yet few people realize that, numerically, the game is not actually centred around the West Coast city.

In fact Ontario has as many players as British Columbia, while there is a liberal spread over the rest of the country. Yet for all that, there has been a gradual migration of top Canadian rugby talent to the top Vancouver clubs such as University of British Columbia Old Boys – or at least there was until the top players moved to play professionally in Europe.

The major miracle, however, is that Canada can deal with a diverse climate which means that summer rugby is the only option for large swathes of the country– or that rugby was ever established in this north American nation in the first place.

Not only do the distances make inter-provincial competition extremely difficult, but with many acres of the country hidden under ice and snow for much of the year, the country has to make do with a "split season".

While becoming increasingly cosmopolitan – especially as Vancouver looks West to the Pacific Rim for its inspiration rather than back to Europe – the game in Canada owes much to the mass emigration from Britain throughout the century.

Indeed, one of the first recorded games of rugby outside Britain – and certainly the first in North America – involved a Canadian side. After five years in the universities, the first cross-border game took place in 1872 when McGill University from Montreal took on the students of Harvard University before both institutions converted to what was to become the rival code of American Football.

Although the code already existed in Canada, the gospel was evangelically spread in the 1880s by A St G Hammersley, an Englishman who played in the first Calcutta Cup match against Scotland at Inverleith in 1871.

Almost thirty years after that first McGill match, a representative Canadian side toured Britain in 1903, winning eight of their 23 matches, losing 13 and drawing two

From there on in, the bulk of international contact was with All Blacks sides returning from Britain, the first of which was the visit of Dave Gallaher's famous "Invincibles" in 1905, but the arrival of a very strong Barbarians party in 1957 also gave the Canadian game a very strong fillip.

The game in Canada is now firmly established. Not only do the Canucks now invariably beat their near rivals the US Eagles in the annual Can-Am Challenge, but they are also prime movers behind the Pacific Rim Championship which has recently expanded to take in the three Pacific Island nations – Fiji, Tonga and Western Samoa – as well as the likes of Canada, Hong Kong and Japan.

Canada's stated aim for the new Millennium is a place in the top ten nations in world rugby – a status it is now right on the verge of achieving.

Italy

Year founded:
1928
Year joined IRB:
1987
Colours:
Blue
No. of clubs:
505

The game in Italy has come on so quickly in the last 15 years that, outside of the Five Nations, Italy are head and shoulders above the rest of Europe. This fact has been recognized by the inclusion of Italian clubs into the top tier of the recently formed European Cup and by the growing number of voices calling for the inclusion of "The Azzurri" in an expanded Five Nations tournament. There are voices that have been vindicated by recent wins over both Ireland and Scotland. If Italy have only come of age as a rugby power recently, then a look back at the history of the country should prove the recent pre-eminence is no fluke. Rugby was first introduced into the small country towns of the Po Valley and Northern Italy in the late 1920s by workers returning from France; and it is still in towns such as Rovigo and Treviso where the game is strongest, helped in

part through the proximity to France's rugby heartland. Enthusiastic approval from Mussolini's cronies in the years leading up to the Second World War also did the game no harm. Yet if it was France who planted the seed and helped nurture it for so many years, it was Italian efforts and a peculiar set of economic circumstances which saw Italian rugby develop a momentum all of its own throughout the eighties. In an effort to promote, sinking money into rugby became virtually tax-free in Italy, and the amounts sponsorship money that came into the sport were huge as companies such as Benetton sponsored club sides. The next step was an influx of foreign stars – many with Italian ancestry because this gave them the same employment rights as Italian nationals – into sides such as Benetton Treviso, and a dramatic rise in standards. Argentina was raided of top players with Italian ancestors, while stars such as Frano Botica, David Campese, John Kirwan and Michael Lynagh also plied their trade in Italy's top flight. Although the rise in standards was not immediate, with the help of top foreign coaches such as Mark Ella and Bertrand Fourcarde, Italy gradually began to develop its own stars. The pace of change is perhaps best illustrated by two meetings with New Zealand at two World Cups: in 1987 the Italians were walloped 70–6, while by 1991 they lost by as little as 31–21 in a close match. By 1994, World champions Australia hosted the Italians and received the shock of their lives when they won the first test 23–20 courtesy of a highly dubious last-minute try, and struggled to win the second 20–7. Italian rugby had arrived. Notwithstanding that some of the best players among Italy's 16,500 registered players in 266 clubs remain foreign-bred – such as Argentinean fly-half Diego Dominguez, South African-born prop Massimo Cuttitta and former Wallaby open-side Julian Gardner – Italy now have at their disposal many truly talented young players, of which utility backs Ivan Francescato and Paolo Vacarri, plus breakaway Carlo Checchinato are examples. after notifying the author.

Japan

Year founded:
1926
Year joined IRB:
1987
Colours:
Red/White
No. of clubs:
4,502

It is fitting that rugby reached Japan less than three decades after the American navy first employed "gunboat diplomacy" to break Japan's isolation from the world.

As with every other facet of Western life, the Japanese took to the sport of rugby with great alacrity, prizing the game for the way in which it enshrined the conflict and courtesy that was a basis for their own Bushido, the code of the warrior.

Although rugby was first played in Japan in Yokohama in the early 1870s when a group of British sailors staged a demonstration match, the game only took hold when introduced to Japan in 1897 by two students who had been studying in London.

After that, rugby swept through the Universities, which remain the heartland of rugby in Japan, and by the 1920s, there were nearly 1,500 rugby clubs in Japan and in excess of 60,000 players.

Despite the intervention of the Second World War, interest has remained amazingly high in Japan, even though their lack of height and weight handicaps the Japanese national sides and makes them peculiarly uncompetitive against top international sides – particularly at the lineout.

It is partly for this reason and partly because of the sheer number of opportunities to play at home, that the Japanese have tended to be a rather insular rugby community.

The first tour to Japan did not take place until 1934, when an Australian Universities side was defeated in four of its nine games and although international contacts have been maintained, Japan have generally fared badly except for a 1990 win over a Scotland XV which was the national side in all but name.

Despite the increasing threat from South Korea, Japan have managed to retain the position of Asian champions, a status that has allowed them to compete at all three World Cup finals, where their solitary success came against Zimbabwe at Belfast's cavernous Ravenhill ground in 1991. Japan have also qualified for the 1999 World Cup.

Stoically true blue amateur, the Japanese have managed to engage in an ingenious form of double-think over the past 30 years, with some of their top companies or universities employing elite players from around the world and then releasing them to play for their company or university sides (i.e. the Japanese top flight).

In this way, players such as Wallaby Ian Williams, Tongan international Sinali Latu and New Zealander Andrew McCormick have ended up playing for Japan, while a whole range of top internationals from Norm Hadley to "Smokin" Joe Stanley have plied their trade for one of the Japanese company sides.

That trend has become more prevalent recently, with the first tie of the 1999 Epson Pacific Rim Championship against Canada seeing Japan fielding five former New Zealanders, all of whom qualified on residency.

The group included former All Blacks Jamie Joseph and Graeme Bachop, while the side was captained by Andrew McCormick, son of the legendary All Black fullback, Fergie.

Rugby in Japan is different from almost anywhere else in the world. With 2,900 clubs and almost 100,000 players it is a huge constituency, while the lack of pitches means that games start at 6 a.m. on grassless grounds and finish late into the night.

Furthermore, it is a game almost devoid of violence: the legend is that when one game between two army units in 1975 got out of hand and had to be abandoned, the units were disbanded, the commanding officer sacked and every played involved banned for life. There has not been a problem with violence since!

The domestic Japanese game is run by Shiggy Konno, a lovable amateur diehard who was educated in Britain and whose favourite anecdote is how he would have become one of the last kamikaze pilots to have died during the Second World War had his plane not run out of fuel.

Namibia

Year founded:
1990
Year joined IRB:
1990
Colours:
Blue/Red/White
No. of clubs:
15

Namibia burst on to the world scene in 1991, when after beating the up-and-coming Italians, the nation from South West Africa defeated the touring Irish in two tests, beating Phil Matthews' men 15–6 in the First Test and 26–15 in the Second during a match in which the Irish were completely outclassed just two months before they started their 1991 World Cup campaign. But if the Irish were caught unawares, it was hardly surprising. Namibia had only pulled away from South Africa to emerge as an independent nation in 1989, and had before that languished in the "B" division of South Africa's Currie Cup.

Yet despite being a backwater of South Africa, Namibia were always tricky opposition. As John Robbie, the former Ireland and Lions scrum-half who made his home in South Africa, said:

"Namibia could never be fancied to beat the big sides such as Transvaal and Western Province, but nobody ever travels to Windhoek expecting anything but the hardest of matches."

Namibia play an aggressive, fast-moving game perfect for the hot and arid conditions. Big, hard forwards like Johann Barnard are complemented by hard-running backs. In this post-Apartheid era, a conscious effort to bring in black and coloured players has resulted in several black caps, of which wing Eden Meyer has been the most successful. However, the Namibian government was threatening to stop the team leaving for the 1999 World Cup finals unless it agreed to play at least six non-white players in every game.

There are now over 50 clubs and 2,000 players in a rural country where players regularly travel huge distances to games. Since independence, Namibia (whose large number of evangelical Christians among their players means on-field prayer meetings before the match, after the match and at half-time) had to make do mainly with matches against Zimbabwe, most of which they won.

The first hitch in Namibian rugby was a shock 13–12 loss to the Ivory Coast at the 1995 World Cup qualifiers. A series of missed penalties in the 16–16 draw with Morocco saw them miss a berth at the finals in South Africa.

Romania

Year founded:
1914
Year joined IRB:
1987
Colours:
Yellow/Blue/Red
No. of clubs:
74

Rugby was introduced into Romania shortly after the turn of the century and quickly became established in Bucharest, where it was enthusiastically taken up by the large number of students who had been exposed to the game in France, and by the capital's burgeoning middle class.

The first British exposure to the Romanian game came in 1954, when Welsh captain Rowe Harding took his Swansea side to Bucharest to play Locomatavia, the Romanian champions.

On his return, Harding spoke at length of a standard of game on a par with that in Britain or the Commonwealth, and a popular enthusiasm for the game unparalleled in Europe outside the Five Nations.

The following year, a Romanian side toured Britain, playing Swansea, Cardiff, Bristol and Harlequins, winning one, drawing two and losing one (to Cardiff by three points). Later that year, Romania defeated Llanelli at a tournament in Moscow, and then beat Cardiff and Harlequins in Bucharest. Only France, who played Romania before almost 100,000 fans in Bucharest, could beat the Romanians, and then only 18–15 after an epic battle.

Since then, however, Romania have been unable to deliver on their early promise. They beat Scotland (1984 & 1991) and Wales (1983 and 1988 in Cardiff), and since their first meeting in 1924, Romania have got the better of France eight times, the last time in 1990 at Auch when legendary No. 8 Hari Dumitras led Romania to a 12–6 victory.

Based around tremendous forward power, the Romanians have the long-term capability to emerge as a real force in European rugby, but Romanian rugby was severely damaged by its association with the dictator Nicolae Caeuscescu.

As one of the sports of choice for Caeuscescu, rugby was in desperate danger of being stigmatised: during the 1991 World Cup, almost 50 per cent of the Romanian squad were officially listed as "locksmiths".

The revolution that saw Romanian lock Viorel Morariu lose his life in the first day of fighting, saw many more casualties among a Romanian rugby community heavily involved with the police and military.

Tonga

Year founded:
   Not known
Year joined IRB:
   1987
Colours:
   Scarlet/White
No. of clubs:
   62

Introduced into Tonga's Tupo College and Tonga College in the 1920s by Irish missionaries, the game is naturally suited to the Tongans, who follow the pattern prevalent throughout the Pacific Islands: huge hits without regard for the life or limbs of either the tackled or tackler.

Some of this is due to the natural strength of the heavily-built Tongans, while the rest is due to a mindset that sees rugby as a game for warriors. Either way, thanks to the New Zealand missionaries who brought rugby to the Pacific, the Tongans have managed to graft no-nonsense Kiwi grit on to a physique that is perfect for the game.

The result, as with the Samoans and Fijians, has been an ability to perform above expectations: a country of 300,000 with less than 65 clubs and 2,500 players just should not be as effective as Tonga have proved themselves to be.

Even then, many of the world's greatest players in recent years – such as the Australians' pile-driving blindside flanker Willie Ofahengaue and the gigantic All Blacks' wing sensation Jonah Lomu – are Tongans by birth and would have made Tonga even more competitive were it not that the overriding aim for young Tongans remains to win an All Black cap.

Although adept at Sevens, as their creditable performances in Hong Kong over the years have proved, the 15-a-side game is more important aspect to the Tongans.

The high point of their history came in 1973, when the touring Tongans beat Australia 16–11, but they now have the chance to play Test rugby on a regular basis after their inclusion in the Pacific Rim Championship, which pits them against the Japanese and Canadians, as well as their near neighbours and natural rivals Fiji and Western Samoa.

Tonga have also qualified for the 1999 World Cup in Wales, beating Georgia home and away at the repechage stage after failing to win automatic qualification through their Pacific Pool.

United States of America

Year founded:
1975
Year joined IRB:
1987
Colours:
Red/White/Blue
No. of clubs:
920

Although a strange form of the game was played at Harvard, Yale and Princeton in the 1840s, rugby was dealt a major blow in 1862 when Yale banned it for being too violent and dangerous.

As rugby began to take hold in the top universities, it also quickly came into competition with American Football, a game based on the rules of rugby and association football as devised by William Gummere of Princeton University.

American Football's first game, between Princeton and Rutgers in 1869, was played at exactly the same time that rugby was first making headway at the American universities, although it was the home-grown code that was eventu-

ally to prevail.

Nevertheless, while rugby failed to match the tremendous growth of American Football, it too was spreading through the American University and College system. The early concentration of players was on the east coast, where the Ivy League universities of Princeton, Harvard and Yale provided the bedrock of the rugby community. Before long, however, the game had begun to be played in earnest in the west coast colleges and, to a lesser extent, in the southern state of Texas.

Although rugby in the USA has always benefited from a large number of players, the geographical difficulties of building the game in such a huge country later led to the rise of "conferences", where the East and the West operated as different blocs. Logistical considerations mean that contacts with other nations at international level have always been problematic, although regular games with Canada have been maintained, while New Zealand and Australia have often played games in California and New York on the return leg from tours to Britain. Dave Gallaher's 1905 "Invincibles" played eleven games in California, while in 1913 the All Blacks won their only full test on American soil by 51–3.

The most amazing feat in American rugby, however, remains the 17–3 defeat of a full French XV in the 1924 Olympic final in Paris by a scratch XV from Stanford University. Such was the reaction from the hostile crowd that the Americans had to literally fight their way from the pitch.

Since then, however, international success has been very limited. Indeed, the US Eagles are now struggling to keep up with the Canadians to the north and the Argentinians to the south – so much so, in fact, that they failed to make the 1995 World Cup finals. Yet all of that may be about to change.

The USA has a huge number of clubs (920) and players (95,000) and the problem has always been how to harness that latent potential. In particular, athletic young Americans have always steered towards American Football, partly because of the financial rewards on offer and partly because of the dubious reputation rugby enjoys in the US because of the over-indulgence of many players in rugby's social side.

The game's failure to have some sort of association with the Olympics has also been a problem for a country obsessed with the four-yearly event.

However, as well as the game going professional and embracing the Olympic concept – 15-a-side rugby is expected to make its Olympic debut before 2010 – new coach Jack Clark has also managed to tie up a $10 million deal with a satellite television company, which has enabled the USARFU to launch a development programme in schools, pay some of the top players and fund international tours. Now that the country has woken up to rugby, it is only a matter of time before the Americans begin to excel.

That process may well be aided by the qualification of the Eagles for the 1999 World Cup and by a $100m deal under discussion with the Fox TV network to set up six professional rugby franchises in the USA.

Were that to happen, the pull on athletic young Americans and the wall-to-wall coverage would surely give the game Stateside the biggest boost in its history.

Western Samoa

Year founded:
1924
Year joined IRB:
1988
Colours:
Royal Blue/White
No. of clubs:
125

Although the game was introduced to Samoa around the turn of the century by New Zealand missionaries, and the union incorporated as long ago as 1927, play was confined to tests against Fiji and Tonga, the first of which took place in 1924 against Fiji and featured a large tree in the middle of the pitch!

It was only in 1986, after Western Samoa toured Wales and lost the Test 32–14, that they emerged as a nation. Prior to the inaugural World Cup in 1987 they had questioned whether they even wanted a national side. Rugby has always been Samoa's national game, but top Samoans wanted to play for the All Blacks, much as Glamorgan cricketers aspire to play for England.

The 1986 tour to Wales changed all that and Western Samoa looked to New Zealand for top players with Samoan antecedents. They struck gold, finding two exceptional youngsters – Michael Jones and Peter Schuster. After missing out on the 1987 World Cup, legendary All Black wing Bryan Williams built a side to challenge for the 1991 World Cup in Europe using a mixture of home-grown backs, such as Brian Lima and Matthew Vaea, and no-nonsense New Zealand-based forwards such as Mark Birtwhistle, Pat Lam, Matt Keenan and Peter Fatialofa.

Once at the World Cup, the shuddering tackles for which they are famous put Wales off their stride in the first game at Cardiff to give the Samoans an unlikely victory. Although Argentina were also overcome, it was the nail-bitingly close finish, a 9–3 loss to future champions Australia established the Samoans. Even a 28–6 loss to Scotland could not dent the impression made by the Samoans.

After 1991 Samoa quickly proved that they were no flash in the pan. Despite a mixed showing in the Super Tens competition and the aberration of a 73–3 shellacking by Australia in 1994, wins were quickly notched up against a touring Scotland XV in 1993 and against a full Wales side in 1994 (34–9).

Further progress was made at the 1995 World Cup where they beat Italy and Argentina, but lost to England and then South Africa in the quarter-final.

Zimbabwe

Year founded:
1896
Year joined IRB:
1987
Colours:
Green/White
No. of clubs:
40

Formed in 1895, and split into northern and southern sub-unions based around Salisbury and Bulawayo in 1952, Rhodesia long had to be content with contesting the "B" division of South Africa's Currie Cup.

Indeed, the country's main claim to fame prior to independence was that it provided several players for the Springboks, the most notable of whom remain Saltie du Rand, the great Northern Transvaal forward and Bok captain who won 21 caps between 1949 and 1956, and Ray Mordt, the bull-necked wing (whose charges were such that he was once famously described by Danie Craven as "a wounded rhinoceros in the body of a man") who won 18 caps and scored 12 tries before he despaired of South Africa's sporting isolation and went to English Rugby League in 1985.

Ian McIntosh, the 1993 Springbok coach and former Natal coach, also hails from Zimbabwe, as does Adrian Garvey, the unfeasibly quick Natal prop who made his name with Zimbabwe at the 1991 World Cup but who now plays for the Springboks.

In a rugby sense, however, independence was a mixed blessing for Zimbabwe. On the one hand, it was able to play against the rest of the world and take its place in the World Cup of 1987, yet on the other it became isolated because it lost its place in the Currie Cup, and some top players formed part of the exodus to South Africa.

Although there are several top black Zimbabwean players such as Richard Tsimba, Bedford Chibima and Honeywell Nguruve, the challenge now is to be able to increase the number of black players, thereby swelling a playing population that stands at 2,000 from 40 clubs. So far, it is a challenge that the multiracial ZRFU are responding to admirably.

Like Namibia, rural Zimbabwe also suffers from the large distances players have to travel. The re-entry of South Africa into mainstream sport will help the cause of rugby in the country inordinately, although it will also mean that any truly talented players – such as Garvey – will probably be lured away to Super 12 fame and fortune, and even to a Springbok berth.

The Famous Players

Which rugby man has never passed a few moments in a bar-room arguing about the selection of the national team, moving almost inevitably on to memories of yesteryear and a comparison of past and present. "Greatest Ever XVs" are compiled and arguments ensue because judging greatness across the ages is a tricky matter, a process without hope of conclusion.

There are no guarantees that George Nepia would wipe the floor with Christian Cullen for instance, or that Wavell Wakefield would be a colossus of the game were he playing today. Differences in the laws, physique and styles of play make such comparisons virtually impossible, if hugely enjoyable. Yet every era has its greats, those players with an indefinable edge who send a tingle down the spine of opponents and spectators, and whose feats are remembered long after the games they played in have faded into history.

Some countries are blessed with more greats than others and here I am thinking primarily of New Zealand and South Africa, countries who seem capable of conjuring up sublimely gifted players almost at will. The number of greats selected for each of the original eight rugby-playing nations has therefore been adjusted so that each country is equally represented as far as possible. Although there are many players of great note to have worn the colours of an "emerging" nation, only the incomparable Hugo Porta has been included because so few have been exposed to all of the top sides over many years.

And while there are countless players from the mists of time who would seem to demand inclusion, I have tried to keep the emphasis on players from the recent past.

Rob Andrew

England
1985–97
Fly-half

When Rob Andrew came on as a replacement for the last ten minutes of England's 1997 Five Nations match against Wales, he added one more cap to his previous total of 70, and prolonged an international career that most assumed had ended in 1995. Andrew was first capped against Romania in 1985 and for much of his career was pigeonholed as a kicking fly-half. Indeed, he carried on an often intense rivalry for the England fly-half spot with Stuart Barnes, a player perceived as an apostle of the running game, throughout his England career. Rather than the cause of England's conservative ten-man game, however, the trusty Andrew was merely its cipher as he turned forward power, possession and pressure into position and points.

Already well ensconced as the England fly-half by 1988, Andrew nevertheless benefited from manager Geoff Cooke's policy of continuity in selection and developed a new confidence which saw him dominate the crucial second and third Lions' Tests in Australia in 1989 after being called out as a replacement. Late in his career, Andrew added top class goalkicking to his tactical kicking repertoire, notching up an England record of 30 points with the boot against Canada in 1994. An intelligent, gritty, consistent footballer who was exceptionally strong defensively, for some reason Andrew never quite received the recognition he deserved for a 13-year career which encompassed 396 points for England, three World Cups and two Lions tours.

After his international career ended, Andrew moved from Wasps to Newcastle, where he became a successful player-coach, winning the Allied Dunbar Premiership at his first attempt.

Gary Armstrong

Scotland
1988–
Scrum-half

Armstrong made his international debut in 1988 in the 32–13 home loss to Australia, but the JedForest scrum-half still managed to shine in his first taste of the big time. That would have come as no surprise to those who knew him best, because despite his apparently painful shyness, Armstrong has proved throughout his career to be almost obsessively focused once out on the pitch. A relatively small man, Armstrong tackles way over his weight and combines this with quick service to his backs and an uncanny ability to break around the fringes just as easily from the first-phase as from ruck or maul. Although Armstrong failed to shine on the victorious 1989 Lions tour of Australia, his gritty nature stood him in good stead when the chips were down in 1990, that famous year for Scotland. Not only was Armstrong a central figure as the Scots pushed the All Blacks to the wire on tour in New Zealand, but he, more perhaps than any other player, was the on-field catalyst for Scotland's 13–7 win in the Grand Slam decider against the Auld Enemy England at Murrayfield. Since then, however, Armstrong has been plagued by injury, missing the entire 1992 and 1995 seasons. But in 1996, following a move to Newcastle – where he quickly picked up a Premiership winners' medal – Armstrong was back in the Scotland side, and in 1999 he captained Scotland to Five Nations Championship glory after a last-minute Scott Gibbs try denied England a Grand Slam.

Jean-Pierre Bastiat

France
1969–78
No. 8

Born in Pouillon, the giant back-row forward was earmarked for greatness from his days with Dax Youth and France Under-19. Initially selected as a second row, the Dax player's speed about the field, handling ability and exceptional rugby brain convinced the selectors to move him to the back row where he was an instant success. Bastiat made his international debut as one of the five newcomers in the French team that beat Romania 14–9 in 1969. With greats such as Walter and Claude Spanghero, Elie Cester, Alain Esteve and Benoit Dauga all contesting back row places, it took Bastiat until the First Test against Argentina in 1974, to break into the national side at No. 8, with Boffelli and Skrela partnering him in the back row. International action was intermittent in 1974 and early '75, but in October 1975 the Bastiat-Rives-Skrela trio made its debut against the visiting Pumas on Argentina's first ever tour to France. The combination proved successful and was retained for the next 14 internationals, including the 1977 Grand Slam. Appointed captain against England in 1978, Bastiat retired at the end of the season, following defeat in the Grand Slam decider in Cardiff.

George Beamish

Ireland
1925–33
No. 8

Recognised as the greatest Northern Hemisphere forward of his generation, No. 8 George Beamish came from a famous rugby family, and was succeeded in the Ireland team by his younger brother Charles, who won 12 caps in the three years following George's retirement. Beamish was the driving force behind the Irish pack for almost ten years after he made his debut as a 19-year-old in the famous draw against the English at Twickenham. A mighty fellow, the Ulsterman stood at a little over 6ft. and weighed in at over 16st. at his heaviest – huge proportions for the time. No matter how heavy Beamish became, however, he remained a great ball player – he was one of the great dribblers of his age – and his inbuilt strategic sense allowed him to dominate proceedings during a period in which Irish teams were fiercely competitive. A natural leader of men, Beamish was quick, fit, immensely strong and led from the front, most notably in 1931 when he led Ireland to their first win at Cardiff Arms Park; and skippered the East Midlands to a win over Bennie Osler's famous Springbok side which was otherwise unbeaten on tour. A distinguished servant of the RAF (he later became Air Marshal Sir George Beamish), Leicester, Ireland and the British Lions, for whom he was the driving force on the 1930 tour to New Zealand, Beamish won 30 caps.

Bill Beaumont

England
1975–82
Lock

Of all the legendary figures in English rugby, none is held in more esteem or more fondly remembered than the 1980 Grand Slam captain, William Blackledge Beaumont (or "Bubble Bum" to his close friends). A stocky, four-square lock who played for Fylde and his beloved Lancashire until his retirement on medical grounds in 1982, Beaumont won a place in all English hearts when he led his country to their first clean sweep for 23 years in 1980, the highlight being a 9-8 victory over Wales courtesy of Dusty Hare's injury-time penalty in a match of sustained and savage commitment. Beaumont won the first of his 34 caps for England in 1975 and when, in 1977, Moseley lock Nigel Horton had to return from the Lions' party in New Zealand, Beaumont was flown out as a replacement. A robust lock who was safe on his own ball at the front of the line-out, Beaumont hit rucks and mauls with huge impact and was, according to team-mate Fran Cotton: "a colossal scrummager". A modest and quietly spoken man, Beaumont had the respect of all the top British players and in 1980 was made the first Englishman to captain the Lions since Doug Prentice in 1930. Although that tour to South Africa was not a successful one, it did little to diminish the reputation of big Bill Beaumont, a loveable bear who characterised all that is good in English rugby football.

Phil Bennett

Wales
1969–78
Fly-half

There could be no more daunting task in rugby than that facing Llanelli fly-half Phil Bennett when he stepped into Barry John's boots upon the great man's retirement in 1972. However, Bennett went on to win 37 caps in his decade-long career. Perversely, it is not necessarily in a Welsh shirt that Bennett is best remembered. His display for the 1973 Barbarians against New Zealand is one of the great performances of all time, while he confirmed his status as a player of genuine world class on the 1974 Lions tour to South Africa. A quiet and immensely modest man by nature, Bennett was a proud Welsh speaker who was able to convey his passion and hwyl to fellow players if required. One of the best known stories about Bennett is the pre-match talk he gave his troops before they ran out to beat England 14-9 at Cardiff Arms Park in 1977 on the way to a Triple Crown. "Look at what these f*****s have done to Wales," he ranted. "They've taken our coal, our water and our steel. What have they given us – absolutely nothing. We've been exploited, raped, controlled and punished by the English – and that's who you're playing this afternoon!"

A brilliant attacking player capable of unlocking even the tightest defences with his pace and innate genius, there were virtually no gaps in Bennett's game.

Pierre Berbizier

France
1981–91
Scrum-half

Pierre Berbizier's evolution from a talented yet undersized centre-cum-full-back into an international class scrum-half was a major factor in France's domination of European rugby in the 1980s. He played centre for the French Juniors alongside Didier Codorniou and after his transfer from his native Lanemezan to Lourdes he played full-back. Coach Jacques Fouroux convinced the talented and unusually serious youngster that he had a future at scrum-half and so, in 1981, he made his debut against Scotland, helping France win not only that match but also the Grand Slam that year. In a career that spanned 11 seasons and included 56 caps, 1987 was undoubtedly the finest year for Berbizier as he helped France to another Grand Slam and then played a leading role as they reached the final of the inaugural World Cup. As so often in French rugby, however, a personality clash effectively finished Berbizier's playing career when a public disagreement with former teammate Daniel Dubroca, then France's coach, led to him being dropped for good in 1991.

Serge Blanco

France
1980–91
Full-back

Venezuelan-born Serge Blanco is undoubtedly one of the most entertaining players the sport has ever produced. Where Gareth Edward's try for the 1973 Barbarians against New Zealand thrilled a generation of rugby enthusiasts, Blanco's last-minute winner against Australia in the 1987 World Cup semi-final sent shivers of excitement down the spines of a new generation. A running full-back of unshakeable elan and panache, Blanco delighted crowds with his sudden changes of pace and direction, and his laid-back joie de vivre. Above all, Blanco was a natural (after all, how many top athletes smoke 40 cigarettes a day and rarely bother to train?). The Biarritz player made his international debut at full-back in a controversial match against South Africa during the sporting boycott in 1980, but it was a 15–0 defeat by Romania three weeks later (the first time France had failed to score in an international since 1964) that threatened to put his career on the backburner. Blanco survived though but was shifted to the wing, from where he played all four games in the 1981 Grand Slam. After dominating the Five Nations for much of the 1980s as a full-back, collecting another Grand Slam in 1987 and winning a World Cup runners-up medal in 1987, Blanco's remaining ambitions centred around the 1991 World Cup. However, following a highly-charged quarter-final against England in Paris in which the French were knocked out, Blanco decided to hang up his boots for good after winning a total of 93 caps.

Naas Botha

South Africa
1980–92
Fly-half

One of the legends of the world game, Northern Transvaal kicking machine Naas Botha is arguably the most prolific kicker in the history of the sport. Certainly, in the thin air on the high veldt of his native South Africa, Botha's ability to punt a ball further than any other player before or since, made him the model for South African fly-halves for many years. In some ways, he was a very limited player of whom Springbok legend Rob Louw once said: "I've played with and against Botha and regard him as extremely overrated ... his poor defence and inability to get involved physically often made him the weak link in the Test matches we played together."

For all that, though, Botha's phenomenal record of success with the Blue Bulls of Northern Transvaal, for whom he contested 11 Currie Cup finals after assuming the captaincy at just 22, has ensured that he has etched himself into South African rugby's record books. And although South Africa's international isolation meant Botha never really got a chance to dominate internationally the way he did domestically, he still rewrote the Springbok record books during his 28 caps. As well as accumulating the fastest-ever century of points when he passed the 100-mark in six Tests in New Zealand in 1981, he also scored 312 points in his 28 Tests. Although a gifted running fly-half in his early years, Botha began to rely increasingly on his boot (which was so widely known that he even spent a few months with the Dallas Cowboys as a kicker). That reputation for a dull, safety-first game, added to the perception of him as a non-tackler, took some of the gloss off an otherwise outstanding career.

Gordon Brown

Scotland
1969–76
Lock

Despite the fact that his older brother Peter was capped for Scotland before him, "Broon Frae Troon", became Scotland's greatest second row. Brown was first introduced to rugby at the age of 12 and, after graduating through Marr FP, he moved onto West of Scotland, and quickly came to the attention of first the divisional and then the national selectors, making his debut on the 1969 tour to Argentina. A buoyant, larger-than-life figure, Brown was an abrasive streamroller of a lock. Unmoveable in the scrum and unfailingly sure on his own ball at the line-out, he also displayed a dynamism in the loose and an ability to look after himself when the going got tough. At 6ft. 5in. and over 17 stone, Brown had trouble maintaining peak fitness so it was hardly surprising that his greatest moments came on tour. Indeed, although Brown was a part of Carwyn James's 1971 Lions' tour to New Zealand – often referred to by experts as the best touring party ever to leave Britain – it was as a cornerstone of the 1974 Lions side that beat South Africa that he really made his name. Also selected to tour New Zealand with the 1977 Lions, Brown thus became the only forward to win selection for all three British Lions' tours in the 1970s.

Maurice Brownlie

New Zealand
1924–28
No. 8

Nicknamed the "moving tree trunk" by Wavell Wakefield, the English captain, Brownlie was the New Zealand rugby colossus of his day, a dominant figure in Hawke's Bay when that province had the first of the great Ranfurly Shield eras and the prime New Zealand forward on their tour of Britain and France in 1924–25. Although Brownlie toured Australia with the All Blacks in 1922, it wasn't until the 1924–25 tour to Britain and France that the back-rower won the first of his eight caps. So successful was that New Zealand side, they defeated Wales, Ireland, England and France (they didn't play Scotland), that they have been immortalised in rugby folklore as 'The Invincibles'. Ironically, Brownlie was said to have played his finest match on that tour when he helped defeat England 17–11 at Twickenham. Perhaps his storming performance was due in part to a desire to avenge his brother, Cyril, who, early on in the match had kicked a player on the ground and became the first player to be sent off in an international match.

Frank Bunce

New Zealand
1992–98
Centre

Even at the very top level, there are some players whose worth only becomes clear when they are not playing. Teak-tough New Zealand centre Frank Bunce is just such a man. Although he appeared to the outside world as a competent performer in every sense, Bunce's value to his teammates was absolutely immense, a point which only became clear when they All Blacks suffered their worst ever season – at one stage losing five games in a row and finishing bottom of the Tri-Nations.

As teammate Jeff Wilson said: "Frank is the sort of player who anchors every side. he was just so important to us – strong in defence and with the sort of experience that meant he took the right option every time."

It was no surprise that Bunce had that well of experience to draw on, because he was 30 before he won his first cap for the All Blacks, against the World XV in 1992. Yet in the space of seven short years, Bunce went on to claim 55 caps in a remarkable career which saw him still at the height of his powers at the age of 36. Even that was reckoned by many to be a conservative estimate – Bunce was famously vague about his age and some believe he was playing for the All Blacks into his forties.

His tally of 20 tries was an amazing feat for a player whose forte was as a destructive tackler and as a mid-field general capable of reading the complex back moves that predominate in southern hemisphere rugby. For all of that, however, Bunce may never have come to the All Blacks selectors' attention had Western Samoa not been at the 1991 World Cup finals in Europe. There the North Harbour centre was a mainstay of the side which impressed so much on their way to quarter-final defeat by Scotland. Within a year he was drafted into the All Black fold and the rest, as they say, is history!

Finlay Calder

Scotland
1986–91
Flanker

As with the Brown brothers before him and the Hastings and Milnes later on, it was sibling rivalry that provided a keen motivation for uncompromising Heriot's FP open-side Finlay Calder. Brother Jim, capped at blind-side before Finlay, was every bit as dogged and determined as his slightly smaller but quicker brother. Yet while Jim was the first Calder to come to the attention of the national selectors – and the most high profile after scoring a decisive try in Scotland's 1984 Grand Slam triumph – it was Finlay who was eventually to eclipse his brother's achievements as captain of the victorious Lions who toured Australia in 1989, and as a vital component of the side which so shocked England with their emotion-fuelled win in the Grand Slam showdown at Murrayfield in 1990. Calder's ability to use his drive, determination and innate knowledge of the game to overcome his undoubted shortcomings – in particular, he was always a bit slow for an out-and-out open-side – helped him become one of the most effective back-row operators of the modern era. If he and the other two members of the Grand Slam back row, John Jeffrey and Derek White, could not impose their own game, they certainly would make sure the opposition could not impose theirs. He retired after the 1991 World Cup having won 34 caps.

Ollie Campbell

Ireland
1976–84
Fly-half

Every era has its memories. If the late 1970s were the days when the Welsh were invincible, and 1980 was the year when Bill Beaumont's England triumphed at last, then the next three years was the era when a willowy Irish fly-half called Ollie Campbell kicked himself into the record books. And Campbell could surely kick. On his first major outing with Ireland, on the 1979 tour to Australia, Campbell established a record by amassing a half-century in just four Tests, and throughout the next five years the sight of Campbell smacking the ball between European uprights was a familiar feature of the Five Nations. Campbell's finest season came during the Triple Crown-winning season of 1982, when he underlined his dominance by scoring 52 of Ireland's 72 points. It would not be fair, however, for Campbell to be remembered simply as a remarkable goal-kicker. Not only could he also kick well from the hand, but once he established himself over long-time rival and silky-smooth runner Tony Ward in the national side, Campbell began to show a penchant and talent for running at opposition defences. A gritty defender, Campbell was also an able orchestrator of his back line, although his failure to do so adequately on either the 1980 Lions tour to South Africa (he was injured) or their 1983 tour to New Zealand means the bulk of his claim to greatness throughout his 22-cap career rests with his right boot.

David Campese

Australia
1982–96
Wing

The most exciting rugby player the world has ever seen, David Campese was quite simply the most outrageous talent ever turned out by the Australians. The boy from Queanbeyan, near Canberra, displayed an unconventional genius on the pitch that won plaudits and brickbats in equal measure. Feted for sublime moments of skill such as the overhead pass which put Tim Horan in for the winning try against the All Blacks in the 1991 World Cup semi-final, Campese was almost as famous for the aberrations which peppered his playing career, such as the unadvised and speculative pass to Greg Martin in the Third Test against the 1989 Lions which sealed Australia's fate. Yet Campese has no regrets, saying that "my first responsibility is to myself – once I get the ball, I don't care whether there are seven people or 70,000 people watching." With a strike rate of two tries every three tests, though, most Wallaby supporters are happy to take the rough with the smooth, especially as Campese holds virtually every record going, including most caps (101), and most tries in Tests (63). An outspoken critic of all things English, Campese's verbal jousts with England's Will Carling were one of the staple diets of Nineties controversy, but once he was on the pitch, there was nobody to touch the New South Wales try-scoring machine. Not searingly fast, Campese had a trademark goose-step which he used to accelerate away, but he was also an unpredictably mazy runner who was virtually impossible to police. "Sometimes even Campo's brain doesn't know where his feet are taking him," said Australian captain Nick Farr-Jones of the Wallaby genius. Campese also outraged some of the game's amateur diehards by flaunting his shamateur status – as someone with Italian antecedents, Campese spent much of his later career playing in Italy, which led him to declare that he was "rugby's first millionaire".

Will Carling

England
1988–97
Centre

England centre Will Carling shall always be remembered as the man who led English rugby's startling revival in the late 1980s. In tandem with coach Geoff Cooke, who appointed Carling to lead England when the then army captain was still a youthful 22, he quickly identified the two pillars that were to make England the dominant force in Northern Hemisphere rugby for the next seven years: consistency of selection and a willingness to play a game based around strong-mauling forwards such as Dean Richards, Wade Dooley and Mike Teague. From the time that Carling made his debut as England captain in the 28–19 win over Australia at Twickenham in 1988 until his retirement as captain in 1996, Carling led his country to an unprecedented period of success, albeit predominantly against Northern Hemisphere opposition, with Grand Slams coming in 1991, 1992 and 1995. Although notable wins were scored against the All Blacks (once), the Australians (twice) and the South Africans (twice), Carling's England were never really a match for the best of the Southern Hemisphere. A powerful runner and a gritty tackler, Carling was one of the mainstays of the English back division alongside Rob Andrew, Jeremy Guscott, Jon Webb and Rory Underwood. The most recognisable and high profile player in rugby, Carling became headline news after a dalliance with the Princess of Wales, but ended his career on a low note when money worries forced him to come out of retirement after his star-studded testimonial match at Twickenham had to be cancelled following public outrage at his public dumping of his girlfriend and mother of his son. He has since re-signed with Harlequins, agreeing a contract which will keep him at the club into the 21st century.

Christian Carrere

France
1966–1971
Flanker

Christian Carrere grew up in Morocco where he played handball. On his family's return to Tarbes, he took up rugby at the junior section of the local club before joining Toulon ,where his athleticism, rugby brain and leadership quickly made the young flanker a household name. A leader of men, fast, fearless and outrageously athletic, Carrere had it all and was clearly destined for great things. In 1966, eight days after his 18th birthday – making him the youngest player ever to represent France – Carrere made his debut against Romania alongside Claude Dourthe and Jean Salut, one of the most talented wing forwards of his generation. The next year, he became the youngest captain of France when he led his men against the visiting All Blacks, and the year after that, he captained France to its first Grand Slam after missing out by one point against Scotland the year before. Carrere, true to the God-like status he enjoyed in French rugby circles, scored the winning try in that 1968 Grand Slam decider against Wales. Carrere went on to win 28 caps until his international career was terminated in strange circumstances in 1971 when he was alleged to have requested an illegal transfer from Toulon to his first club, Tarbes.

Thomas Castaignede

France
1995–
Fly-half

The impish Thomas Castaignede is not a French back of the old school. He's no rangy runner like a Villepreux or Maso; has no siege-gun boot like a Laporte or Camberabero. Yet for all that, the little man from Toulouse with the trademark shock of peroxided hair has become one of the great French players if, for no other reason, because his instinctive love of the game and capacity to take chances is breathtaking. Castaignede first showed what he was capable of in an incredible series against New Zealand in 1995, but it was for his remarkable match-winning drop-goal against England in 1996 that he became instantly recognisable. With France fighting England for European top dog status, and their frenetic match at the Parc des Princes about to end as a 12-12 draw, the young Castaignede demanded the ball and then dropped a sublime goal to seal France's dramatic win. Cocksure and self-assured, Castaignede can play anywhere in the backs, and even looked good during France's horrible 1998-9 season which saw them finish bottom for the Five Nations for the first time since 1969. Although just 24 when the 1999 Five Nations finished, Castaignede had already won 25 caps and scored almost 200 points, including nine tries.

Ken Catchpole

Australia
1961–68
Scrum-half

The memory of outrageously gifted scrum-half Ken Catchpole is all too often obscured by the horrific manner in which his Test career was prematurely finished in the 1968 Bledisloe Cup clash in Sydney. With Australia, and Catchpole in particular, frustrating the All Blacks, the diminutive scrum-half was caught in a ruck and driven into the splits position by All Black legend Colin Meads. When play moved away Catchpole remained prone, his leg tendons and muscles so badly damaged that his career was over. After making his New South Wales debut aged 19 against a 1959 Lions side containing men such as Tony O'Reilly and Peter Jackson – and ending up on the winning side in the only Lions' defeat in Australia that tour – Catchpole made his international debut against Fiji in 1961 before being given the job of coach and captain of Australia for the tour to South Africa the next year. Catchpole's finest hour came on the 1966–67 tour to Britain, when he was in superlative form as he master-minded the 23–11 destruction of England at Twickenham, before inspiring his forwards to a 14–11 win in front of 50,000 screaming Welshmen at the Cardiff Arms Park – the first time Australia had ever beaten Wales. Catchpole won 27 caps, 13 as captain.

Bill Cerutti

Australia
1928–37
Prop

Somehow the time-honoured phrase "larger than life" doesn't quite do justice to Bill
Cerutti. The ever popular prop was more of a "huger than life" sort of man. A man who
lived life to the full, Cerutti has provided a template for generations of bad boy props;
a slugger who got his retaliation in first in the darker recesses of the forward confrontation and then drank his way to eternal friendship with his fellow combatant afterwards. An immensely popular man, Cerutti wrung every last bit out of his life and only
gave up playing when dismissed as a 43-year-old while also doubling as an Australian
selector. For all his attributes off the pitch, however, it was on the pitch where "Wild
Bill" Cerutti really did his talking. A huge man, his technique was also faultless, and
he was never bettered in the set-piece. Cerutti began his career against the All Blacks
in 1928, but it was his seven Tests against the South Africans – and the legendary prop
Boy Louw in particular – which really tested him; a test he passed when Louw insisted
on moving sides to get away from the mad Italian-Australian. Indeed, the only regret
Cerutti ever expressed about his rugby career, in which he won 21 caps, was that he
missed out on tours to Britain in 1927 (too young) and 1939 (too old).

Don Clarke

New Zealand
1956–64
Full-back

To a generation of New Zealanders, Clarke was known simply as "The Boot", the full-back who would kick the goals to win the Test matches. Introduced into Test rugby halfway through the tempestuous 1956 series against South Africa, Clarke had the sort of impact that continued throughout his 31-Test career. In his first Test, the third against the Springboks, he scored eight points in New Zealand's 17–10 victory. From then until his retirement in 1964, Clarke missed only one Test, and that was because of injury. His most celebrated kicking display was in the First Test against the Lions in Dunedin in 1959 when the Lions scored four tries, but Clarke, with his straight-line, toe-kicking style, kicked a world record six penalties to ensure an All Black win. Clarke was more than just a kicking machine, however. He was big for a full-back and strong in the tackle or on forays into the backline, and he also had uncanny ball skills honed from his many years as a first-class cricketer. Colin Meads once remarked that Clarke had "unworldly" hands and was, without doubt, the best full-back of his generation. Clarke's brother Ian was a durable prop for New Zealand on both the 1953–54 and 1963–64 tours of the UK, Ireland and France and won three caps. Three other brothers all played rugby for Waikato, the five of them appearing in one game in 1961.

Bert Cooke

New Zealand
1924–30
Centre

It was instructive that when the New Zealand Sports Hall of Fame was formed in 1990, one of the first rugby players to be inducted was Bert Cooke, even though few of the selectors had seen him play and none had the benefit of video archives to assess his undoubted brilliance. Cooke is still regarded as one of the finest backs to have played for New Zealand, though his career was brief by modern standards. On the 1924–25 Invincibles' tour of Britain and France, Cooke played in 25 of the 30 games and scored 23 tries, the highest tally. He continued that sort of form against New South Wales in 1926 but was unavailable for the All Blacks' tour of South Africa in 1928. The last of his eight appearances for New Zealand came in the Fourth Test against the British Isles in 1930, scoring two tries in the final Test. Cooke turned to Rugby League in 1932 and played for New Zealand against Great Britain and Australia. After the Invincibles' tour, Cooke was described in a booklet as the most brilliant back in the team: "As swift as a hare, as elusive as a shadow, strikes like lightning, flashes with brilliancy, Cooke is the shining star of the side."

Fran Cotton

England
1971–81
Prop

Born and raised in Wigan, the heart of Rugby League country, Cotton's father and brother were noted professionals with Warrington, and Cotton's boyhood heroes were Rugby League legends Billy Boston and Bev Risman. Yet Cotton become a major force in Union as a player with England and the Lions, and as a businessman (he owned Cotton Traders, who at one stage supplied kit to half of the world's top national sides). He was also chosen to be the 1997 manager of the British Lions' tour to South Africa. At 6ft. 2in. and over 17stones, he had all the raw materials for a prop, but it was his innate strength, inner drive and technical appreciation that helped him accumulate 31 caps. One of the fittest players of his generation, Cotton was also one of the most versatile and because of his technical acumen became as proficient on the tight-head as he was on his more accustomed loose-head. Cotton's top-level career began as a 23-year-old when he led the North to a famous victory over the 1972 All Blacks at Otley – the first time an English province had beaten the All Blacks. Over the next decade, until his retirement in 1981 after an on-field heart attack, Cotton was a central figure in British rugby. The first choice Lions tight-head in South Africa in 1974, Cotton also played three of the four Tests in New Zealand in 1977 as a loose-head, and returned to South Africa with the 1980 Lions' tour.

Benoit Dauga

France
1964–72
No. 8

Nicknamed the "Big Brother" and once described by Jean Prat as the best forward produced by French rugby, Benoit Dauga governed the aerial battles of the 1960s and early 1970s with an iron hand, both figuratively and literally. The rugby writers had run out of metaphors to describe the 6ft. 5in. colossus: the strongest, most gifted, fastest, most astute, hardest, most perceptive, meanest. All were true. A uniquely talented player, and one that the peerless Mervyn Davies described as the best No. 8 he ever played against, the Mont de Marsan utility forward won the first of his 63 caps against Scotland in 1964. Despite losing 10–0 in Edinburgh, Dauga retained his position in the side right through until the 1968 Grand Slam. After that, however, while still in the side, the French hit a mini-trough, a 2–0 series defeat against the All Blacks starting an undreamt-of run of seven consecutive losses. Dauga became captain of France in the Second Test in South Africa in 1971 and skippered his country in six consecutive Tests before his last international selection, against Wales in Cardiff in 1972, brought to an end one of the most remarkable careers in international rugby. Having played in every position in the second row and back row, Dauga would have gone on to win more caps had it not been for a running row with incoming captain and No. 8, Walter Spanghero, who immediately dispensed with Dauga's services.

Gerald Davies

Wales
1966–78
Wing

Gerald Davies was unquestionably the finest Welsh wing of the modern era, a player of such style, verve and potency that he was one of the mainstays of the outstanding Welsh sides of the 1970s. Along with Gareth Edwards, Phil Bennett, J.J. Williams and J.P.R. Williams, Davies formed the backbone of one of the most outstanding back divisions ever seen as the men in red dominated the British rugby scene in the 1970s. Blessed with outstanding pace and a lethal side-step, Davies began international life as a centre before switching to wing during the 1969 tour of New Zealand. The effect was mesmerising. Given extra space and time, Davies gave full rein to his creativity and sheer speed becoming one of the most effective and feared finishers in world rugby. By the time he retired in 1978, he had scored 20 tries in 46 internationals. At the his peak, with the British Lions in 1971, Davies destroyed New Zealand defences, and was one of the most impressive components of the best back line ever to leave Britain. Had he not declined to tour in 1974 or '77, he would undoubtedly have become the Lions' most capped winger. A quiet, thoughtful academic, Davies is now a rugby correspondent for *The Times*.

Jonathan Davies

Wales
1985–97
Fly-half

A gifted young fly-half in the classic Welsh mould, Jonathan Davies came into Welsh rugby just as it began to enter a prolonged period of darkness. With expectations still high from the successes of the 1970s and early 1980s, results became increasingly hard to fashion out. Third place in the 1987 World Cup erroneously convinced many in Wales that the game was in a healthy state. A semi-final 49–6 thrashing by the eventual winners New Zealand was repeated the following year when the touring Welsh were humiliated 52–3 and 54–9 in a two-Test whitewash. With constant carping and finger-pointing by top administrators, Davies became increasingly disillusioned and left for Widnes Rugby League club at the end of 1988. Once in League, Davies prospered. His creativity, good hands, pace and wonderfully accurate kicking stood him in good stead for both Widnes and Great Britain, and once he bulked up to become a better defender he became one of League's greats. With the move to professionalism in 1995, Davies was lured back to Cardiff RFC, seven years after his switch. Despite his advanced age of 33, he won three more caps and played against England in 1997 in the last major international to be staged at Cardiff Arm's Park.

Mervyn Davies

Wales
1969–76
No. 8

Although he later became quite possibly the best No. 8 Britain has ever produced, Mervyn Davies started his career in inauspicious circumstances as a 22-year-old when he arrived at London Welsh unheralded and with no rugby pedigree. Quality will out, however, and within three months, "Merv the Swerve" was in the Wales side which defeated Scotland 17–3 at Murrayfield. He went on to win 38 caps for Wales - captaining them to a Grand Slam in 1976 - and eight for the Lions, before a brain haemorrhage in a 1976 Schweppes Cup semi-final tie put him out of rugby forever and almost killed him. By modern standards Davies' 6ft. 4in. physique wasn't awe-inspiring, but his strength and athleticism compensated for his lack of bulk. Moreover, Davies was a Great precisely because he allied his incredible physical talents with an almost unprecedented degree of foresight which allowed him to overcome virtually the only flaw in his make-up, a lack of really top gear acceleration.As effective in attack as in defence, Davies added an extra dimension to the line-out play of both Wales and the British Lions. In fact, both New Zealand's Colin Meads and South Africa's Morné du Plessis identified Davies' contribution at the back of the line-out as one of the biggest single reasons why the Lions' backs received such a limitless amount of quality ball from the set-piece in 1971 and 1974.

Henry Oswald de Villiers

South Africa
1967–70
Full-back

Henry Oswald de Villiers, or "HO" to his hordes of admirers, would probably have established himself as the greatest in a long line of marvellous Springbok full-backs but for a serious knee injury that ended his career aged 25. Even despite the setback, though, the dark-haired De Villiers did enough in 14 Tests to vie for that accolade, scoring tries that were unbelievable for stunning strength and vision from deep-lying defence. He was brave and immovable under the high ball and a fearless tackler. An added goalkicking gift made him the complete footballer. Rugby skills came easily to this product of famous Dale College in King Williams Town, a conveyor belt for many fine South African sportsmen. De Villiers crowned his Test debut against the French in 1967 with a sparkling display in a 26–3 victory. He was one of seven new Springbok caps that day and one of the nucleus of the team which was to carry South Africa into an exciting era in the 1970s prior to Apartheid-induced world sports isolation. Blessed with a desire to attack from anywhere, De Villiers never neglected his defensive work and some of his finger tip catches under fierce pressure during the UK tour of 1969–70 made him the individual star. Then came the knee calamity and it was all over by 25.

Wade Dooley

England
1985–93
Lock

When the England squad for the 1985 season was announced at a press conference, the first question from the assorted journalists present was "Who is Wade Dooley?" Eight years and 55 caps later on, however, there was no mistaking the man who had been plucked from the obscurity of fourth division rugby with lowly Preston Grasshoppers. Dooley, a 6ft 8in policeman weighing in at almost 19 stone, went on to form the heart of the outstanding England pack which won back-to-back Grand Slams and made it to the 1991 World Cup final. An ultra-physical player, Dooley was a fearsomely strong man who was tailor-made for the muscular mauling game that became England's trademark in the late Eighties and early Nineties. Although he had a variety of second row partners in his early Tests, after 1988 he formed a very durable partnership with another English great and fellow copper Paul Ackford, until "Ackers" retired after the 1991 World Cup. Dooley, who jumped at No.4 in the lineout, had many great moments, but he will probably be best remembered for the 1989 Lions tour to Australia. With the Wallabies winning the First Test, England decided to try to physically overwhelm the Aussies, and in two gruelling Tests, Dooley the enforcer led a frightening and controversially violent forward effort which saw the Lions literally batter the series from the Wallabies' grasp. Dooley's career, however, ended in unfortunate circumstances when, on the 1993 Lions tour to New Zealand, he had to return home briefly for a family funeral only to then be told that meant he had disqualified himself from any further involvement in the tour.

Frik du Preez

South Africa
1960–71
Lock

Big Frik du Preez was a larger than life figure whose legend looms large among South Africa's rugby followers even now. The second row amassed 38 Test appearances in his international career, beating the 1968 Lions almost single-handedly and setting a record for appearances since equalled only by flanker Jan Ellis. His total of six overseas tours, which started in 1961 and stretched for the next twelve seasons, is also a record and he wore the famous jersey an unprecedented 87 times. Yet while Du Preez set impressive statistics and records, they never matched the impressiveness of the man himself. One of the most cherished images in Springbok rugby is of Du Preez bursting through, ball in one hand, his giant strides carrying his powerful frame at a deceptively fast pace, a mop of black hair flopping in the wind. His greatness has been established beyond all doubt, though a few detractors would point to a lazy streak in his make-up that hinted at his marvellous sense of humour and relaxed attitude to life off the pitch. It is frightening to imagine what heights he might have scaled had he possessed the dour uncompromising attitude to rugby of some of the other giants of the game. He eventually sought fulfilment in a farming life in the semi-desert of the Kalahari.

David Duckham

England
1969–76
Wing

Every country needs its heroes, and in wing David Duckham, 1970s England found a role model for a new generation. A player of such overwhelming flair and on-field charisma, Duckham was even able to overcome a chronic shortage of ball to emerge as arguably the best player ever to pull on an England shirt. At a time when England were at their lowest ebb, even the opposition feared the Coventry express. "David's approach to rugby was almost Welsh," wrote Welsh legend Gareth Edwards, "and his skills were certainly recognised on our side of Offa's Dyke. Big, aggressive and with a chilling sidestep, he was one of the great attacking wings of mine or any other day." Duckham may have won 36 caps for England, but his greatest hours did not come in either a Coventry or an England shirt. No, it was in the shirts of the British Lions and the Barbarians which Duckham will remain in the immortal memory. In the victorious 1971 Lions tour to New Zealand – a tour which represented the high point of British backs play – Duckham arguably outshone even luminaries such as Gareth Edwards, Mike Gibson, JPR Williams and Gerald Davies. His six tries against Buller on that tour are still a Lions record. Arguably his greatest single match, though, was that famous 1973 match between the All Blacks and the Barbarians, the 1971 Lions in all but name. During that game, Duckham was uncontrollable, even for the great Bryan Williams. It was completely fitting that it was Duckham who, with the score at 17-11, jinked his way past five defenders before off-loading the ball to JPR Williams for the final score.

Willie Duggan

Ireland
1975–84
No. 8

Rarely can one man have spawned more anecdotes than the back-rower from Kilkenny, Willie Duggan. Every contemporary to have laced up boots in the Emerald Isle seems to have a stock of stories about this legend-in-his-lifetime, a man whose off-field feats appear as famous as those on it. That is some going, for Duggan was one of the most fearless, passionate players ever to play for Ireland. From the time that he pulled on the Ireland shirt in the famous win over England in 1975, Duggan careered around world rugby fields with a wanton abandon that made him one of the least popular opponents of all time. A large man with famously huge hands – his nickname was "spade hands" – Duggan was noted for his storming runs and committed tackling. A useful line-out forward, Duggan had a quick temper is remembered for his role in a punch-up between the Welsh and Irish packs in 1977 that saw both him and Geoff Wheel dismissed. In tandem with the lightning-quick Fergus Slattery and the more cerebral talents of the great blind-side John O'Driscoll, Duggan completed an extremely effective back-row trio. In 41 caps for Ireland and four for the 1977 Lions in New Zealand, the "Blackrock bomber" established himself as the epitome of the Irish back-rower. As whole-hearted as Bill McKay, Duggan was also as skillful as Jimmy Farrell. Almost as famously, he was also notoriously genial and popular when the after-match festivities began.

John Eales

Australia
1991–
Lock

One of the most complete second-rowers of all time, John Eales burst onto the international scene in 1991 and later that year had a World Cup winner's medal to show for his efforts. Since then, despite a break for a shoulder injury in 1993, Eales has continued to develop into the best lock in the world. At 6ft. 7in., he is not particularly tall for an international level lock, yet combines sublime timing with an impressive standing jump to dominate taller opponents at the line-out – England's Martin Bayfield, for instance, was completely outplayed when the two first met in 1991 despite the fact that Bayfield stands 6ft. 10in. tall, while Eales counts New Zealand's Ian Jones his trickiest opponent. Hugely mobile in the loose, Eales is also a genuinely talented footballer who has taken to acting as a stand-in place-kicker at Test level with a remarkable degree of accuracy (he boasted a 100 per cent success rate during the 1991 World Cup, making two conversions from the touchline). Now firmly in place as the Wallaby captain, Eales will be only 29 at the 1999 World Cup and when World Cup 2003 comes around don't bet against the Queensland lock being present.

Gareth Edwards

Wales
1967–78
Scrum-half

In his 53 caps for Wales over 12 years and ten Lions caps over three tours, Edwards proved himself the best scrum-half ever to play in the northern hemisphere and only Australian Ken Catchpole has ever been referred to in the same breath as Edwards by contemporaries. An accomplished gymnast and sprinter, Edwards had great upper body strength and pace to burn off a standing start, as he showed when scoring that memorable try for the Barbarians against the 1973 All Blacks. A Welsh cap at 19, a Lion and captain of Wales at the tender age of 20, by the time Edwards came of age he had already established himself as a world-class No. 9, even if many of his Lions team-mates on the 1968 tour of South Africa considered him "selfish and inclined to keep the good ball for himself" in the words of South African writer Chris Greyvenstein. Yet Edwards was nothing if not eager to learn and soon became the complete player, whether in the colours of Cardiff, the Lions or Wales. In 1971 he was outstanding in New Zealand alongside Barry John, while in 1974 he was at his imperious best in South Africa partnering Phil Bennett. Edwards combined remarkable strength with incredible physical resilience – he won all 53 of his Welsh caps without missing a game. Robust in defence, Edwards had superb balance, remarkable hands and was a master of the grubber kick. His tally of 20 tries has only been bettered by Ieuan Evans.

Mark Ella

Australia
1980–84
Fly-half

It is perhaps one of rugby's greatest tragedies that Mark Ella retired aged just 25 after winning only 25 caps. Probably the most naturally gifted fly-half the game has ever seen, Ella had just reached the peak of his powers, leading the hugely entertaining Wallaby side of 1984 on an unbeaten Grand Slam tour of Britain. Had Ella carried on playing, he may well have become the most accomplished player the game has ever seen, and his decision to retire prematurely caused widespread consternation through-out the rugby world. One of three Aboriginal brothers to play for the Wallabies, Mark Ella was discovered by Randwick coach Bob Dwyer – now in charge at Leicester – and drafted into the first grade – along with his twin Glen and younger brother Gary – at just 17. Using looping moves they had perfected as schoolboys, the three brothers revolutionised back play at the top Sydney club, introducing the flat back line that has since been adopted by the Wallabies as something akin to a national style. Standing unusually close to the scrum-half and moving the ball quickly, Ella developed a style of playing virtually on the gain line that brought results at Test level as spectacular as when he first used them in the Under-15s.

Jan Ellis

South Africa
1965–76
Flanker

Raised in the vast emptiness of South West Africa (now Namibia), flame-haired flanker Jan Ellis was a highly individualistic loner who preferred to sit with a book or write a letter home while on tour. An aloof man who alienated many in South West Africa for his perceived brusque manner, the social side of rugby, after-match functions and partying, were not for the man they called "Red Devil". A rangy flanker best remembered for his surprisingly fast loping run, ball held arrogantly in one hand, mowing a path through would-be-tacklers, Ellis is regarded as one of the best flankers ever to play for South Africa. Ellis played hard, and he played to win: to a man as focused as he was, everything except winning was superfluous. Ellis was lucky in that throughout his 12 straight years as a Springbok regular after his debut against the All Blacks in 1965, his two usual back-row partners shared his playing philosophy, making the loose forward trio of Ellis, Piet Greyling and Tommy Bedford an outstanding one. Ellis worked in marvellous tandem in 24 Tests with Greyling on the blindside, twelve of those with Bedford at No. 8 and won 38 Test caps.

Jannie Engelbrecht

South Africa
1960–69
Wing

The "Prince of Wings", in full flight Jannie Engelbrecht was a truly awesome sight to behold, running with the ball tucked under his right arm with his head tilted at a slight angle, a high-knee action eating up the ground. As if mesmerising would-be tacklers, the pacy swerve took him to the bulk of his eight tries in 33 Tests, although his detractors always suggested this was too sparse a return for a player of his undoubted pedigree. Seldom, however, did they pay more than lip service to the brilliant corner-flagging cover defence that prevented as many tries as he scored. Engelbrecht played all his rugby at Stellenbosch, in the country's hotbed of backline play, where he came under the wing of his lifelong mentor, Dr Danie Craven. His record of 33 Tests for a wing has only recently been equalled by James Small. After being a permanent right wing fixture, unless injured, Engelbrecht played his last Test against the touring Australians in 1969 and missed the demonstration-marred tour to Britain later that year. He turned successfully to administration and is currently president of the Stellenbosch club. His sojourn as a successful Springbok team manager, however, ended in acrimony after a messy public dispute with SARFU president Dr Louis Luyt.

Eric Evans

England
1948–58
Hooker

Eric Evans was a late starter who won his first cap as a hooker against Australia in 1948 at the age of 26, but failed to impress and only managed to regain his place in the England starting line-up – this time back in his proper position of hooker – for a solitary Test against Wales in 1950, before becoming a fixture from 1951 until his retirement in 1958. As a player, Evans was extremely fit and his shock of blond hair was a regular feature of three-quarter movements and the early stages of any break-down. Yet he was also one of the finest hookers England have ever possessed, particularly in the days when suppleness and flexibility were vital as the props went nose to ground as often as possible. An exuberant man both on and off the pitch, Evan's leadership style was to expect every man to follow his example or expect a tongue-lashing if they didn't. It was not always popular, but it was effective: as early as 1948 Evans led Lancashire to a 5–0 victory in the County Championship final, while his record as England captain in 13 of his 30 internationals was outstanding and included a Grand Slam in 1957.

Ieuan Evans

Wales
1987–1999
Wing

It is a measure of the class of Llanelli, Bath, Wales and British Lions wing Ieuan Evans that he has been able to prove his undoubted quality despite his international career coinciding with the worst period Wales have ever had to endure. Indeed, Evans' career started in 1987, the year when a crushing World Cup defeat at the hands of the All Blacks brought Wales's decline into stark relief, and it continued through horror spots such as the 1988 whitewash tour to New Zealand, the 1991 drubbings in Australia and the World Cups of 1991 and 1995. Worse still, injuries – particularly one to his shoulder – hampered his progress, yet Evans was one of Wales's most devoted servants, its longest-serving captain and most capped player. Modest and ever pleasant, Evans was as constant off the pitch as he was on it. A solid defender, the Welsh wing was outstandingly quick, and possessed a shimmy that helped him score a record 32 tries in his 71-Test career, another Welsh record. Evans has a hat-trick of Lion's tours, having toured Australia in 1989, New Zealand four years later and South Africa in 1997. He finished his career with a two-season stint at Bath before announcing his retirement in 1999.

Nick Farr-Jones

Australia
1984–93
Scrum-half

During the decade between his first and last caps, Sydney University scrum-half Nick Farr-Jones dominated the world of scrum-halves. Australia's most capped scrum-half with 63 caps, Farr-Jones was also a natural leader, who took a young Wallaby side to the World Cup final in 1991 where they beat hosts England. By the time Farr-Jones arrived at Sydney University as a law student, it was obvious that he had all the attributes needed by the modern scrum-half. Tall and exceptionally strong, Farr-Jones played in attack and defence like an extra back-row forward. Alan Jones recognised Farr-Jones's potential and drafted him into the national squad in 1984, at the age of 22. He was impressive on that year's Grand Slam tour of Britain; his quick brain, slick service and ability to take the pressure off Mark Ella were major contributors to the whitewash, and he remained a fixture in the Wallaby side until his retirement in 1993. Controversially made captain in 1988, Farr-Jones formed an inspirational management team off the pitch, alongside coach Bob Dwyer, and he played a major part in the radical reshaping of the Wallaby pack following the physical battering and series defeat inflicted by the all-conquering Lions in 1989.

Sean Fitzpatrick

New Zealand
1986–1997
Hooker

New Zealand rugby's most durable forward who played in a record 92 Tests. But more significant than the statistics was his competitiveness, a dedication to fitness and his technical skills that kept younger challengers and opponents at bay. Fitzpatrick, the son of 1953–54 All Black Brian Fitzpatrick, had a fortuitous All Black debut in 1986. Most of the leading All Blacks had been suspended for their rebel tour to South Africa and the original choice for the Test against France was injured, so he was called in as a late replacement. It was the beginning of an extraordinary career and there was more luck for Fitzpatrick, when the All Blacks' World Cup captain in 1987, hooker Andy Dalton, was injured and Fitzpatrick went from the prospect of a Cup as understudy to playing in every match. Fitzpatrick took over the captaincy of New Zealand in 1992 and, despite leading them to the 1995 World Cup final, considered the effort a failure such is his desire to be a winner. Driven by an ambition to become the first New Zealander to win a Test series in South Africa, Fitzpatrick stayed on as captain for the 1996 season and achieved his dream in August of that year when the All Blacks took the series 2–1. He led them unbeaten through 12 Tests in 1997 before reitiring because of a knee injury.

Grant Fox

New Zealand
1985–93
Fly-half

Grant Fox was a scoring machine for New Zealand in his 46 Tests in the 1980s and 1990s and the All Blacks many times had reason to be grateful for his presence. For all the goalkicking records Fox holds it would be a mistake to dismiss him as just a goal-kicker, however gifted. He was a perfectionist and a tactician, advising and cajoling the backs, planning moves and then ensuring their accurate execution; and he was seen as the brains of the All Black backline. New Zealand coaches found they could not do without him. John Hart, when he first coached the All Blacks on a tour of Japan in 1987, dropped Fox and Laurie Mains, when he took over in 1992, also tried other fly-halves, but Fox proved to be as indispensable as it's possible for a rugby player to be. Fox made his All Black debut on the 1985 Argentina tour and became the regular fly-half in the 1987 World Cup, remaining one of the dominant figures for the All Blacks.

Jean Gachassin

France
1961–69
Utility back

Jean Gachassin was one of the most gifted and versatile three-quarters of the 1960s. He made his international debut at the age of 20 against Scotland and retired somewhat prematurely at the age of 28 after winning 32 caps. His devastating pace and brisk side-step, combined with a high level of skill and unusual intuition, made him one of France's trump cards during this decade. However, it took him a while to establish his credentials in the highly competitive French set-up, and he never fully established himself in any one position, playing at wing as well as fly-half, centre and full-back in his eight-year international career. Gachassin started his club career with Vichy, and after a spell with Bagnerre, he joined Lourdes with whom he won the French Championship in 1968. Throughout his playing days, Gachassin was known as "Peter Pan", a reference to his diminutive physique; he stood 5ft. 4in. tall and tipped the scales at a modest 10stone. Yet what he lacked in physical presence he more than made up for in courage. On retirement he became coach of the Stade de Bagneres club.

John Gainsford

South Africa
1960–67
Centre

Call it the killer instinct, call it what you will: John Gainsford had that controlled fury and deep burning desire to win, and carried them into big matches like a boxing champion stepping into the ring. Those qualities turned the big thrusting centre into the best in the world in his heyday, which was to stretch for seven years from his debut in 1960 against Scotland. He notched up eight scorching tries, two of them in the miracle of Christchurch in 1965 when Gainsford helped turn a 16–5 half-time deficit into an unlikely 19–16 South African win over the All Blacks, until the selectors decided he had lost his cutting edge and dropped him for the final Test of the winning series against the French in 1967. After playing 71 matches for South Africa, scoring 31 tries, 17 of those on the tour of Britain and France in 1960–61, the heavily-built 6ft. 1in. wing felt embittered about being discarded mid-series and never played for the Springboks again. He continued to captain Western Province, and later went on to be a successful wine producer on the Cape.

Tim Gavin

Australia
1988–
No. 8

Tim Gavin will long be remembered as one of the most effective Wallaby forwards of the modern era, a workhorse No. 8 who learned his trade the hard way, playing lock in his early internationals. Although already a Wallaby by the time the 1989 Lions came to town, Gavin was yet another player to benefit from the series defeat which effectively marked the end of rival back rower Steve Tuynman's Test career. After that Gavin was a regular fixture with both New South Wales and Australia, becoming as much of a talisman for the Wallabies as Dean Richards became for England. In fact, Gavin rates his much-vaunted performance in the 40–15 defeat of England shortly before the 1991 World Cup as his greatest moment, because it saw him eclipse the great Englishman who had been the hammer of the Wallabies two years earlier while wearing a Lions shirt. The accolades for that game – and indeed for his monumental effort against the Springboks in 1993 – are perhaps all the more significant because Gavin missed out on a World Cup winners medal through injury. At 6ft. 5in., Gavin was always a threat at the line-out, while his huge upper-body strength always made him a presence at breakdown.

Danie Gerber

South Africa
1980–92
Centre

From the time he made an impression on Bill Beaumont's 1980 touring British Lions as a 22-year-old Junior Springbok, Daniel Mattheus Gerber, better known to the rugby world simply as Danie, was destined to make his mark. After 24 Tests and a South African record 19 tries, Gerber was regarded as one of the greatest backs of the modern era, scoring tries that few others could emulate. His blistering speed, allied to huge piston-like thighs, made him hard to tackle and there were many memorable efforts among his tally for the Springboks. He scored a hat-trick of tries in the 35–9 Second Test win over John Scott's England side at Ellis Park in 1984, exhibiting the startling quickness off the mark, magnificent co-ordination and ability to maintain speed over a distance which made him such a feared opponent. Gerber's Test career was marked by his partnerships in midfield with two brothers, Willie and Michael du Plessis. He played in eight Tests with the former and six with youngest brother Michael. A natural athlete, Gerber turned, on his rugby retirement, to working as a sports organiser and coach among the disadvantaged peoples of Port Elizabeth and retains his keen interest in all sports.

Mike Gibson

Ireland
1964–79
Centre

Although Barry John is often thought of today as the most feted back ever to issue from the British Isles, many of his contemporaries are equally adamant that the greatest British three-quarter of the post-war years was Ireland's Mike Gibson. He possessed fierce mental and physical resilience, allied to a brilliant playmaking mind. A rather singular man and strict teetotaller who has kept a determinedly low profile since retiring, Gibson was noted for his rigorous, structured approach to fitness, and for intensive pre-match planning in an era before this became the norm. A model of consistency throughout his 69 caps for Ireland and 12 for the Lions over five tours between 1966 and '77, Gibson actually started his Test career at fly-half in the famous 18–5 win at Twickenham in 1964. The qualities that made the Ulsterman a fine fly-half made him a great centre, particularly outside Barry John on the 1971 Lions tour to New Zealand, when he was at his peak. Strong in the tackle and quick to spot a gap, it was Gibson's mindset that really gave him the edge. His perception always put him in the right place at the right time, while his quick hands and wonderful passing frustrated opponents and gave team-mates valuable time and space in which to work. Gibson always looked good himself, but one of his great skills was to make every player around him look good too.

Sid Going

New Zealand
1967–77
Scrum-half

Going was regarded as an unorthodox player and a great improviser, who often played as if he was a one-man tactical band. He was a master of the dummy, feint and slight of hand and, at times, passing the ball to his fly-half seemed the option of last resort. He was also a goalkicker during his 29-Test-career, often used when the kicks required were of prodigious length. Much of the jiggery-pokery that was a hallmark of Going's game was developed at his club, Mid-Northern, and his province, North Auckland, with brothers Brian, who was a fly-half, and Ken, an All Black full-back on the centenary tour of Ireland in 1974. The trio developed a series of cut-outs and scissors, double-scissors and triple-scissors that mesmerised opponents and often confounded their team-mates as well. Going's early All Black career was as understudy to Chris Laidlaw and his Test appearances came only when Laidlaw was either unavailable through exams or injured. But by 1971 Going was the incumbent No.8.

Jeremy Guscott

England
1989–
Centre

Jeremy Guscott has dominated English three-quarter play since his debut for England and the Lions in 1989 and remains indisputably the finest English centre of the modern era. Indeed, there are virtually no weaknesses in Guscott's game; he is so quick that Jack Rowell was able to play him on the wing to great effect in 1997, while he remains one of the most technically outstanding tacklers in the game, a fact he demonstrated most effectively against Canterbury in 1993 when a performance of immense grit single-handedly secured a much-needed win for the beleaguered Lions. In addition, his exceptional acceleration mark him out as the one English back consistently able to prise open tight drift defences from first phase possession, a useful skill in a period dominated by forward-orientated tactics. Guscott's skills were also complementary to those of his long-term England centre partner Will Carling. Carling provided the brawn, Guscott provided the pace and the tries. Despite being a proven try-scorer, Guscott's talents have remained largely under-utilised by England in an age when muscle and the direct route were often the favoured approach. However, Guscott has been one of the major influences in Bath's dominance of English league rugby in the 1990s, that has seen the West Country club win five league titles and five Pilkington Cups. Capped eight times by the Lions over three tours, Guscott was in great form during the 1998-9 season, scoring England's only try in their superb win over South Africa at Twickenham.

Andy Haden

New Zealand
1977–85
Lock

One of the ironies of Haden's All Black career is that he is remembered as much for events off the field as for those on it, and even the match memories include the controversial. Haden served an apprenticeship on the All Blacks' tour of the UK, Ireland and France in 1972–73 but was not picked for the All Blacks again until 1976, finally making his Test debut against Phil Bennett's Lions in 1977. He went on to win a total of 41 caps before his retirement in 1985. Often controversial and always colourful, Haden was one of the pioneers among New Zealanders playing the off-season overseas, initially in France, and then in Italy and Britain. For a time, he played on Saturdays for Harlequins in Britain and on Sundays for a club in Italy, actions which did not endear him to officialdom. His alleged dive in an effort to earn the All Blacks a last-minute penalty against Wales in 1978 ensured him an enduring notoriety in Britain. Though the All Blacks won the match 13–12 because of a last-minute penalty, English referee Roger Quittenton always maintained it was against Welsh lock Geoff Wheel who was marking Frank Oliver, and had nothing to do with Haden's theatrics. Haden's amateur status was often questioned and once investigated by the NZRFU, but in an ironic twist, the poacher became the gamekeeper in the late 1980s when Haden was appointed the NZRFU's first marketing agent.

Gavin Hastings

Scotland
1986–95
Full-back

Probably the greatest Scottish player of this or any other generation, Gavin Hastings has a rugby CV that is second to none in world rugby. After making his debut against France in 1986 along with brother Scott, he went on to win 61 caps in a career that saw him become a Grand Slammer with Scotland in 1990, a Lion in 1989 and captain of the Lions in New Zealand in 1993, and until he was recently overtaken by Neil Jenkins, the highest international points-scorer in the history of the British Isles with a remarkable tally of 733 points. Yet even that doesn't tell the full story of a career that was successful from day one. Hastings captained the first Scotland Schoolboys side to win on English soil; he captained the victorious Cambridge University side in 1985; he won the Gallaher Shield in his year off with Auckland University; and he was captain of the first Scotland side to win at the Parc des Princes. For all that, though, Hastings achieved his unparalleled success while still retaining the laid-back manner which helped put teammates at ease. A born leader, he nevertheless inspired others through words not deeds. As Ian McGeechan said of him: "Gavin is a big man in every sense. His greatest asset was his ability to engender confidence in those around him and to lead by example when the opposition had to be taken on. In New Zealand they considered him simply the best fullback in the world." An immensely strong man with a physically imposing 6ft 2in frame, Hastings was as assured in attack as he was in defence. Despite not possessing blistering pace, there was not a weakness in Hastings' game.

Scott Hastings

Scotland
1986–97
Centre

Scott Hastings is remembered by those present when he first entered the Scottish squad set-up in 1986 as one of the most cocksure personalities they had ever met. And while that wild joie de vivre and natural ebullience has sometimes since overspilled off the pitch, on it they have been a positive boon. In his early days Scott Hastings was most notable for his searing pace, straight-running and ability to break the gain line virtually every time he received the ball. It was not long, however, before his bullocking runs from centre were complemented by the stonewall defensive qualities which were to remain the salient quality in his game as his pace faded later on. Hastings's finest moments came early on during his career specifically while on tour with the Lions in 1989, if there is one moment for which he will long be remembered it was during the 1990 Grand Slam decider, the proudest day in Scottish rugby history. English winger Rory Underwood had scythed through the Scottish defence when Hastings managed to drag him down short of the line when a try had seemed inevitable. Scott won his 62nd cap on tour against New Zealand in June 1996, thereby overtaking brother Gavin's record of 61 appearances and becoming Scotland's most capped player. with 65 caps

Tim Horan

Australia
1989–
Centre

Like so many of Australia's current greats, Queensland centre Tim Horan entered the international fray in the fallout that followed the 1989 series defeat by the British Lions. The stocky centre was joined that year by Jason Little, a lithe Queenslander who had grown up alongside Horan as a schoolboy on the Darling Downs, and together the two formed one of the most enduring centre partnerships of all time, with both winning the majority of their 50-odd caps alongside each other. An untried teenager when Bob Dwyer elevated him to Wallaby status against the All Blacks in 1989, Horan soon justified the faith shown in him and by 1991 was one of the main reasons behind Australia's World Cup triumph. A bustling centre who is rock solid in defence and has the speed to exploit any half gap in attack, Horan has proved a consistent try-scorer, grabbing 16 tries in his first 30 Tests. Horan sustained a potentially career-ending knee injury in the 1994 Super 10 final against Natal which sidelined him for a year. Yet by 1998 Horan was back to his best in the Australian side, showing his versatility, too, by playing a couple of games at fly-half.

Andy Irvine

Scotland
1972–82
Full-back

Looking back at the history of the game, there is a temptation to view world-class attacking full-backs in the same way as the local bus: you wait for ages and then two arrive at the same time! Yet if Andy Irvine MBE, one of the first real superstars of the game North of the Border, spent much of his rugby career in competition with that great Welsh full-back JPR Williams, that does little to diminish the impact he had upon Scottish rugby throughout the 1970s. First capped against the All Blacks in 1972, Irvine played 52 times for his country in a career that spanned ten seasons. Yet despite his many caps, Irvine was notoriously frail under the high ball, and even his staunchest supporters could not pretend that he was the most defensively sound of Scotland's recent full-backs. For all that, though, the Heriot's FP star was a potential match-winner for club or country, especially after the unbeaten 1974 Lions tour to South Africa, when he absorbed many of the moves and patterns of play and grafted them onto his own natural flair and love of counter-attacking from deep.

Peter Jackson

England
1956–63
Wing

Once described as "the old dancing master a cross between Nijinsky and Stanley Matthews", Coventry wing Peter Jackson was one of the great entertainers in a career that spanned eight seasons, 25 caps and three of the best tries ever seen in internationals. A charismatic player, Jackson was a cult figure at Twickenham from the moment he made his debut in the narrow 8-3 defeat at the hands of Wales in 1956. With an amazing sleight of hand, a wonderful side-step and divine sense of balance, the speedy Jackson was a confirmed crowd pleaser throughout his career, with his finest hour coming when he ran through seven tackles in the dying seconds to score a try in the corner and snatch an unlikely win over the 1958 Wallabies. That try was never bettered by Jackson, although his spectacular efforts for the Lions in the First and Fourth Tests in New Zealand in 1959 must come close. Indeed, Jackson's driven performances on that tour – where he finished as the second highest scorer behind prolific Irishman Tony O'Reilly, crossing the line 19 times in 18 games – confirmed him as a player of the highest calibre. Slight and pallid due to a childhood kidney complaint, Jackson's combination with fly-half Richard Sharp was at the heart of England's Championship triumph of 1963 when only a 0-0 draw in Dublin prevented them from winning the Grand Slam.

Dickie Jeeps

England
1956–62
Scrum-half

Courageous, gritty and with remarkable physical resilience for a small man, Dickie Jeeps was the perfect scrum-half during seven years in which he was generally reckoned the best No. 9 in the world. His rise to prominence was remarkably swift after his debut for the British Lions against South Africa in 1955 as an uncapped 24-year-old. During the drawn series, Jeeps provided fly-half Cliff Morgan with inch-perfect service while also halting the Springbok forwards in full charge to help the tourists to a famous victory in the First Test. That was to be the first of Jeeps' 13 appearances for the Lions (he also toured New Zealand in 1959 and South Africa in 1962), a record bettered only by Willie John McBride. A great thinker on the game, Jeeps possessed an ebullience and inner strength that earned the undying respect of team-mates and commentators by consistently proving himself willing to take enormous punishment rather than pass on bad ball to his fly-half. In addition, Jeeps was blessed with outstanding leadership qualities which saw him captain England 13 times out of his 24 caps. The key member of England's 1957 Grand Slam side, Jeeps retired in 1962 and became President of the RFU in 1976–77.

John Jeffrey

Scotland
1984–91
Flanker

No matter how much the average Scotsman enjoys beating England – and every red-blooded kilt-wearer loves nothing better – there are few to whom it means more than John Jeffrey, the Borders farmer whose one regret about his farm is that "If I stand on a hill I can see England". To Jeffrey, giving the Auld Enemy a stuffing was everything, and he in turn became synonymous with cross-border raids against England, whether it be as a vital cog in the 1990 Grand Slam winning side or as the man who famously dented the Calcutta Cup after an impromptu game of Tag after the 1988 post-match dinner! A lean blind-side flanker of 6ft 4in who lived more on guile and guts than sheer speed, the blond thatch belonging to "The Great White Shark", as Jeffrey is universally known, was one of the most galvanising sights in Five Nations rugby throughout the 1980s and early 1990s. When he retired in 1991, Jeffrey had won a then record 40 caps for Scotland as well as touring Australia with the 1989 British Lions.

Neil Jenkins

Wales
1991–
Fly-half

ust 19 when he made his debut for Wales, Neil Jenkins is possibly the best goal-kicker the world has ever known. Despite playing for Wales during a period when the country has been at its weakest, Jenkins has still managed to amass 64 caps and 726 points, making him the second highest international points-scorer in the history of the game behind Australia's Michael Lynagh (Gavin Hastings has scored less than that for Scotland, although his Lions total pushes him up to 733). For many years despised as simply a kicking machine in the land where running fly-halves in the image of John and Bennett are the norm, Jenkins has long had to put up with a procession of challengers for his No.10 shirt. Yet the quiet, flame-haired lad from Pontypridd has just got on with his game and proved his worth, even coming in at fullback for a season when his kicking skills were considered indispensable. As Wales have rallied in the late Nineties, however, it has become clear that Jenkins was not responsible for the non-functioning of his country's backline, and that with a pack going forward and backs of the calibre of Robert Howley and Scott Gibbs around him, Jenkins is a superb midfield general. Indeed, in one of the greatest games of rugby ever seen, when Wales beat England in injury-time to deny them a Grand Slam in 1999, it wasn't just Jenkins' faultless eight-from-eight kicking which caught the eye, but the way in which he set up the first crucial try for Shane Howarth.

Barry John

Wales
1966–72
Fly-half

Unless you are Welsh, Barry John is arguably the greatest fly-half the rugby world has ever seen. If you are a Welshman, he is undoubtedly the greatest fly-half the rugby world has ever seen. What is not in doubt is that between 1970-2, when John was at the peak of his powers, he was the greatest rugby player alive. King John, as he was dubbed in New Zealand, almost single-handedly destroyed the All Blacks on the Lions 1971 tour to the Land of the Long White Cloud. At a time when British rugby ruled the world, John ruled British rugby. When he retired prematurely at the tender age of 27 with only 25 caps to his name, the Welsh rugby public was aghast. They were right to be; they would never see his like again. As his successor, Phil Bennett, once said of him: "King John was a one-off genius. He had an arrogance which put him in a class apart from his contemporaries, but it was arrogance in the right manner, a self-belief that gave him the confidence to try things that other players simply would not imagine." John wasn't faultless, and wasn't overkeen on tackling, but he had wonderful vision, faultless tactical acumen and a burst of speed that would let the wonderfully balanced runner scythe through even the tightest of gaps. John also had the most cultured boot of his generation, whether from hand or in kicking for goal in his round the corner style, and scored 181 points on that Lions tour to New Zealand. As well as gaining Lions glory, John also helped Wales to their first Grand Slam for 19 years in 1971

Martin Johnson

England
1993–
Lock

Captain of the 1997 Lions to South Africa, Leicester lock Martin Johnson established himself as a great player after his strong performances as a tyro replacement for Wade Dooley on the 1993 Lions tour to New Zealand. With only one cap to his name Johnson came into the Lions' side and along with Martin Bayfield dominated the line-out in the Second Test, sending the British to a much deserved victory. Since then, Johnson has gone on to establish himself as the dominant front five forward in Northern Hemisphere rugby, winning 30 caps at the relatively tender age of 27. Possessing a startling standing jump and wonderful timing, Johnson is most conspicuous as a ball winner at the line-out yet he is a far more complete player than that. Fast for a big man at 6ft. 7in. and 18 stone, and with sure hands, Johnson is as adept at playing the mauling game as he is playing in a looser rucking role. Rugged, well-co-ordinated and athletic, the only weakness in his game remains a short fuse: two off-the-ball incidents in separate 1997 Five Nations games resulted in two England tries being disallowed. Nevertheless, he is now managing to graft a greater contribution in the loose onto his outstanding set-piece and mauling game, as proved when he won the 1998-9 Allied Dunbar Player of the Year award.

Ken Jones

Wales
1947–57
Wing

The only Welsh winger who could hold a candle to Gerald Davies, Newport flier Ken Jones combined his rugby career with life as an international athlete. A sprint champion in the Far East during the war years, Jones also won the Wales 100 yd. sprint title seven times, and collected a silver medal at the 1948 London Olympics. Yet Jones had far more to offer than scintillating pace. He was also supremely competent in all the basic skills and was well-known for his ability to catch poorly directed passes while travelling at top pace. Never a side-stepper, Jones was the possessor of a frightening swerve which he combined with his sheer pace to ease himself around hapless opponents, even at international level. It was this elusive quality which brought him 17 tries for Wales in 44 Test matches, 43 of which were played consecutively. Many of the tries he scored were at crucial moments, such as the famous instance when he latched onto captain Clem Thomas's hack out of defence to score the try which beat the 1953 All Blacks. However, it was as a wing for the 1950 Lions to New Zealand that Jones proved his ability to live with the best. So outstanding were his displays that he was named as one of the New Zealand Rugby Almanack's five players of the year, an honour which was a fitting tribute to a man who tackled like a madman and scored 16 tries in 17 games.

Michael Jones

New Zealand
1987–
Flanker

When two coaches as different in outlook as Laurie Mains and John Hart describe Michael Jones as the best forward in the world, it has to be something more than coach's hyperbole. Jones has had an extraordinary international career that started in 1986 when he represented Western Samoa, the county of his birth, against Wales. His performance in that match so impressed the New Zealand selectors that they persuaded the 22-year-old flanker, who had lived in Auckland since childhood, to play for the All Blacks in the 1987 World Cup. That was the start of a magnificent career, interrupted for a year in 1989 by a serious knee injury, that took in the 1991 World Cup and has to date earned Jones 50 caps. Respected on the pitch by both friend and foe, Jones has achieved legendary status off the pitch as well for his refusal to play on Sundays because of religious beliefs. His insistence on observing the Sabbath cost him his place in the 1995 World Cup squad such were the number of games scheduled for Sundays, but he forced his way back into the side and played a prominent part in the historic series win against South Africa in August 1996. Although Jones continued to turn out for Auckland in the 1999 Super-12 competition, it seems likely that his 55-cap career (including 13 tries) is at an end.

Andre Joubert

South Africa
1989–
Full-back

Andre Joubert's silky skills have earned him the accolade as the Rolls-Royce of full-backs. Quietly spoken and now in his 1930s, he was something of a late bloomer in international rugby, due mainly to South Africa's isolation. Joubert won the first of his official Test caps against Australia in 1993, when he was already aged 29, although he had played for South Africa in the rebel Tests against the World XV in 1989. It took Joubert several post-isolation seasons to establish himself ahead of other talented full-backs such as Gavin Johnson and Theo van Rensburg, but consistently impressive performances during the 1995 World Cup consolidated his reputation as one of South Africa's most influential players. There is little doubt that Joubert would have been a colossus in any era but the recent law changes which have added such a new dimension to an attacking full-back running from deep defensive positions have enhanced Joubert's contributions to the Springbok cause. A strong runner and prolific try-scorer, Joubert is the complete footballer.

Ken Kennedy

Ireland
1965–75
Hooker

Back in the days when it was a question of "how low can you go?" in the front-row, Ulster hooker Ken Kennedy was an undisputed king of the limbo routine. So much so, in fact, that many of his contemporaries swore he could hook a ball with his nose if he needed to! Supple, strong and incredibly fit, the CIYMS dynamo was an ever-present in the loose for Ireland for 11 seasons. He made his debut as a 24-year-old in 1965 and finally retired in 1975 after winning his 49th cap in the 32–4 humiliation by Wales at Cardiff Arms Park. A deadly accurate line-out thrower who profited from the presence of "Wiggs" Mulcahy and Willie John McBride at various stages in his career, Kennedy was nevertheless a bit on the small side, even for hookers of that era. Although this meant added mobility in the loose – and Kennedy could often have been mistaken for a back-rower – it also meant problems for him when the game was a very tight one. Although Kennedy thrived in the Five Nations, he never made much impact for the Lions when faced by the huge maul-based New Zealand pack in 1966, while by 1974 he was forced to play second fiddle to Welshman Bobby Windsor in South Africa.

Tom Kiernan

Ireland
1960–73
Full-back

There was little reason to presume that Tom Kiernan would go on to become Ireland's most capped full-back of all time when he made his debut against England at Twickenham in 1960. Yet, 14 seasons later, with 54 Irish caps and two Lions tours under his belt, the quiet and self-effacing Munsterman had established himself as one of the most efficient and dependable Test players in the history of Irish rugby. An outstanding place-kicker who scored over 150 points for his country, Kiernan was also an astute kicker from the hand and had shrewd positional sense. A natural footballer with an even temperament well suited to international rugby, Kiernan tackled well and came into the line with real purpose, even if his slight lack of pace was a handicap in this area. Kiernan's influence continued well after his retirement in 1973. Not only was he a mentor to his nephew Michael, an accomplished Irish back who won 44 caps as a kicking centre with a penchant for attack in the 1980s, but Kiernan has remained a mover and shaker in the game's halls of power. Now one of the main driving forces behind the burgeoning World Cup organisation, Kiernan became president of the Irish Rugby Union in 1989.

David Kirk

New Zealand
1985–87
Scrum-half

As Rhodes scholar, medical doctor, business executive and would-be politician, Kirk did not fit the All Black imagery, yet he led New Zealand to one of its finest rugby triumphs, victory in the first World Cup in 1987. Kirk's career was also relatively brief. He was first an All Black, as the No.2 scrum-half on the tour of England and Scotland in 1983, a ranking he retained in Australia the following year. He won the first of his 17 caps in 1985 against England, the same year that he opted out of the rebel tour to South Africa. Kirk was made captain of the "Baby Blacks", the team that beat France when the Cavaliers were unavailable, and he retained the job when they returned for a series against Australia. He was replaced as captain by Jock Hobbs for an end-of-year tour of France and then by Andy Dalton as leader of the inaugural World Cup squad. Fate intervened, however, and when Dalton pulled a hamstring before the first cup match Kirk took over the captaincy. He led the team throughout the Cup campaign, coach Brian Lochore deciding against reintroducing Dalton for the later matches when he had regained fitness. One of the enduring images of the World Cup, and of New Zealand rugby generally, is of Kirk holding aloft the Webb Ellis Trophy, then drawing in Dalton to share the moment with him.

Ian Kirkpatrick

New Zealand
1967–77
Flanker

One of the greatest flankers to have played for New Zealand, Kirkpatrick's place in history suffers because he was captain on the 1972–73 tour of the UK, Ireland and France, a tour rooted in the controversy over the banishment of prop Keith Murdoch after a fracas with a security guard in a Cardiff hotel. That is a harsh judgment, especially since Kirkpatrick played no part in the decision to send Murdoch home. For happier reasons, Kirkpatrick is remembered not only for his 39 caps but for displacing the great Kel Tremain in the Test team in France in 1967, for scoring three tries when he went on as a replacement against Australia in 1968 and for a 60-metre solo try against the Lions in Christchurch in 1971, the only Test of that series the All Blacks won. Kirkpatrick was controversially dropped as captain (and replaced by Andy Leslie) for the 1974 tour of Australia and responded by playing what many observers regarded as his finest Test, the first against the Wallabies in Sydney, in strong winds and driving rain. His final Test series was against the Lions in 1977 and despite continuing fine form, he was left out of the team to tour France later that year. Kirkpatrick added another controversial chapter to his career when in 1986 he managed the rebel All Black team in South Africa, the Cavaliers.

John Kirwan

New Zealand
1984–94
Wing

New Zealand's leading try-scorer in Tests with 35 from 63 matches, his try total is almost double that of the previous record-holder, Stu Wilson. Kirwan was 19 when the Auckland coach, John Hart, spotted him and placed him in the side with immediate, stunning effect, prompting comparisons with another electric Auckland wing of a decade earlier, Bryan Williams. Kirwan was first chosen for the All Blacks for a series against France in 1984 and went to Australia with New Zealand later that season, but a shoulder injury cut short his tour. He returned to the All Blacks in 1985 for the two-match series against England and was chosen for the aborted tour of South Africa. He and scrum-half David Kirk were the only two members of that team not to go on the rebel tour the following year. Kirwan's speed and strength, allied with sidesteps off either foot, body swerves and a fiendish fend, made him a devastating attacking wing, perhaps best exemplified by a 90-metre try against Italy in the opening match of the 1987 World Cup. Injuries, including a ruptured achilles tendon on the tour of Wales and Ireland in 1989, were all that kept Kirwan out of the All Blacks until 1993 when coach Laurie Mains, in a controversial decision, left him out of the team to tour England and Scotland, promoting Kirwan to say publicly that Mains "had lost the plot". Kirwan retired from Rugby in 1994 and played Rugby League in 1995 and 1996 for the Auckland Warriors

Jack Kyle

Ireland
1947–58
Fly-half

It would not be over-egging the pudding to say that only Barry John stands comparison with Jack Kyle in the history of fly-half play since the end of the Second World War. A diminutive genius, he dominated Irish back play from the time that he sliced through the French defences in 1947 until he hung up his boots after beating Scotland 12–6 a record 52 caps later. Under Kyle, Ireland achieved a level of dominance in Europe which they have never threatened to repeat since his retirement. He brought Ireland their only Grand Slam in 1948, while the next year only a 16–9 defeat by France denied back-to-back clean sweeps. Kyle was perceptive in attack, quick to spot a gap and even quicker to zip through it. He seemed to be able to turn matches with moments of brilliance plucked out of the ether, yet he was also able to dictate the course of tight matches with raking punts that landed inches short of the touchline. Kyle endeared himself to those around him by making the ball work to give them space, and he was certainly no shirker – he was a lightweight who packed a heavyweight tackle. The Belfast doctor even won the admiration of the Kiwis, who rated him one of the best players ever to tour New Zealand, even though his Lions side failed to win any of the four Tests there in 1950.

Chris Laidlaw

New Zealand
1964–70
Scrum-half

An outstanding scrum-half for New Zealand in the 1960s, Laidlaw played for his province, Otago, for South Island and for New Zealand Universities in his first year out of school. He was the youngest player on the All Blacks' 1963–64 tour of the UK, Ireland and France and played his first Test on that tour, against France. Barely 20, the tour established him as New Zealand's first-choice scrum-half, a standing he retained for the rest of his career, including full series against South Africa in 1965, the Lions in 1966 and the tour of Britain in 1967. He captained the All Blacks against Australia in 1968 when regular leader Brian Lochore was injured. After completing a Rhodes Scholarship at Oxford University, Laidlaw returned to New Zealand and won the last of his 20 caps on the 1970 tour to South Africa. Laidlaw was a scrum-half of the classic mould, with a long, quick pass, a deft kick over the top of forwards and brought a tactical vision of the game. In an age when it wasn't the done thing to do, Laidlaw wrote a book Mud In Your Eye, which was critical of Rugby administration. He also condemned South Africa's Apartheid system though he himself was criticised for playing against South Africa for Oxford and for touring there. Laidlaw was later a diplomat as New Zealand high commissioner to Zimbabwe and had a prominent role in the multi-racial talks that led to the formation of the South African Rugby Football Union. He was also, for a term, a Labour member of the New Zealand Parliament.

Roy Laidlaw

Scotland
1980–88
Scrum-half

Every country has, at some stage, a double-act which sees two players, through sheer longevity, become mentioned in the same breath. England had Dooley and Ackford, Wales had the Viet Gwent (the Pontypool front row of Faulkner, Windsor and Price) and Australia had Lynagh and Farr-Jones. One of the most enduring partnerships of all was that of Jed Forests's Roy Laidlaw and Selkirk fly-half John Rutherford. For nigh on a decade, the two were immovable at half back for Scotland. Unlike most of the other famous pairings, however, it was Laidlaw and Rutherford's differences, rather than their similarities, that melded them into an outstanding partnership. On the one hand, there was the peerless Rutherford, all grace and poise, who could glide through tackles and drill a ball onto a sixpence in the opposition's 22. On the other, there was Laidlaw, a gutsy little fighter in the classic Borders mould. The pair played together on 35 occasions, a world record for a half-back partnership. They also teamed up for the British Lions in the Third Test against New Zealand in 1983.

David Leslie

Scotland
1975–85
Flanker

Every team needs a nutcase, a player who – no matter how urbane and civilised off the field – cares so little for his own physical well-being that he is prepared to sacrifice himself every time he laces up his boots. David Leslie was such a man. Throughout his career, he was consistently the most focused and fearless player in a Scottish squad which had far more than its fair share of fearless breakaways. One story is instructive. So uncompromising was Leslie that shortly after his retirement when he returned to his alma mater, Glenalmond College near Perth, to play in an old boys match alongside David Sole, the body count was so high that the College's Master-in-Charge had to appeal to his guest's better nature – difficult for a man who knew no way other than full bore until full-time. For all his intensity, Leslie found it hard to establish himself in the Scottish side until late on in his career. First capped against Ireland in 1975, he didn't become a regular in the side until 1981. When he finally decided to hang up his boots in 1985 he had won 32 caps.

Brian Lochore

New Zealand
1964–71
No. 8

Lochore first gained national acknowledgement in 1963 when he was on the shortlist for a home series against England and he made his debut at the end of the year on the tour of the UK, Ireland and France, playing in the England and Scotland internationals. A No. 8 of power and perception, he had a tigerish strength in rucks and mauls and was blessed with deceptive speed. Lochore became All Black captain in 1966, after Wilson Whineray's retirement, and continued to lead with dignity and success, retiring after the tour of South Africa in 1970. But he was persuaded to come back in 1971 and play, at lock, in the Third Test against the Lions when he won his 25th and last All Black cap. Lochore turned to coaching and was an immediate success with his Masterton club team before doing the improbable when he coached his province, Wairarapa-Bush, into the first division. He was fast-tracked onto the national selection panel and was coach of the 1985 All Black team that was stopped from going to South Africa. He coached a team of All Black newcomers to beat France in 1986 when most of the established All Blacks were under suspension for their rebel tour of South Africa, and in 1987 he coached the first team to win the World Cup. Lochore continued to serve Rugby in a variety of less high-profile roles and in 1995 he was brought back as campaign manager for the World Cup and was widely regarded as being one of the main reasons for that team's outstanding play.

Jonah Lomu

New Zealand
1994–
Wing

Although Jonah Lomu is still only 24 and does not have an unblemished record of success, he is nevertheless worthy of inclusion for the impact he made upon the 1995 World Cup. In one month of mayhem in South Africa, the 6ft 5in, 18-stone wing was well-nigh unstoppable. He almost single-handedly sunk Ireland and Wales, and then let rip on hapless England. Within one minute of the kick-off in that semi-final, Lomu had literally run over Tony Underwood and run through the challenges of Tim Rodber and Rob Andrew to score an outrageous opening score that set the scene for England's destruction. Just for good measure, Lomu also scored another try halfway through the second half. Although South Africa marked him out of the game in the final, the huge Tongan-born All Black had etched his huge frame onto the mind of every rugby fans in the world. Overnight, he had become the biggest superstar in the sport. Although he has failed to live up to that early promise – especially when a kidney infection in 1996 put him out of the game for 18 months and threatened to end his career – Lomu is nevertheless getting back to the sort of bull in a china shop form which he displayed in 1995. Huge and incredibly fast, Lomu can still display dodgy hands and tactical naivete at times, yet he remains as powerful and dangerous as he was when a schoolboy. Back then he was a second row, and England Schools reckoned him so dangerous that they asked the New Zealanders not to play him because the genuinely feared for the health of their forwards. Personal problems dogged his performance in 1998 but by 1999 he was looking sharp playing for the Chiefs in the Super-12.

Michael Lynagh

Australia
1984–95
Fly-half

Australia's most capped fly-half, with 72 Tests to his name, Lynagh is also the most prolific points-scorer in international Rugby, amassing 911 points before his retirement after the 1995 World Cup. Although he made his debut in 1984 against Fiji as a 21-year-old, it was later in that year on the Grand Slam tour of Britain that Lynagh came of age. Despite being unable to shift the great Mark Ella from the No.10 spot, he demonstrated his versatility by playing at inside centre. Lynagh will be best remembered working in tandem with scrum-half Nick Farr-Jones, who also first made his mark in 1984 before going on to play in 47 Tests alongside Lynagh. Farr-Jones's efficient service and attacking ability took a good deal of pressure off his fly-half, allowing him to stand virtually on the gain line in attack. Although Lynagh could take on opposition defences one-on-one, as he brilliantly proved when scoring a famous injury-time winning try against Ireland in the 1991 World Cup quarter-final, he was better as a player who gave the dynamic runners such as David Campese the space and time in which to work. In the summer of 1996 "Noddy" announced his shock move to London club Saracens where he linked up with Phillipe Sella, one of his former adversaries. They formed a majestic partnership, culminating in Saracens winning the 1998 Cup final.

Jo Maso

France
1966–73
Centre

Perpignan and Narbonne centre Jo Maso won his 25 caps in spite of rather than because of the system. Arguably the most gifted centre of his generation, maso was regarded by the connoisseurs as the heir apparent to Andre Boniface, the legendary French centre of the late fifties and early sixties. Nevertheless, Maso had a chequered international career at a time when the French panel of selectors was dominated by safety-first former forwards. Dropped for a variety of ridiculous reasons, some of which included having long hair and being too worried about his clothes, Maso's long absences were a mystery top rugby supporters outside France. A formidable footballer with a formidable turn of pace, fine hands and a dangerous outside break, Maso also displayed a languid character when faced with the incomprehensible selection criteria of the national panel. Only 22 when he made his debut against Italy in 1966, Maso's Test career spanned eleven seasons yet saw him win only 26 caps before he finally called it a day at the end of the 1973 season.

Willie John McBride

Ireland
1962–75
Lock

Willie John McBride is the most capped forward in the history of the British Lions. The other bruisers loved him, because he was the rock in the middle of it all. If something was going down it was usually an opponent on the end of one of McBride's hits. The Ballymena hardman left behind him a number of beaten bodies during those 17 caps for the Lions and 63 caps for Ireland. Colin Meads, the ultimate enforcer, reckoned that McBride hit him with the hardest punch he ever received.

A strong scrummager, a powerful mauler, a bodyguard, McBride was the tightest of tight forwards. The fulfilment of McBride's reputation was his captaincy of the unbeaten Lions tour to South Africa in 1974. McBride had been on two previous losing tours of South Africa and knew the Springbok mentality. He decided that the Lions would be the intimidators this time around and the outcome was the notorious call of 99. McBride reckoned there would be trouble, so on a call of 99 everyone on the team was to join in the fight. That way the referee would have to send off everyone or no one. Half way through the tour the South African forwards were frightened. One of their supposed hard men actually ran away from a fight. Under McBride's captaincy the Lions ducked nothing and nobody, which is why the South Africans, regarded them as the greatest team to tour their country. The broke the image of South African physical superiority forever and are still rated by South Africans as the best side ever to tour there. McBride was a good captain who had respect because he never let anyone else fight his wars. As a player his strength was strength.

Ian McLauchlan

Scotland
1969–79
Prop

As the richly deserved epithet "Mighty Mouse" would indicate, Ian McLauchlan was both small for a prop, but also remarkably strong. Certainly, McLauchlan was not the conventional size and shape for a loose-head prop in the 1970s, but in many ways it was precisely the combination of an amazing power to weight ratio plus his ability to get under his opposing tight-head that made him such an effective performer in the tight. McLauchlan, however, was also outstanding in the loose and prospered as a member of the Lions party which tore across the hard grounds of the South African Veldt in 1974. As a larger than life character, he played best in the most intimidating circumstances, which is why he was so effective in Paris, Cardiff and on the 1971 Lions tour of New Zealand where he played all four Tests. During his ten-year career, McLauchlan won 43 caps, captaining his country in 19 of those matches and recording ten victories, making him Scotland's most successful captain. After his retirement the Scottish Rugby Union showed their gratitude by banning him for publishing a his autobiography.

Colin Meads

New Zealand
1957–71
Lock

By modern standards, 6ft 4in Colin "Pine Tree" Meads is no giant. By any other standard, however, Meads stands astride the game like a colossus. The King Country farmer is a national institution in New Zealand and the most influential forward of his or any other generation. Immensely strong and durable – legend has it that he trained by running up hills with a sheep tucked under each arm – Meads also possessed the right mental attributes for the game. Fit, uncompromising and mentally impregnable, Meads was also a former No.8 and had wonderful hands and great tactical awareness. But it was as the All Blacks' fearsome enforcer that Meads was best known. Lions hard man Willie John McBride hit him once, but then explained afterwards that you can only die once, so he wanted to die famous as the only man with the guts to whack the hardest man in rugby. Aggressive, fiercely proud of wearing the silver fern of New Zealand and a shrewd, mobile footballer, Meads was part of a strong pack featuring other greats such as Ken Gray, Wilson Whineray, Brian Lochore and Kel Tremain. Meads also played 14 of his 55 caps alongside his younger brother Stan, a player of some standing who helped Colin inflict a 4-0 whitewash on the 1966 Lions. It was after defeat by the 1971 Lions that Meads decided to call it a day after 15 seasons at the sharp end of New Zealand rugby.

Murray Mexted

New Zealand
1979–85
No. 8

In the process of winning 34 caps as an All Black, Mexted brought a new dimension to the play of the No. 8, his style never better demonstrated than in his First Test, against Scotland at Murrayfield in 1979. He won the ball toward the back of a line-out, then broke through the line, ball in one hand, and with long strides and side-steps, scored a try without the Scottish defence laying a hand on him. Mexted's height of 6ft. 5in. made him an ideal line-out ball-winner but he also had a fitness level and athleticism that made him seem, at times, to be an extra back. Playing Rugby was his joy and his vocation and at a time when many All Blacks complained of too much touring, Mexted was always available and always picked, playing series against Australia (1980, 1984), the tempestuous series against South Africa in 1981, the 4–0 series win over the Lions in 1983 and the tour to England and Scotland in 1983. Mexted was picked for the 1985 tour of South Africa and when that tour was abandoned, he went instead on the rebel Cavaliers tour in 1986, retiring after it. He also played club Rugby in France and was one of the first New Zealanders to play club Rugby in South Africa. Mexted married a Miss Universe, Lorraine Downes, in 1986. His father Graham had been an All Black in 1950 and 1951.

Iain Milne

Scotland
1979–90
Prop

In many ways, "The Bear", as Iain Milne was affectionately known, was one of the great anomalies of Scottish forward play, a lumbering bull of a man whose greatest strength lay in his sheer strength. Although a capable footballer, it was Milne's destiny to build up a reputation as a formidable scrummager; the type of man even the Paparembordes of the world thought twice about taking issue with. But then, as Milne himself says, it was his ability to provide a solid tight platform that would allow Scotland to play No. 8s such as Derek White and Iain Paxton in the second row so that they could play a more fluid style and get away with it. Milne, who played for Heriot's FP and Harlequins, won a total of 44 caps before he retired following the 1990 tour to New Zealand. His younger brother Kenny, with whom he scrummed down with in his last Test appearance, won 39 caps as a hooker.

Ray Mordt

South Africa
1980–84
Wing

Powerfully built Rhodesian right wing Ray Mordt ran his way into Rugby folklore when he scored back-to-back hat-tricks of Test tries, crossing three times in the Third Test against the All Blacks in Auckland in 1981 and against the US Eagles a week later. However, at the time his amazing record was overshadowed by wider political events. The Auckland Test became known as the "crazy Biggles" Test because an anti-Apartheid activist circled Eden Park in a light aircraft dropping flour bombs on the players and threatening to crash the plane into the crowd if the New Zealand Air Force tried to force him down, while the Test against the Eagles was held in virtual seclusion on a polo field after the date and venue were changed to avoid anti-Apartheid campaigners. As powerful as John Kirwan and as difficult to stop as Jonah Lomu, the stocky Mordt is still a legend in South Africa, where he was once memorably referred to as a "rhino in a man's body." Yet while he certainly possessed his fabled strength in abundance, it was speed, fearlessness and wonderful sense of balance that marked him out, allowing him to play in 18 Tests and score a total of 12 tries for South Africa. Those qualities were also much in demand elsewhere, and when South Africa's growing isolation reached the point of no return, Mordt packed his bags and joined Wigan Rugby League Club 1984.

Cliff Morgan

Wales
1951–58
Fly-half

The star attraction for Cardiff, Wales and the British Lions, Cliff Morgan was a fly-half capable of sparkling genius in attack and dogged resistance in defence. In tandem with Cardiff and Wales immortals Clem Thomas and Bleddyn Williams, he helped Cardiff become the dominant force in Welsh Rugby, and was a key factor in both Cardiff and Wales's win over Bob Thomas's All Blacks in 1953. Morgan was also a member of the Welsh Grand Slam side of 1952, and went on to lead his country to the Five Nations crown in 1956. For all the plaudits he won for his displays on British soil, however, it was as a British Lion that Morgan will be best remembered, not least because he remains the only Welshman to have captained a side to victory over the Springboks on South African soil. That 9–6 Third Test win in Cape Town came against all the odds, and put the Lions 2–1 up in a four-Test series that was eventually drawn. His feats in 1955 led the 'Boks of the time to label him the best fly-half ever to have visited the Republic, and it is certainly true that South Africa was the perfect environment for the quicksilver Morgan. With 29 Welsh caps to go alongside the four he won for the Lions, Morgan retired from Rugby in 1958 to enter the world of media. He proved as successful in the world of broadcasting as he was on the rug by field, eventually becoming the BBC's head of Outside Broadcasts.

Graham Mourie

New Zealand
1977–82
Flanker

A flanker with a cool, analytical brain and an astute captain on and off the field, Mourie led New Zealand successfully through a period when the All Blacks' dominance was under severe threat. He was first picked to lead a New Zealand 'B' team to Argentina in 1976 and won the first of his 21 caps against Phil Bennett's 1977 Lions. At the end of that year, he took over the captaincy for a tour of Italy and France and the following year was again leader when the All Blacks achieved the Grand Slam in Britain and Ireland for the first time. Injury and farming commitments interrupted Mourie's career, but he returned to Britain in 1979 to lead the All Blacks on a tour of England, Scotland and Wales. In 1981, he caused a storm in New Zealand Rugby when he refused to play against South Africa on its controversial tour, but he returned for an end-of-year tour of Romania and France. In his last season, 1982, he led the All Blacks to a series win over Australia. Mourie wrote a book at the end of that year and, unusually for the time, told the NZRFU he was keeping the profits. He was therefore banned and was only reinstated in 1994 when he publicly advocated the appointment of John Hart as All Black coach. Mourie's tireless play, his inspiring leadership and his moral stance on South Africa ensured his place in New Zealand Rugby history.

Karl Mullen

Ireland
1947–52
Hooker

In a country that has sent forth more British Lions captains than any other, Old Belvedere hooker Karl Mullen remains the best and most successful captain Ireland have ever produced. In a career spanning just six seasons and 25 caps, Mullen took Ireland to their solitary Grand Slam in 1948, the Triple Crown in 1949 and led the 1950 Lions in in the shared series against Australia and New Zealand. While the legendary Ireland fly-half Jack Kyle marshalled the backs for Ireland and the Lions, the indefatigable Mullen spurred his forwards onto ever greater efforts. Unfortunately, the Lions pack available to Mullen, while strong enough to dispatch the Wallabies in both Tests, lacked the mettle to live with an All Black side that had revolutionised loose play by adopting the rucking game as coached by Vic Cavanagh and practiced by Otago. The result was a 3–0 whitewash on the Lions' visit across the Tasman Sea. A shrewd tactician, Mullen was a step away from the traditional blood and thunder, up and at 'em approach to captaincy generally favoured by the Irish. Although thick-set and technically outstanding at the set-piece, Mullen's own ability to keep up with a running game played at a frantic pace tended to influence the style of play he advocated, and for most of his representative career his main concern was unleashing the creativity of Jack Kyle and his talented back-line.

Noel Murphy

Ireland
1958–69
Flanker

A flanker of fire and incredible persistence, Cork Constitution battler Noel Murphy was almost an ever-present for Ireland through 12 seasons, during which time he won 49 caps for Ireland and the Lions. From the time that Murphy made his debut, aged just 20, in the famous 9–6 win over the touring Wallabies in 1958, he quickly established himself as one of the most consistent performers of his generation. A fiery character, Murphy was also a naturally gifted footballer who could play either open-side or blind-side with equal alacrity. An intelligent player who rarely took a wrong option, Murphy was a canny and strong defender who also excelled as an outstanding runner in attack. Although Murphy never managed to win a Triple Crown, he did prove that he could make the step up to a higher level when he toured with the 1959 and 1966 Lions to Australasia, excelling on the successful tour of '59 before being part of a side eclipsed by All Black forward power seven years later. Murphy retired in 1969, after he was famously decked by a Welsh forward in Ireland's disappointing 24–11 loss. He retains a keen interest in Rugby administration and has worked in a coaching or managerial capacity for Ireland and the Lions as recently as 1995.

George Nepia

New Zealand
1924–30
Full-back

Although he only won nine caps Nepia is one of the most revered figures in All Black history. A member of the 1924–25 "Invincibles" tour to Britain and France, he played in all 30 matches on the tour plus another two in Canada on the way home. He also played in four matches in Australia and two in New Zealand as a warm-up for the tour. As a 19-year-old Nepia won much praise for his kicking, tackling and fielding of the ball. In the 13 months after his debut, Nepia played 39 consecutive matches for New Zealand but he played only another seven for the rest of his career. He couldn't go on the All Blacks' tour of South Africa in 1928 because he was a Maori, while injury restricted his appearances in Australia in 1929, but he was back to play all four of the Tests against the British Isles in 1930. He tried unsuccessfully to make the 1935–36 team for Britain and captained a New Zealand Maori team to Australia. He switched to Rugby League with Halifax in 1936 and played for New Zealand at League in 1937. He returned to Rugby Union in 1947, at the age of 42, and in 1950 he became the oldest man to play in a New Zealand first-class match when he led the Olympians club against Poverty Bay

Bob Norster

Wales
1982–89
Lock

One of the great forward confrontations in the Northern Hemisphere throughout the late 1980s was between Wales's lock Bob Norster and England's Wade Dooley. Only 6ft. 5in. tall, Norster was the perfect technician, a spring-heeled line-out jumper with immaculate timing who ensured Wales a constant supply of quality line-out ball. In the opposite corner was 6ft. 8in. Dooley, a streetwise bruiser who ruled the line-out jungle through a mixture of brute force and determination. Despite his prodigious talent, Norster was in many ways atypical of Welsh tight forwards during the 1980s. A mobile lock who preferred a fast rucking game to the more static mauling game favoured by the Gwent forwards, Norster was also a scrupulously fair player who shied away from niggle and confrontation. After serving as understudy to Allan Martin, the Cardiff man made his debut in the 34–18 home humiliation at the hands of an Andy Irvine-inspired Scotland. Although Welsh defeats became depressingly regular throughout the 1980s, Norster was still able to provide Wales with a lifeline to possession, and was to prove his credentials independently when he emerged as the single most important Lions' forward on the 1983 tour to New Zealand. In all, Norster won 34 caps for Wales, equalling his mentor Allan Martin's record, and three Lions' caps (two against New Zealand in 1983 and one against Australia in 1989).

Gwyn Nicholls

Wales
1896–1906
Centre

The man who helped usher Wales into their first "golden era" of 1900-1911, when they won the Triple Crown six times, and the first Welshman ever to represent the British Isles, Gwyn Nicholls remains one of the founding fathers of Welsh rugby. A strong-running threequarter who was capped 28 times for Wales and the Lions, Nicholls was brave in the tackle and had outstanding on-field judgement. He was also a potent attacking weapon and an intelligent captain for both Wales and Cardiff. After making his debut against Scotland in 1896, he established himself as one of the best backs in Britain, touring New Zealand with the British Isles side in 1899 and playing in all four Tests as well as ending the tour as top scorer. Already a member of the Triple Crown-winning sides of 1900 and 1902, Nicholls led Wales to a Triple Crown in 1905 and then onto a famous 3-0 win over the New Zealanders, a feat he almost repeated with Cardiff before the visitors eventually triumphed 10-8. Despite Nicholls' continuing brilliance for Cardiff, the following season saw his international demise when an 11-6 defeat by Ireland was followed by an 11-0 defeat by the first Springbok touring party, led by Paul Roos. Despite masterminding Cardiff's emphatic 17-0 thrashing of the same Springboks, Nicholls was deemed to have passed his sell-by date and was never again selected by Wales.

Tony O'Reilly

Ireland
1955–70
Wing

One of the most colourful characters ever to play for Ireland (an accolade in itself), Tony O'Reilly also ranks – alongside Mike Gibson and Jackie Kyle – as one of the three best backs Ireland has ever produced. By the tender age of 18, O'Reilly had made his international debut and arrived in South Africa as first-choice wing for the 1955 Lions. At 6ft. 2in., 15 stone, and with a blistering turn of speed, O'Reilly's impact was similar to John Kirwan in 1987 or Jonah Lomu in 1995. Difficult to put down and fiercely determined, he proved the sensation of the tour, returning with two tries in four internationals and the undying admiration of the Springboks. O'Reilly's outside career boomed, but business and Rugby were incompatible, limiting him to 29 Irish caps, and he was never at his best on the European stage. Further proof of O'Reilly's greatness came in 1959, on the Lions tour to Australasia, when he scored four tries in six Tests. All told, O'Reilly scored 38 tries for the Lions, a record unlikely to be beaten. His Test career ended in off-beat fashion, seven years after his last cap. On a business trip to London in 1970, he was called up after right-wing Bill Brown was injured in training before the Twickenham game. Overweight and nowhere near match fit, O'Reilly's main contribution to the game was to raise Irish morale by pitching up in his chauffeur-driven Rolls Royce!

Willie Ofahengaue

Australia
1990–
Flanker

From the time that "Willie-O" made his first huge hit on All Black flanker Alan Whetton during the opening play of the first Bledisloe Cup Test in 1990, Australia knew it had unearthed a real gem. But if Ofahengaue was to become one of the greats of Australian Rugby, it owed as much to luck as judgement. Tongan-born and raised, the 6ft. 4in. Ofahengaue toured Australia as a New Zealand Colt in 1988 only to find himself denied entry back into New Zealand by customs officials. The All Blacks' loss was the Wallabies' gain, however, as the ARFU successfully petitioned the government to allow Willie-O to be allowed to stay in Sydney with his uncle. From that moment on, with the exception of an injury-plagued 1993, Ofahengaue became central to Bob Dwyer's plans, providing him with a dynamic breakaway who could be relied upon to cross the gain line every time he took the ball on, while also acting as an extremely effective stopper on the blind-side. Ofahengaue also did much unseen work, and Australia's try in the 1991 World Cup Final was typical. At a line-out ten metres from the England line, Phil Kearns threw the ball over the fourth man in the line to Ofahengaue, who was then rolled round into midfield towards the England try-line, from where prop Tony Daly emerged as the try-scorer, the only one of that final. Injury prevented Ofahenagaue from taking part in the 1996 Tri-Nations series and although he won several caps in 1997, with a fresh crop of talent installed in the Australian back-row, his international days are probably numbered. He has been used more lately, both for New South Wales and Australia, as a super-sub, coming on for the last 30 minutes of matches.

Phil Orr

Ireland
1976–87
Prop

One of the key players in Ireland's Triple Crown campaign of 1983 was gargantuan loose-head prop Phil Orr, a rock in the Ireland front-row for 12 seasons after coming on as a replacement in Paris to win his first cap in 1976. While fly-half Ollie Campbell provided the finishing touches during that 1983 campaign, it was generally recognised that it was a series of gutsy performances from an adrenaline-fuelled Irish pack that turned the screws throughout that season. Few forwards were more adept at applying telling pressure than Orr; his contribution in the loose was never overwhelming, but his scrummaging ability was legendary. A phenomenally bright man, Orr shared many of the attributes and the technical excellence of his predecessor Ray McLoughlin, but tended to have a more laid-back demeanour, and he lacked McLoughlin's obsessive tendencies. Not that Orr was not dedicated, quite the reverse. His thick mop was always in the thick of the action, and throughout his 58 caps for Ireland he displayed a consistent fervour and desire to win that made him one of the great Irish props.

Robert Paparemborde

France
1975–83
Prop

One of the all-time great scrummagers, Robert Paparemborde had a fearsome reputation as a tough man to get to grips with. This was due, in large part, to the fact that his shoulders seemed to come all the way up to meet his head – as England prop Mike Burton once said, if he had a neck, then there was certainly no way of telling. A big man, although not quite in the same weight class as monsters such as his long-time international tight-head partner Gerard Cholley, Paparemborde allied a supreme technique at the set-piece with a fierce determination and surprising agility. That many opponents were surpised by his agility, however, is more down to their lack of homework: as a top class handball player and judo black belt, Paparemborde's athletic qualities were hardly well hidden. Paparemborde began his international career the hard way, on the whitewashed tour to South African in 1975, but soon established himself as the cornerstone of the feared French pack of the late 1970s, playing in all four internationals as France won their second ever Grand Slam in 1977. An ability to bore in at the hooker was an invaluable part of his repertoire, yet the Pau hardman was never a dirty player. Having won a record 55 caps including a second Grand Slam in 1981 when he announced his retirement, Paparemborde remains France's most capped prop forward.

François Pienaar

South Africa
1993–1996
Flanker

François Pienaar is a strange rugby player: a man almost as important for what he represents as for how he plays the game. Pienaar is the exciting new Afrikaner face of South African Rugby which profited from the country's democracy both during and after its wonderful World Cup triumph of 1995. As the most identifiable face of the tournament, Pienaar's massive contribution as captain on and off the field, stretched into homes of all colours and cultures. He became a role model for young, disadvantaged blacks and helped enormously to spread the game into the townships and non-white areas. After 29 Tests as captain from his debut against France in 1993 – a record eclipsing the previous best held by Dawie de Villiers – his controversial axing by new national coach Andre Markgraaff before the 1996 tour to Argentina and France caused a national uproar. Upset at his treatment, Pienaar took advantage of the new professional era and made a lucrative move to London club Saracens where he is now coach, acknowledging in the process that his international days could well have come to a premature end. He led them to cup success in 1998 and the following season guided them to the top six and qualification for the European Cup.

Simon Poidevin

Australia
1980–91
Flanker

Australia's most capped flanker with 59 caps, New South Wales back rower Simon Poidevin was also one of the fittest players ever to wear the green and gold. An urbane, sophisticated stockbroker off the pitch, Poidevin was the original "100 per center" on it, yet he was not a selfish player and never lost sight of his belief that his role was to help others play the game. This attitude, combined with his incredible levels of fitness and speed to the breakdown, created a flanker who snaffled countless tries out wide while also acting as a linkman to provide endless quick ball to his backs. In other words, he was the perfect flanker for the game Australia have adopted in modern times. Captain of the ill-fated tour to Argentina in 1987, after which he temporarily retired, Poidevin rates winning the World Cup in 1991 and the Bledisloe Cup on New Zealand soil in 1986 as the high points of his career. The best summary of Poidevin was that by Mark Ella in his autobiography Path to Victory: "Simon is such a perfectionist that it's almost a disease. Not only is he the best rugby player in Australia, but he's also the most determined."

Hugo Porta

Argentina
1973–90
Fly-half

Hugo Porta is the CB Fry of Argentina – the consummate all-rounder. There is little doubt that he could have been whatever he wanted to be. Educated at the De La Salle monastery school in Buenos Aires, where he also played soccer, he was advised to go pro and was offered a contract by Boca Juniors, the Argentinian equivalent of Manchester United. Porta, though, preferred to study law, and by 1970 was the fourth-choice Pumas scrum-half. Welsh visionary Carwyn James, who saw Porta play in 1980, wrote: "To study the craftsmanship of a great player is a privilege. Everything that happened around Hugo Porta was contested at a much lower level of skill and intellectual awareness. For a critic or coach or ex fly-half, it was a question of having one's faith restored in the aesthetic and artistic possibilities of back play." A stocky player with a lightning turn of pace over 15 yards, Porta did more than any player to usher Argentina on to the world stage. Against France in 1977, he kicked all 17 points in a 17-17 draw, and did the same in the 1985 21-21 draw against the All Blacks. In between, he helped defeat Australia in Brisbane in 1983, the French in 1985, and he lead a Jaguars side to South Africa in 1982, where they astounded the hosts by winning the Second Test. He later became Ambassador to South Africa and then his country's Minister of Sport. Porta scored 530 points for the Pumas in his 57-cap, 20-season career.

Jean Prat

France
1945–55
Flanker

Jean Prat was the man who finally put French Rugby on the map. A wing forward and captain emeritus, Prat missed only three games in an illustrious international career during which he played 51 Tests for France over an eleven-year period. Born in 1923 on his father's farm, within sight of the Lourdes Rugby club, the man nicknamed "Monsieur Rugby" became the catalyst of a revolution in French Rugby, largely described as the "Lourdes Phenomenon". Under his visionary leadership, the Lourdes club won six Championship titles in ten years, the last three with him as player-coach after his retirement from international Rugby in 1955. Prat was first capped on New Year's day in 1945 against the British Army team at Parc des Princes. The game was a watershed in French Rugby history, hence the decision to award caps against a Services side. It was France's first game since matches were suspended in 1940 (and it was against the same opponents at Parc des Princes), 13 new caps were awarded on the day and it heralded the resumption of the relations with the Home Unions severed in 1931. Jean Prat became captain in 1953 against Scotland and he scored a then record 146 points for France before his retirement in 1955.

Graham Price

Wales
1975–83
Prop

If Fran Cotton ranks as the greatest British loose-head of the modern era, then Welshman Graham Price certainly ranks as the greatest tight-head. In 41 caps for Wales and 12 consecutive Tests for the Lions on tours in 1977, '80 and '83, Price proved himself the strongest and most formidable scrummager in international Rugby against the best the Southern Hemisphere had to offer. Perfect technique, a huge reservoir of natural strength and a grimly determined mindset were the tools of the trade for Wales's most capped prop. In tandem with his two Pontypool front row teammates – fellow Lion Bobby Windsor and Charlie Faulkner, or the "Viet Gwent" as Max Boyce christened the threesome – the softly-spoken Gwent strongman dominated Welsh front row play in the late 1970s and early 1980s. Not that the Price was just a scrummager, as he showed in his debut at the Parc des Princes in 1975 when French No. 8 Jean-Pierre Bastiat spilled the ball just outside the Welsh '22 and Price hacked it downfield before falling on it for a try that sealed a 25–10 win. Some would argue that his decision to retire in 1983 at the age of 32 was premature, but Price continued to play for his beloved Pontypool as late as 1989 when he packed down against the touring All Blacks.

Dean Richards

England
1986–96
No. 8

"Deano", as No. 8 Dean Richards is widely known, was the single most influential forward in the Northern Hemisphere from his debut in 1986 until the last of his 48 caps against Ireland a decade later. A huge bear of a man whose lumbering gait belied a shrewd rugby brain and a determination to win at all costs, Richards' preference for the rolling maul coincided perfectly with England's priorities and strengths in the late 1980s as the Leicester man became the driving force behind England's gargantuan and unstoppable pack. Despite his less than athletic frame, Richards always seemed to be in the right place at the right time because of his knack of knowing where the ball would end up. He regularly took games by the scruff of the neck as he drew the ball into his mighty mitts and dragged team-mates along with him. Never happier than when engaged in a war of attrition, as England looked to play a more expansive game Richards' lack of speed was perceived as a deficiency rather than a virtue. It was this attitude that led Richards to be dropped for the 1991 World Cup campaign where he was replaced by Mick Skinner. A marvellously intuitive player and a cult hero wherever he played, the shy and retiring Richards also won six caps for the British Lions.

Jean-Pierre Rives

France
1975–84
Openside flanker

As a player Rives contained all the elements that make French rugby so exciting. On the one hand he represented the dash and verve of the outstanding threequarters that seem to grow on trees in France, while on the other hand he was as teak hard and uncompromising a forward as France has ever produced – and for a country which puts its forwards through the most brutal school of domestic rugby in the world, that made him pretty tough. Rives was a man who combined the silky skills of the threequarters with a love of no-holds barred close-quarter combat. Rives was highly visible thanks to his shock of blond hair, which was invariably streaked with blood, so reckless was the Toulouse man with his personal safety. In the gargantuan world of Seventies French forwards, Rives looked out of place at just 5ft 10in, but more than made up for that by his lightning speed and ferocious courage. For many of his 59 caps (34 as captain), during which he won two Grand Slams, one as captain, Rives worked in tandem with blindside flanker Jean-Claude Skrela and lumbering No.8 Jean-Pierre Bastiat. It was a great partnership to which Rives brought pace, superb distribution skills and a unquenchable will to win. As Gareth Edwards said: "I was never taken in by Jean-Pierre's warmth, charm and flashing smile off the field, for once the whistle went he was a hardfaced enemy with a will of steel, an opponent who went all out to win. At set-pieces in the four internationals I played against him, we were never more than a yard or two apart and I could feel the hostility radiating from his berth."

Laurent Rodriguez

France
1981–90
No. 8

A durable, robust bruiser, Laurent Rodriguez was a man of huge strength whose charges from the back of the scrum would take three or four players to stop. Although particularly in vogue during the time when coach Jacques Fouroux was obsessed with fielding gargantuan packs, the "Bull of Dax" was always far more than just a big man. A skilled ball player, he showed an acute tactical sense during a career that brought him 56 caps. Although never an instigator of the rough stuff, Rodriguez was more than able to hold his own as the Wallabies first found out during the bad-tempered series of 1981 in which he made his debut. Drafted into the side immediately after the 1981 Grand Slam, Rodriguez was to win the ultimate European prize in 1987, capping a magnificent 12 months for the Dax player. First, in 1986, Rodriguez had been outstanding when the French beat the All Blacks 16-3 in a frenzied assault during the Second Test in Nantes. So gruelling was the rugby that New Zealand legend Buck Shelford, who required 22 stitches in his scrotum after the match, called it the hardest match he had ever played in, adding that he was convinced that the French must have been "on something" to play with such sustained savagery. A year later, another Rodriguez crowning moment occurred when he was instrumental in France's injury-time 1987 World Cup semi-final win over Australia in one of the great contests of all time.

Olivier Roumat

France
1989–
Lock

Up until the age of 18 Olivier Roumat channelled all his sporting energies into basketball. Then one day his father – a former player with Mont de Marsan and now an official at the famous Dax club – persuaded him to take up the game. At 6ft. 7in., weighing over 17 stone and with a basketball player's hands, Roumat took to the game with alacrity and, at the age of 22, made his debut against the All Blacks. The most consistent line-out jumper in France for many years, Roumat soon became a regular feature of the second row, although he did miss the 1992 tour to Argentina after being sent-off for stamping whilst playing for the World XV against the All Blacks in the 1992 Centenary Celebrations. Roumat has had his share of periods out of favour – such as when he played for Natal for a season against the wishes of the French Federation – but has also had some glorious successes against the cream of the Southern Hemisphere. Those finest moment include leading France to a series win over South Africa (the first on South African soil since 1958), captaining France during the shock win over the world champion Wallabies in Bordeaux in 1993, and then in 1994 the awesome achievement of being part of the only side except the 1937 Springboks to win two Tests in a row in New Zealand.

Mannetjies Roux

South Africa
1960–1970
Centre

Mannetjies Roux, the popular name of Francois du Toit Roux, was a brilliant individualist and yet another product of the celebrated Stellenbosch factory line where Danie Craven rolled out world class backs with almost indecent speed. A small, agile man and a darting, nippy runner, Roux was also a killer tackler with a big heart, often taking on and bringing down forwards twice his size. But it was an infamous tackle on British Lions' star Richard Sharp which won him international notoriety because of the fractured cheekbone suffered by the England fly-half in the incident during the 1962 tour match against Northern Transvaal. Putting Sharp – the only British back capable of unlocking the Springbok defences – out of commission earned him the label in the Fleet Street press as the "Monster", a sobriquet hardly fitting a man standing 5ft. 8in. and 13 stone in a dripping wet shirt. Roux was to go on to a distinguished career of 27 Tests, 21 at centre and six on the wing, his less preferred position. An accomplished try-scorer, the pick of his bunch was try against the Lions in the Fourth Test in 1962 when he sidestepped and waltzed through six tackles to score. Mannetjies ended his career on a high note as a star of the 3–1 series win over the powerful 1970 All Blacks.

John Rutherford

Scotland
1979–87
Fly-half

Outside Wales, perhaps only the Irish pair of Tony Ward and Ollie Campbell were able to hold a candle to fly-half John Rutherford, the man who dominated Scottish back play for most of the 1980s. Rutherford was peerless when halfback partner Roy Laidlaw dogged it out in front of him (they played together a record 35 times for Scotland) and gave the Selkirk man time by providing quick ruck and maul ball as the Scots tried to play a fast-moving game. Deceptively quick and a natural athlete, he was able to hoof the ball prodigious distances or beat a man one-on-one, seemingly at will. Allied to a keen Rugby intellect, Rutherford was Scotland's star turn throughout the 1980s. Surprisingly durable for a slender man, Rutherford was an ever present from his first cap in 1979 – the year when Scotland lost five Tests – until injury finally finished him off during the 1987 World Cup opener against France. His high points were a Grand Slam in 1984 and playing for the 1983 Lions in New Zealand, even if it was at centre outside Ollie Campbell in a whitewashed side.

Ken Scotland

Scotland
1957–65
Full-back

Like Gavin Hastings against France nearly three decades later, Ken Scotland started his international career on a high note, scoring all six points in his country's win over France. Yet although Scotland made a huge impact as he won his first cap aged 19, it could all have been so different. Until circumstances caused his selection at full-back for the Scottish Trial earlier that year, Scotland had always played fly-half. That experience of playing fly-half added another dimension to his game, and he soon emerged as the first true attacking full-back in an age where a safety-first attitude and a large boot were the most important attributes for any No.15. Although he struggled to establish himself at Cambridge University, it did give him a chance to work in tandem with Scotland's visionary fly-half Gordon Waddell, also at Cambridge, on the move where the full-back came into the line at speed between fly-half and inside centre. Novel at the time, it is now the staple diet of attacking full-backs the world over. Scotland made the cut for the 1959 Lions tour to New Zealand, playing five of the six Tests despite going as second choice to Welshman Terry Davies. The Fourth Test win is still regarded as the high point of an outstanding career in which one man redefined the role of full-back, winning 27 caps in the process.

Philippe Sella

France
1982–95
Centre

Agen centre Philippe Sella retired from international Rugby in 1995 as the most capped player in the history of the game after wearing the French jersey in a total of 111 full Tests. A stocky player whose prodigious strength in defence was allied to a blistering turn of pace in attack, Sella was also remarkably consistent, his durability leading to a run of 45 consecutive Tests at one stage, while he scored tries at a steady rate throughout his career, finishing with a tally of 30. Sella made his international debut, aged 20, on the wing in a rare defeat by Romania in 1982, although he was not in any state to care after being concussed and spending the night in a Bucharest hospital. Sella also played a number of games at full-back. The milestones in an unparalleled career are too numerous to all be listed, but scoring a try in each of the four matches of the 1986 Five Nations and playing in every game of the 1987 Grand Slam would certainly be among them. Sella also took part in the first three World Cups, finished runner-up in 1987, was knocked out by England in the quarter-finals in 1991 and avenged the misfortunes of 1991 by beating the English in the play-off for the bronze medal in 1995. Except for the very early years of his career when he played amateur Rugby League in Clairac and a couple of formative seasons with Valance D'Agen, Sella remained faithful to the Agen club until 1996 when, with the game now fully professional and having made the decision to retire from international Rugby, Sella joined the north London club Saracens in 1996 and spent two years with them, helping the club win the English Cup Final in 1998.

Richard Sharp

England
1960–67
Fly-half

Although Richard Sharp was given his international debut only because of an injury to incumbent fly-half Bev Risman, the Cornishman did not need to be asked twice and delivered a mesmeric performance full of poise and menace to destroy Wales 14–6. Given his imperious form and the understanding he had clearly developed with scrum-half Dickie Jeeps, Sharp retained his place even when Risman was ready to return and was considered one of the key figures in England's 1960 Triple Crown. When Risman switched codes the next season, Sharp assumed the mantle of the saviour of English back play, and when the Lions side was selected for the 1962 tour to South Africa, the rugged former Commando's name was the first on the teamsheet. Yet a head-high tackle by Springbok centre Mannatjies Roux in an early match of the tour smashed Sharp's cheekbone and the Bristol player had to wait for the chance to show the South Africans his elusive running or ability to shift up a gear and squeeze through the smallest of gaps. Although Sharp recovered to play in the final two Tests, the Lions back play was pedestrian without him and the tourists failed to win a Test. Sharp led England to the Five Nations Championship in 1963, including the historic 13–6 win in Cardiff, but that effectively marked the end of his career apart from his 14th and final cap in the 23–11 trouncing by Australia at Twickenham in 1967.

Wayne Shelford

New Zealand
1986–90
No. 8

"Buck" Shelford was one of the All Blacks who had a long wait for his Test debut. He was first chosen for New Zealand on the tour that never was, the 1985 visit to South Africa that was cancelled because of court action. He made his debut on the replacement tour to Argentina but had to wait for a Test debut until the retirement of Murray Mexted. His first Test was in France in 1986 and he thereafter became one of the most popular rugby players in New Zealand, crowds loving his no-nonsense style and his utter commitment. He played in all but one match when New Zealand won the World Cup in 1987 and when David Kirk retired, Shelford took over as captain, leading New Zealand through its unbeaten run in the late 1980s under coach Alex Wyllie. He was controversially dropped after a successful but hard-fought home series against Scotland in 1990, prompting a wave of "Bring back Buck" sentiment throughout New Zealand that was unprecedented. But the selectors decided 22 caps were enough for Shelford and so, disillusioned, he moved to England to coach Northampton.

Jean-Claude Skrela

France
1971–78
Flanker

Skrela made his international debut in 1971 in the Second Test against South Africa in Durban. Skrela replaced Walter Spanghero, who had been dropped after a disappointing First Test. The Toulouse prodigy managed to hold his Test berth through the two-Test autumn series against the Wallabies, before he was replaced by Beziers's Olivier Saïsset. From then until the 1975 Five Nations, Skrela's performances for France were intermittent as he fought a four-way competition for an international berth with Bié-mouret, Boffelli and Saïsset. By 1975 Skrela had established himself in the French side and in 1977 played no small part in helping France win the Grand Slam. Yet he retired prematurely at the end of the 1978 season when he was twice overlooked for the captaincy of France. Although leaving on a losing note when Wales denied France their second Grand Slam in a row, Skrela scored his only international try of a 46-cap career that day. He then embarked upon a successful coaching career, taking up the post of coach of France in 1995. He guided them to Grand Slams in 1997 and 1998.

Andrew Slack

Australia
1978–87
Centre

One of the Rugby's thinkers, as a player Slack was a talented play-maker whose intuitive knowledge of the game helped him dictate the pace of the proceedings. He was lucky to have gifted individuals such as Mark Ella, Nick Farr-Jones and Michael Lynagh around him, for they fed off his organisational skills and sheer will-to-win as he lived off their creativity. That was one of the reasons that Slack became one of Australia's best captains: he knew what made players tick, who gelled with whom, and worked accordingly. An intelligent, straight-down-the-line man, Slack enjoyed the respect and trust of his team-mates, which impacted upon the way he led the side. He never shouted, he never screamed and he never had to raise his voice – he was the sort of man whose quiet instructions were listened to and then followed. A man who once said he would rather win a game 3–0 than lose 60–59, Slack was also dedicated to winning and managed to pass that on to his charges – it obviously worked because, under his leadership, the Wallabies completed a Grand Slam tour of Britain in 1984 and wrested the Bledisloe Cup from the All Blacks on New Zealand soil in 1986. It was disappointing that after winning 39 caps, Slack retired on a low note following Australia's 22–21 bronze medal play-off defeat against Wales in the 1987 World Cup.

Fergus Slattery

Ireland
1970–84
Flanker

Over the years, Ireland have produced many barnstorming forwards, men like George Beamish, Bill McKay, Ken Goodall and Jim McCarthy. But no Irish back-rower ever managed to fuse speed, fire and commitment quite as successfully as open-side flanker Fergus Slattery. At his peak, only Frenchman Jean-Pierre Rives of his contemporaries occupied the same stratosphere as the Blackrock flier. A fitness fanatic and doggedly determined tackler, Slattery's keen rugby brain ensured perfect lines of running and an extremely high count of hits on fly-halves. In an international career spanning 14 years, Slattery captained his country 17 times – including the victorious 1979 tour to Australia – and won 61 caps for Ireland, a record for a flanker, yet it is as a Lion that Slattery will be best remembered. In 1971, as a 21-year-old, injury and the dominance of Welshman John Taylor meant that Slattery did not face the All Blacks in a Test. Three years later, though, Slattery was at his phenomenal best as the Lions stormed through South Africa unbeaten. Much of the credit for that success was down to the forwards who, for virtually the first time since the 1890s, were able to dominate the mighty Springbok forwards on their own soil in South Africa. On the hard grounds of the high veldt, Slattery was outstanding, playing a central role in all four Tests. He threatened to have the final say when he touched down just before the whistle went in the drawn Fourth Test, but the referee controversially ruled no try.

David Sole

Scotland
1986–92
Prop

Loose-head prop David Sole is another of those players who is remembered and virtually defined by one moment: in this case it was when he made the decision for his side to take the now famous walk onto the pitch for the Grand Slam decider against England at Murrayfield in 1990. As a statement of resolve, it was a masterstroke from which the English never recovered as they lost the most high-profile game in Five Nations rugby history. It also cemented Sole's name in Scottish folklore. But if Sole if remembered for that day, it was only a snapshot in an illustrious career that brought him 44 caps. As well as captaining a Scotland Grand Slam side, Sole was also a key component of the British Lions side which stormed through Australia in 1989. That tour, in particular, was one suited to Sole, who remains probably the greatest ball-handling prop of the modern era. Relatively small for his position, there was a constant question-mark over Sole's scrummaging ability, especially after England's pack destroyed Scotland in the tight during the 1991 World Cup semi-final. Sole, though, makes the point that he never conceded a push-over try in his career. It is a point of honour for Sole, one of the game's most softly-spoken and considered men off the field and one of the most inspirational and thoughtful captains and players on it.

Walter Spanghero

France
1964–73
No. 8

The most famous member of a Rugby dynasty who dominated French rugby during the 1960s and 1970s, Walter Spanghero represented France 51 times in the decade between 1964 and his retirement in 1973. Despite being only 6ft. 1in. tall, Spanghero was a bull of a man; immensely strong, frighteningly committed and one of the most physically intimidating forwards of his generation. The Narbonne bruiser made his debut in France's memorable 8–6 win over South Africa in Springs during a one-off Test in 1964. During that match, Spanghero formed a second row pairing with another outstanding converted No. 8 of the time, Benoit Dauga, which lasted until March 1967 when Spanghero was injured and pulled out of the Italian game. They resumed their partnership in the Second Test of the 1967 South African tour, but this was going to be Spanghero's penultimate game at lock forward. In the Third Test he joined the back row, to become one of the best and most influential No.8s in the game. He played in all four matches of the 1968 Grand Slam and became captain of France in February 1972. His younger brother Claude won 22 caps between 1971 and '75 while the senior Spanghero, Jean-Marie, and the youngest, Gilles, were useful club players who repre-sented the two family clubs of Narbonne and Castelnaudary.

Joe Stanley

New Zealand
1986–90
Centre

Joe Stanley was one of the most underestimated yet effective achievers of the great All Blacks team of the late 1980s that went, under coach Alex Wyllie, 20 test matches without defeat. A dependable centre with outstanding peripheral vision, he was introduced to the All Blacks in 1986 for the Test against France, when most of the leading All Blacks were ineligible following the rebel Cavaliers tour to South Africa. He retained his place with marked effect, giving the All Blacks a midfield solidity that had previously been questionable and giving his wings welcome opportunities. A quiet, unassuming man, Stanley never gave interviews reputedly because in the early stages of his career he had been misquoted by a journalist. "Smokin' Joe" Stanley was one of the outstanding players in New Zealand's World Cup win in 1987 and remained an essential cog in the All Black game plan for the rest of the 1980s. Like his captain and close friend, Buck Shelford, Stanley was dropped after the 1990 series against Scotland. Capped 27 times by the All Blacks, the hole left by his his departure was plain to see during the 1991 World Cup when the New Zealand backs looked a sorry sight as they were comprehensively beaten by Australia in the semi-final.

Alan Tait

Scotland
1987–
Centre

Kelso centre Alan Tait is one of an elite band who has been capped for Britain at Rugby League and Rugby Union, and one of the few Scots to have made the move from Union to League. First capped during the 1987 World Cup, when he came on as a replacement in the 20-20 draw with France, Tait had only won eight caps when he went to League in 1988. A stocky, muscular runner and a superb defensive tactician, Tait was superbly suited for the League code and played in tandem with other exiles such as Jonathan Davies. When the barriers between the codes came down after 1996, Tait was one of the first players to come back. But he had not yet made it back into the Scotland set-up when he was called by the Lions' Scottish coaching duo, Telfer and McGeechan, to join the party to go to South Africa in the summer of 1997. A sledge-hammer tackler with a keen tactical sense, Tait made it into the Test side as a winger, playing in both of the wins and scoring one of the tries which won the series. Although he wasn't expected to make it into the 1999 Scotland Five Nations side, an injury to Jamie Mayer was enough to see the rejuvenated old-stager pick up four more caps – to take his caps to 22 and try-total to 14 – as Scotland topped the Championship.

Gary Teichmann

South Africa
1995–
No. 8

Thrown the biggest hospital-pass in the history of South African rugby, quietly-spoken No.8 Gary Teichmann had little choice but to get on with the job. "It was, though, hardly the best way to get the job," said Teichmann. He is, of course, referring to the way in which he was made Springbok captain after the controversial decision to drop Francois Pienaar, the clean-cut player whose lifting of the 1995 World Cup in South Africa made him about the most popular white man in the country. Since then, however, Teichmann has proved all of the doubters very wrong. A tidy, committed player with a decent turn of pace but an outstanding tactical brain, Teichmann has gone from something approaching national pariah to become the most successful captain in the history of South African rugby. Not only are South Africa the Tri-Nations champions, but they achieved the feat undefeated. Against the best in the world, South Africa put together a record-equalling run of 17 unbeaten Tests, a sequence which only came to an end when an exhausted touring party lost the last match of their European tour by a score at Twickenham. Now South Africa's most-capped captain.

Kel Tremain

New Zealand
1959–68
Flanker

Kel Tremain was one of the finest flankers in world Rugby in the 1960s and seemed to epitomise the New Zealand spirit of unflagging energy and unwillingness to compromise. He made his debut against the 1959 Lions and for the next decade, the All Blacks seldom took the field for an international without him. Though not regarded as a big forward, he was an asset in line-outs for New Zealand and especially in the driving move that came to be known as the "Willie away", named after his first captain Wilson Whineray. Tremain scored ten tries in 38 Tests, which was then an All Black record. He captained New Zealand once in a Test, against France in 1968, but that was his last series. It was a major surprise the following year when he was omitted from the All Black side to play Wales and by the end of the year he announced his retirement. Tremain turned to administration and became chairman of the successful and innovative Hawke's Bay union and a member of the NZRFU council. He was being touted as a future NZRFU chairman when he died suddenly in 1992.

Rory Underwood

*England
1984–96
Wing*

With 85 caps, Rory Underwood is the fourth most-capped player of all-time and the English record holder, not only for caps won, but for tries scored. His total of 49, including five against Fiji in 1989, a feat that equalled Dan Lambert's 1907 record, is unsurpassed in English Rugby. Underwood was first capped as a 20-year old against Ireland in 1984. Since then he has managed to juggle his life as an international Rugby star with his career as a fighter pilot in the RAF. Indeed, were it not for his flying commitments that prevented him touring with England to South Africa in 1984 and Argentina in 1990, Underwood would have more caps in his collection. Although justifiably criticised in the past for defensive aberrations - Wales have made him look inept on a couple of occasions - Underwood is devastatingly quick once the ball is in his hands. Two Lions' tours (Australia in 1989 and New Zealand in 1993) bear testimony to the quality of his try-scoring ability. His younger brother, Tony, has also played on the wing for England and when, in 1993, they lined up against Scotland in the Five Nations, they became the first brothers to appear in an England Championship side since the Wheatleys in 1938.

Roger Uttley

England
1973–80
Utility forward

A player who earned his spurs as a young lock in 1973 and 1974, Roger Uttley will be best remembered as a blind-side flanker after winning four caps in that position for the victorious 1974 Lions in South Africa. Originally selected as a lock for the 1974 series, as the tour progressed it became clear that Uttley was ideally suited to play the blind-side stopper role that Derek Quinnell and Peter Dixon had so admirably performed three years earlier in New Zealand. Tall at 6ft. 5in., raw-boned and utterly committed, Uttley was also superbly fit and strong, making up for a lack of genuine pace with a shrewd rugby brain, unstinting effort and an ability to make a difference when he did arrive at the breakdown. Sound in defence, Uttley was perfect material for the Lions adding the necessary physical edge to Fergus Slattery's pace and Mervyn Davies' ball-handling excellence. After 1974, however, Uttley's career was blighted by injury, and he was never to tour with the Lions again. He eventually retired in 1980 after he had helped England to their first Grand Slam for 23 years. The final 30–18 win over Scotland at Murrayfield was his 23rd cap for his country, of which 11 were won at second row, seven at No. 8 and just five caps on the blind-side.

Joost van der Westhuizen

South Africa
1993–
Scrum-half

Joost van der Westhuizen quickly established himself as the highest profile Springbok of the modern era after a spectacular 18 months in which he came from second grade university Rugby to become one of the most sought-after players in the world. Van der Westhuizen burst spectacularly onto the scene as part of the impressive class of '93 given its head in Argentina, and went on to have a spectacular year as first Scotland and then England were treated to outrageous individual scores. Yet if Van der Westhuizen became famous for his audacious tries, it was for his defence that his team-mates valued him every bit as much. Never was this more true than in the 1995 World Cup final against New Zealand, when the Northern Transvaal man was conspicuously quickest and most effective at bringing down the raging All Black giant wing Jonah Lomu. Van der Westhuizen may not have the finest pass in the world, and his options were certainly wild in his early years, but as a scrum-half prepared to spot a gap and accelerate through it he has no equal. Added to his good looks and star quality, it was a combination which drew Rugby League agents like bees to honey. In another era, Van der Westhuizen may well have been lost to the Union code, but with the Rugby union professional era ready to explode into being, the man with the Midas touch decided he could stay at home in Pretoria and have the best of both worlds. He won his 50th cap against England in 1998 and had scored 25 tries in that time.

Pierre Villepreux

France
1967–72
Fly-half

One of the finest exponents of the attacking game in his playing days, following his retirement Pierre Villepreux became the leading advocate of total rugby, the new game involving all 15 players in both attack and defence. An unconventional and passionate man, Villepreux has dedicated himself ever since to spreading the gospel of running rugby, and in 1997 was finally employed by France in an official capacity after already working with both the Italian and English national sides. Villepreux started his career at his local club, Brive, but became best known as a long-striding full-back for Toulouse. He succeeded Claude Lacaze in the French team in 1967, but was replaced by Jean Gachassin for the Welsh game in the Five Nations. The two-match experiment with Gachassin at full-back was deemed a failure, and the selectors brought Villepreux back for his first Five Nations match in Ireland two weeks later. Until the retirement of Angouleme's Lacaze in 1969, Villepreux was never able to claim a regular spot in the French side and missed the 14–9 win over Wales at Cardiff Arms Park, when France claimed its first Grand Slam in 1968. However, by the time Villepreux won the last of his 34 caps in 1972, beating Australia 16–15 to take the series at the same time, he had already assured his position as one of the greatest French backs ever.

Piet Visagie

South Africa
1967–71
Fly-half

Piet Visagie seldom received rightful acclaim as an international fly-half of repute. Somehow the freckle-faced player from unfashionable province Griqualand West always seemed to have to achieve the impossible before general acceptance of his talents, although a cursory glance at his Springbok record proves the doubters wrong. Until Naas Botha came along, his tally of 130 points in 25 Tests and a total of 240 in 44 matches for his country, was a record. Essentially regarded as a defensive, kicking fly-half – as opposed to his main rival of the day, Transvaal's mercurial Jannie Barnard – the Griquas' pivot kicked well with either foot and was a drop-goal expert who slotted five in Tests. Visagie could also make clean breaks as he proved in the 1969 series against the Wallabies when he scored tries in the Second and Third Tests of the series. On three occasions he topped 12 points in internationals, with his best all-round display coming in the series-clinching final Test in 1970 against the All Blacks when his solo try launched the Springboks to a 20-17 victory.

Tony Ward

Ireland
1978–87
Fly-half

There have been famous fly-half rivalries, such as that between England's quicksilver Stuart Barnes and metronomic kicker Rob Andrew, or that between Scotland's equivalents Craig Chalmers and Gregor Townsend, but the very public rivalry between Tony Ward and Ollie Campbell was probably the most intense contest for a No.10 shirt ever. It was a rivalry which has seemed to define Ward's career, the enterprising artist who lost out to Campbell, but never quite faded away. Nevertheless he earned but 19 caps in a decade-long international career. Ward burst on to the scene against Scotland in 1978, and for two years lorded it over European Rugby, being widely described as the best fly-half in the world, as he thrilled crowds with searing breaks and spontaneous brilliance. Yet for all that, the Irish selectors had him marked down as an individualist and, on the 1979 tour to Australia, dropped him in favour of the more reliable Campbell. Ward was stunned, the Wallabies were stunned and Irish rugby was in uproar, with every bar-room divided in a debate that raged for the next seven years. Yet campbell was an unmitigated success on that tour, leaving Ward in the international wilderness. The high point of Ward's career came in 1980, during the Lions' First Test against the Springboks – he had been flown out as a replacement for the injured Campbell – when he scored a record 18 points. Yet for one of Ireland's most naturally gifted footballers, his career yielded scant reward for so much talent.

Peter Wheeler

England
1975–84
Hooker

Capped 41 times by England, Peter Wheeler had all the mental attributes which go to make up a superb hooker. But he also managed to combine his fire and determination with a technical excellence that made him a truly outstanding competitor. His line-out throwing, in particular, was peerless and he was a solid scrummager who more than pushed his weight and who had lightning reflexes at the strike (in only his third inter-national he took four strikes against the head in England's 23–6 victory over Australia). Wheeler won seven caps for the Lions in the 1977 and 1980 tours. Unfortunately both were dogged by controversy and the Lions' performances suffered as a result. As captain of the Leicester Tigers, Wheeler led them to a hat-trick of national cup victories between 1979–81 and it was said that only his outspoken nature stopped him being awarded the captaincy of his country. That was an omission remedied in 1983 when just one week short of his 35th birthday he led England against the touring All Blacks, a match which an inspired England won 15–9. Wheeler is now president of top Midland's outfit Leicester and has been largely responsible for help-ing the club make such a successful transition from amateurism to professionalism, including the capture of the 1999 league title.

Wilson Whineray

New Zealand
1957–65
Prop

Whineray was a loose-head prop who won the first of 32 caps for New Zealand in 1957 and was made captain the following year for a series against Australia. He was then 23 and the youngest All Black captain for 30 years. He subsequently captained New Zealand against the Lions (1959), South Africa (1960), France (1961), Australia (1961–62), England (1963) and South Africa (1965) in addition to the 1963–64 British tour. When he scored the last of the All Blacks' eight tries against the Barbarians at the end of that tour, he was carried from the Arms Park and the crowd spontaneously sang, "For He's A Jolly Good Fellow". Whineray played for several New Zealand provinces but mostly for Auckland. Though a prop, he played successfully toward the end of his career as a No. 8 for Auckland and the All Blacks. Whineray became a successful businessman and director of several companies and was appointed by the government to chair various committees, including the Hillary Commission, the overall funding body for New Zealand sport.

J.P.R. Williams

Wales
1969–81
Full-back

John Peter Rhys Williams, universally known by the acronym J.P.R., became the iden-
tikit attacking full-back in the 1970s. Big, fast, fearless and utterly committed,
Williams was first spotted as a 19-year-old full-back on tour with a Wales development side in Argentina in 1969; he was quickly drafted into the senior side to make his
debut in the 17–3 win at Murrayfield. Williams's 15 stone frame, allied to strong running, was enough to unsettle any defence and he quickly became one of the most
potent threats in Wales's attacking armoury. Yet there was far more to Williams than
attacking prowess. Famous for his aggressive tackling, he was also rock-solid under
the high ball and positionally immaculate. Williams was fortunate to be a part of
Welsh back divisions that were truly gifted. He remains Wales's most capped full-
back with 55 caps and eight for the Lions. In a 12-year career he won the Triple Crown
six times, the Grand Slam three times and was only on a beaten Lions Test team once
in eight starts (Second Test against New Zealand in 1971). Almost as importantly to a
Welshman, he played England 11 times and was never on the losing side!

Jeff Wilson

New Zealand
1993–
Wing

Born in Invercargill, on the southern tip of New Zealand, Jeff Wilson has come to occupy a central role in the current All Black side. A footballing winger who fuses lightning pace with a keen tactical sense and a great boot, Wilson is the consummate all-rounder. Indeed, that is true in more than one way – the Otago wing or fullback is also a distinguished cricketer who opened the New Zealand bowling attack while still in his teens. It is no exaggeration to say that he is probably the most complete foot baller in world rugby at the moment, even if his talents are sometimes overshadowed by the more unmissable attributes of teammates Jonah Lomu or Christian Cullen. It says much for Wilson that since his debut he quickly became a regular in the All Black side which so impressed on its way to the 1995 World Cup final. Since then, even when the All Blacks faltered during 1998-9, Wilson still impressed, and the sight of his blond shock tearing down the wing was one of the few bright spots in an otherwise dreadful year for New Zealand rugby. Fast approaching a half-century of caps and thirty tries, and yet still only 25, Wilson will undoubtedly enter the New Zealand Rugby Hall of Fame before his playing days are done.

Stu Wilson

New Zealand
1977–83
Wing

One of the fastest and most explosive backs New Zealand Rugby has seen, Wilson played for the All Blacks between 1976 and 1983 and when he retired was the country's leading Test try-scorer with 19 in 34 Tests, a record subsequently broken by John Kirwan. Wilson made his debut on a New Zealand second team tour of Argentina in 1976 and made his Test debut in France the following year. He was a crucial figure on the All Blacks' Grand Slam tour of Britain and Ireland in 1978 and scored New Zealand's only try in the Welsh Test. His position in the All Blacks was unchallenged throughout his career and in the latter part of it, he was joined on the left wing by his Wellington teammate Bernie Fraser, with whom he later combined in a joint biography, Ebony and Ivory. Wilson's finest series was the 4–0 blackwash of the 1983 Lions, during which he broke Ian Kirkpatrick's Test try-scoring record. Regular captain Andy Dalton was unavailable for the tour of England and Scotland at the end of 1983 and Wilson was made captain, an experience he acknowledged he didn't enjoy. The Scottish Test was drawn and the England Test lost. Wilson, an extrovert and a natural comic, was regarded as too much of an individual to be a good captain and wing.

Peter Winterbottom

England
1982–93
Flanker

Few players in the world have been held in such high esteem either during their playing days or after their retirement as Peter Winterbottom, England's most capped
flanker. From 1982, a vision of the Yorkshireman's blond shock of hair screaming
towards them ready to deliver one of his telling, heavy tackles dominated the night-
mares of fly-halves the world over, for Winterbottom was a rugby nomad who plied
his trade wherever he felt most comfortable. By the time he retired in 1993 with 58
England caps and seven Lions appearances to his name, the Straw Man had spent time
in New Zealand with Hawke's Bay and, more spectacularly, with Transvaal in South
Africa, where the man is regarded as a living legend. At 6ft. 2in. and 15 stone, Winterbottom was the perfect build for open-side and although he lacked the handling skills
of the naturally gifted footballer, he gradually learnt how to mitigate these faults in his
game and he became one of the core members of the outstanding England pack of the
late 1980s and early 1990s. Although bedevilled by injuries throughout the late 1980s,
Winterbottom's England career spanned 12 years and he was as effective on his last
Lions' tour to New Zealand in 1993, as he had been on his first in 1983.

Keith Wood

Ireland
1994–
Hooker

Ireland and British Lions hooker Keith Wood has been one of the most distinctive figures in European rugby throughout the second half of the Nineties. It may be his distinctive bald pate that spectators see leading from the front, but Wood is in every way
a leader of men. The son of former Ireland and Lions prop Gordon Wood, the hooker
came up through the Garryowen club in Limerick, where his father was a stalwart until
his untimely death a few years ago. Fast and furious and fearsomely committed, Wood
is a hooker who plays the game like a flanker. His charges are often Ireland's primary
attacking option, while at his new club, Harlequins, his crashing sorties have become
his trademark. But it was with the 1997 British Lions to South Africa that Wood truly
came into his own. A motivator of men and an unquenchable spirit, Wood was one of
the few men to go toe-to-toe with the huge Springbok packs. His mobility was particularly important, although his game approach eventually cost him dear, sparking a
recurrence of the shoulder problems that have plagued his 24-cap career.

The Famous Coaches

Carwyn James once memorably defined the coach's role as follows: "The coach must resolve all that is difficult to resolve into something simple." Stunningly simple, yet stunningly true. Coaching has long been about the art of the possible, so the best coaches have invariably proved to be men who empathise with players and who understand their potential while also understanding their deficiencies.

As well as being a visionary with the ability to analyse and communicate, the great coaches have acted as mentors. The two are not synonymous. The great Danie Craven of South Africa, for instance, was a mentor to generations of players, but not a coach in the way that we understand it. But it is not possible to be a truly great coach without being a mentor, a man who players respect and have faith in. Welshman Carwyn James was just such a man. Although he never coached Wales, as coach of the 1971 Lions to New Zealand and the great Llanelli side of the 1970s, he had a level of success unprecedented in British coaching – and the players at the time place a good deal of the credit for their success in his coaching methods and quiet powers of motivation.

Another man of the same ilk was South African Izak van Heerden. Like James, his genius was never rewarded with the stewardship of his national side, but his intuitive analysis of the game and the principles he laid down are as valid today as they were in his heyday of the 1960s. Indeed, Springbok coach Kitch Christie openly acknowledged that his game-plan for the 1995 World Cup campaign was based on the principles laid down by Van Heerden 30 years before.

As the great thinkers of rugby football, New Zealanders have made a huge contribution to the development of the game, and none more so than Vic Cavanagh in the 1930s and 1940s. A rugged loose-forward with Otago in his day, where Van Heerden later developed a game with mauling at its centre, Cavanagh laid down the foundations for the intense rucking game that has been the model for New Zealand rugby ever since.

In that, he shares much with Ian McGeechan, the recent Scotland and British Lions coach, who qualifies as a great through his ability to develop a similar pattern of play which has seen Scotland make the most of meagre resources. That in itself is enough for McGeechan to make the cut, yet his versatility in taking the 1989 Lions to a series win in Australia – and adapting his ideas so that he centred his approach around the strong mauling English forwards of that time – and then doing the same eight years later with the British Lions in South Africa, assures him of his place.

Lastly, New Zealand's John Hart, the man who engineered Auckland's record Ranfurly Shield run and coached the All Blacks to an unprecedented series whitewash of the Spingboks in South Africa, deserves his place among coaching's greats despite the dismal season that he endured with the All Blacks in 1998-9.

There have been many other great coaches who do not feature here. Australia's Grand Slam coach Alan Jones and World Cup-winning coach Bob Dwyer both merit consideration, as do New Zealand's Charlie Saxton and Maurice Trapp. Geoff Cooke, who did so much to revive English rugby in recent times, the Ireland duo of Ray McLoughlin and Syd Millar, Scotland's Jim Telfer and South Africa's World Cup-winning Kitch Christie or Tri Nations-winning Nick Mallett all also deserve a place in the coaching hall of fame.

Vic Cavanagh

Father of the rucking game

Born:
June 19, 1909, in Dunedin

Died:
July 20, 1980, Dunedin

Nationality:
New Zealander

Teams coached:
Southern, Otago

Teams played for:
Otago (wing-forward)

Honours won:
Ranfurly Shield

Vic Cavanagh, the founder of the modern rucking game, is recognised as the best New Zealand coach never to coach the All Blacks and one who laid down principles generally followed in New Zealand rugby since the Second World War.

Cavanagh, who played in the old position of wing-forward for Otago in the early 1930s, also played cricket for Otago and was 12th man for New Zealand against MCC in 1933. His father, Vic Senior, coached the University and Southern clubs in Dunedin as well as Otago and was coaching University while his son coached Southern.

Cavanagh's greatest period was as Otago coach in the immediate post-war period when the province successfully defended the Ranfurly Shield in 17 matches and New Zealand rugby argued about whether: "the Otago game", as developed by Cavanagh, was good or bad. The New Zealand selectors must have thought it was good because when the All Blacks went to South Africa in 1949, 11 Otago players were in the side.

Although considered the best man to coach the All Blacks on that tour, Cavanagh was passed over in favour of Alex McDonald, a 1905 All Black who was then in his sixties. The All Blacks lost all four Tests to the Springboks, and Cavanagh thereafter refused to have anything to do with national rugby, remaining a trenchant critic of the

New Zealand Rugby Union until his death in 1980.

His coaching method was founded on the simple basis of forwards gaining and retaining possession, then bringing backs into play. Under him, forwards' body positions were crucial and Otago was renowned for its rugged, fierce rucking.

With the grounds in the South Island wetter than other parts of the country, Cavanagh's rucking concept was ideal. Otago forwards bulldozed over the top of the ball as soon as the opposition came into view. The physical momentum of the tactic overwhelmed all Otago\s adversaries.

It was used to great effect against the 1950 British Lions who were beaten 23-9 by Otago, an experience they admitted to finding "humiliating and discouraging".

After his retirement from coaching, Cavanagh wrote a series of articles about his beliefs and principles, and even now they could serve as a textbook for any coach.

"I believe it is impossible for a team to be successful over a long period unless it is able to build up, by a series of attacks, such unrelenting pressure that the opponents wilt sooner or later and allow the attackers in for tries," he wrote.

"Although the Otago forwards have had a large part in the tactics recently, the backs have scored the tries. I believe this is a sound method as the backs are faster and better handlers and, broadly speaking, it is their function to score tries. Give me an orderly and organised team, working in unison, helping one another, and I think they would score tries which would bring any crowd anywhere to its feet."

Ron Elvidge, the Otago and New Zealand midfield back, recalled Cavanagh's team talks as being models of clarity and recall. "He had a photographic memory, total recall of almost entire matches," he said.

Cavanagh became general manager of the Evening Star newspaper in Dunedin and the newspaper's boardroom often became a rugby forum when visiting rugby teams were in town. Among the coaches to seek him out was Carwyn James, the coach of the 1971 Lions, the first Lions side to take a series from the All Blacks. James and Cavanagh were closeted away in the boardroom for several hours before the Lions' First Test win in Dunedin.

John Hart

The Coach who won in South Africa

Born:

Auckland

Nationality:

New Zealander

Teams coached:

Auckland, New Zealand Colts, New Zealand

Teams played for:

Otahuhu, Stratford, Waitemata, Auckland (scrum-half)

Honours won:

Tri-Nations Series, Ranfurly Shield

In New Zealand's rich rugby tradition, there is still one benchmark by which all players and coaches judge themselves: their record against the Springboks. On that score alone, John Hart deserves his place in the All Blacks hall of fame, particularly given the controversial circumstances under which he took a young tour party to South Africa in 1996.

Hart had been selected as coach following the resignation of Laurie Mains in the bitter aftermath of the 1995 World Cup, when tactical naivety had allowed South Africa to snatch an extra-time victory in the final. A three-Test tour to South Africa was hastily arranged, following on the back of the 1996 Tri-Nations Series.

This was not Hart's first experience with the All Blacks. He had been backs coach during the 1991 World Cup, forming an uneasy alliance with Grizz Wyllie, yet the Tri-Nations Series and tour to South Africa was a chance for the prodigal son of New Zealand coaching to show what he could do. In just two months, the All Blacks defeated Australia twice and then beat South Africa five straight times – the last three in South Africa.

But if Hart cemented himself into New Zealand rugby history on that tour, it was an honour that had been brewing for many years. A scrum-half with Otahuhu, Stratford, Waitemata and Auckland, Hart displayed the virtues of shrewdness, thinking on his feet and an ability to inspire those around him that were later to stand him in good stead as a coach.

Although Hart never pulled on the black shirt, his experience at Auckland, year after year the most formidable side in New Zealand, gave him a priceless insight into what was needed to succeed at the top. By the time he gave way to Maurice Trapp in 1986, he had already established a legacy of success – in his five-year reign, Auckland played 90 games and lost only 11. Although Auckland is the most populous province in New Zealand, Hart's success was down to shrewd man-management and keen eye for talent.

Yet throughout his time with Auckland, New Zealand Colts and then the All Blacks, it was not just Hart's ability to gain results that marked him out, but his manner. An erudite and articulate man who doubled as a successful businessman, Hart successfully managed to draw together New Zealand's rugby public as he forged one of the best All Blacks sides of all time.

A high-flying businessman, Hart's independence and willingness to speak his mind often threatened to see him alienated on a whole range of topics.

His high profile stand on the rebel tour to South Africa and on Buck Shelford's sacking led to him being controversially rejected as All Black coach in 1988 and 1992, but rugby needed John Hart more than John Hart needed rugby and by 1995 he was back at the helm. In his last period of isolation in 1993–94 when a series of losses led to signs being erected in Auckland reading "Another Hart-less Performance", the subject of John Hart was a constant bone of contention between north and south islanders.

But Hart was perfectly suited for the new professional era – as he showed in 1996-97 by guiding New Zealand through what was arguably their toughest ever season. Only one defeat in seven full internationals against the might of both South Africa and Australia tells its own story.

Although his All Black side endured a terrible record of failure in 1998-9, when the departure of Sean Fitzpatrick, Frank Bunce and Zinzan Brooke ripped the guts out of his team, most of New Zealand has little doubt the little man will be back in time for the 1999 World Cup.

Izak van Heerden

The thinking-man's coach

Born:
> August 1910 in Durban

Died:
> June 1973

Nationality:
> South African

Teams coached:
> Natal, Argentina

Izak van Heerden was years ahead of his time, yet in terms of national rugby recognition in his own country, the former Natal mastermind was almost a forgotten man. It is true, that during his innovative days at the helm of Natal, then one of South Africa's less powerful provinces, Van Heerden reigned supreme.

It was not unknown for the scholarly-looking coach to arrive at practices straight from his school-mastering duties at Durban High School in tweed jacket or conservative dark suit. If this was considered eccentric, it became one of the many foibles that grew with the reputation. But there is no doubt that Van Heerden suffered at the hands of the crass thinking of the time, unless a coach had played for the Springboks, he should be disqualified from being South Africa's coach.

But if he was a neglected visionary in his own land, Van Heerden became a helping hand greedily grasped by others. He became a mentor for Argentine rugby after he first flew to Buenos Aires to help them prepare for their first trip to South Africa during the 1960s.

It was the start of a long and happy relationship, especially as Van Heerden virtually invented what we now term the "tight loose", an area in which the Argentines still excel. The Pumas repaid the initial debt by beating the Junior Springboks at Ellis Park, and their emergence as one of the better modern rugby nations is due largely to the talents of the quiet Durban schoolmaster and rugby tactician.

His celebrated work, Thinking Rugby, has become the game's bible for coaches around the globe. Several strategies devised by Van Heerden during his rise to prominence when he masterminded Natal's win over the touring Australian Wallabies in 1953, to his death some twenty years later, have become part of the high-speed, high-intensity modern game.

The late Kitch Christie, the man who guided South Africa to their 1995 World Cup triumph, was a committed Van Heerden disciple, having studied and used many of his methods. If Christie was the most prominent of Van Heerden's followers, many others adopted him as a role model and his fame as a rugby coach grew in Britain as reports filtered through about the rugby guru with the golden touch.

Somehow, however, all these acknowledgments worked against him in his native South Africa. Petty jealousies overtook his growing reputation and, apart from one series against the British Lions in 1962 in which the Lions were comprehensively outplayed, losing the series 3-0, Van Heerden's massive input was not required by South Africa. Yet his footsteps laid a path for others, like Christie, to follow.

His unique ability to create scoring opportunities by playing 15-man rugby, even with limited possession from tight phases, made him a formidable adversary. Among the great players who went through Van Heerden's hands were Springboks like Tommy Bedford, Keith Oxlee, Trix Truter and Snowy Suter.

As a player himself, Van Heerden had only moderate success. He was a loose forward, and once he had turned to coaching he brought perhaps the most insight to an appreciation of back-row play.

Kitch Christie revealed that he grafted much of his mentor's thinking on loose forwards onto his World Cup blueprint. "Most of what you hear the modern coaches saying and the phrases they use were first coined by Izak."

Carwyn James

Welsh visionary

Born:
1929

Died:
1983

Nationality:
Welsh

Teams coached:
Llanelli, Rovigo, Wales and the Barbarians, British Lions

Many coaches place a firm belief in luck playing a part in their team's progress. Carwyn James did not come into that category. For him preparation for every eventuality would negate the need for good fortune.

James was a very good player, although never in danger of being a great. Capped twice by Wales in 1958, against Australia at centre and France at stand-off, the Llanelli man was to make his indelible mark on rugby history as the coaching mastermind that gave form to the most outrageously talented tour party ever to leave the British Isles, the Lions of 1971 and the finest British side ever to play on home soil, the 1973 Barbarians.

Shy, unprepossessing and noticeably diffident as a young man, by the time James came to accompany Doug Smith on his first Lions tour to New Zealand in 1971, he had developed into an inspirational motivator of men and a shrewd compiler of game plans. With raw material like Barry John, Gareth Edwards, Mervyn Davies, Willie John McBride, Mike Gibson, J.P.R. Williams, J.J. Williams, Phil Bennett, Gordon Brown et al, James was able to produce sides able to compete in the harshest of rugby environments – New Zealand and South Africa.

Always a man who preferred pulling players in the direction he wanted, rather than trying to push them, James became a master not only at motivating players at the peak of their rugby careers but also of adapting game plans around the players available. Of all those players, it was a skinny kid from Cardiff via Llanelli called Barry John who stood out as the player around who James would base his whole game plan. "The King", as the fly-half was later to become crowned, responded in kind to establish himself as the lynchpin around which the 1971 Lions' triumph was forged.

But if James was able to inspire great players with quiet phrases such as his now famous aside to Phil Bennett – "now go and show the world what all of Stradey [Llanelli's home ground] knows" – then he was also capable of being extremely hard-headed when the situation warranted.

Before the second Test against New Zealand in 1971, James took Barry John out for a beer. Over a game of pool, James told John he wanted him to destroy the All Black full–back Fergie McCormick during the impending second Test. John did as he was told with a series of tortuous kicks that broke McCormick. He never played for New Zealand again.

Whether it was dealing with the media, or resisting the NZRFU's desires to appoint a referee who had once raised arms in triumph when the All Blacks had slotted a dropped goal, James could be stoically stubborn. As a street-wise coach, there were few to match a man better known for his fondness for back play.

James coined the now infamous phrase "Get your retaliation in first", during the often brutal Lions' tour of 1971, and he was also responsible for unleashing Derek Quinnell at All Black scrum-half Sid Going, a confrontation which was to be a turning point on that same Lions' tour. An ardent Welsh nationalist, James turned down an MBE.

Ian McGeechan

Master of psychology

Born:

1946

Nationality:

Scottish

Teams coached:

Scotland, British Lions (3 tours), Northampton

Teams played for:

Headingley, Scotland (32 caps), British Lions (8)

Honours won:

Grand Slam 1990 (with Scotland) Division 2 (with Northampton); two winning tours with the British Lions (1989 and 1997)

There is no more graphic an illustration of the flaw in rugby's traditional maxim that a good big 'un will always get the better of a good little 'un than Scotland and Lions centre Ian McGeechan. At 5ft 9in and 11st 7lb, "Geech" was nothing if not little, yet there can be few, if any, opponents who ever really got the better of him.

As a player, the softly-spoken McGeechan was a playmaker par excellence. Not the most physically imposing player in defence, he had very quick hands, skirted the off-side line and was a technically outstanding tackler. His greatest on-field achievement was to play in all four Tests as Willie John McBride's unstoppable 1974 Lions rampaged their way around South Africa.

Yet while McGeechan certainly rates as one of the best players ever to pull on a Scottish shirt, it is for his contribution as a coach that he will be best remembered. Although he moved straight into coaching at international level, eschewing an apprenticeship as a club coach, McGeechan was an instant success within the Scotland coaching set-up.

One of the game's most original and innovative thinkers, McGeechan explained his philosophy simply: "The challenge is to merge a group together to play one way and to have an identity. I lay down a tactical framework and say 'this is what I want you to do and this is how I want you to do it'. Then it is up to the players to adjust."

McGeechan's philosophy of "horses for courses" was one which proved spectacularly successful during his time with Scotland. In conjunction with Jim Telfer, McGeechan pioneered the fast-rucking style of play based around an abrasive backrow that has now become his national side's hallmark.

McGeechan immediately appreciated that Scotland's small pool of players and lack of muscular front five forwards meant that a style of play had to be developed which would make the most of the fast-flowing style of Scottish club rugby. So effective was the style imposed by McGeechan and Telfer that Scotland were able to prosper while at the same time mask the deficiencies of players struggling to compete at international level.

In 1995, a year after McGeechan retired as national coach, he became Director of Coaching at Northampton. Already destined for relegation from England's first division, the free-running style McGeechan imposed upon the Saints' youthful players saw them sweep all before them on their way back to the first division, where they subsequently consolidated their position in the top flight.

Yet it has not been just the Scots and Northampton who have benefited from McGeechan's coaching ability. During the first of his three Lions tours as a manager, when he coached the party to Australia, his ability to change tack in mid-tour and construct a side based around the strong-mauling English front-five led to a famous series win. McGeechan was back with the Lions in 1993 during the tour to New Zealand where the series was lost 2–1 after the Lions had battled back to level the series having lost the First Test 20–18.

In 1997 came arguably his finest hour when McGeechan coached the Lions to a 2–1 series victory against the Springboks. Asked to explain the reasons behind the Lions' 1997 success, McGeechan said: "We've tried to be positive and bold about everything we've done. We've encouraged the players to play open football."

That was also the abiding principle behind his masterminding of the Lions' stunning 2-1 series win over South Africa in 1997, when the tour party played a brand of attacking rugby that many thought beyond British and Irish players. McGeechan's legacy will be that when muscle was the answer in 1989, he used it; and when he needed to out-think the opposition in 1997, he was able to do that, too.

Wavell Wakefield

The First True Coach

Born:

1898

Nationality:

English

Teams coached:

Cambridge University, RAF, Leicester, Barbarians

Teams played for:

England (31 caps), Harlequins, Cambridge University, RAF, Barbarians,

Leicester

Honours won:

Grand Slam 2, Triple Crown 4 (as player)

Sir Wavell Wakefield might have been the man who gave truth to the myth of a rugby superman: the sort of man who could play, think, administer and charm all in the same afternoon. In fact, Wakefield performed all those functions over a lifetime, yet in rugby terms his was the most remarkable lifetime in rugby history. It would be no exaggeration to say that no man since William Webb-Ellis has done as much to give us the game we recognise today.

As a player alone, Wakefield did enough to enter any rugby hall of fame. A break-away with a breathtaking turn of pace, plus amazing strength and stamina, by the time he retired he had amassed a record 31 caps. Not only that, but he had managed that between 1920–27, during a period of unprecedented England domination of the Five Nations. As well as captaining his country to the Grand Slam in 1924, Wakefield also led two Triple Crown-winning sides. Whether wearing the colours of Harlequins, Cambridge University, RAF, Leicester, the Barbarians or England, Wakefield was probably the outstanding player of his generation.

But as an administrator, Wakefield was also way out of the ordinary. An ebullient and charismatic man, he quickly rose to the top and eventually became President of the Rugby Football Union.

In addition, Wakefield became a Conservative MP shortly after his retirement from the game, entering parliament at the age of 37. In 1963 he became the First Baron Wakefield of Kendall.

Yet it is neither for his on-field contribution or for his administrative genius that Wakefield will be remembered, but for his revolutionary changes that changed forward play forever. Until Wakefield arrived on the scene, the general form was for players to arrive at the scrummage or line-out as soon as possible and prepare for the set-piece in the order in which they arrived. Back row forwards operated on their own, independent of their fellow back-row forwards, in an ad hoc, haphazard manner.

What Wakefield did was to develop forward play into a highly specialised science by allotting each forward a specific function at the scrummage and in loose play. In addition, he also turned the breakaways from three disparate individuals playing games not related to each other into three-pronged tactical team with specific functions both in attack and defence.

Wakefield also reorganised centre play, removing the practice of playing three interchangeable centres and replacing them with a centre pairing – which later became inside centre and outside centre – plus a specific, dedicated fly-half.

When one looks at the other great coaches of all time selected, perhaps the most amazing thing about Wakefield, was that he built up all of his tactical acumen – and applied it – while he was playing. In this, as in virtually every other aspect of his staggering rugby life, he was unique.

The Great
Rugby Clubs

and provincial teams

While the armchair fan is content to watch the occasional international, the true "rugger-man" knows his Bath from his Beziers. The grass-roots are where provide the glamorous and gritty internationals. The next section provides insights into who and what makes the game great.

Agen

France

Founded:
   1900
Stadium:
   Stade Armandie
Colours:
   Royal Blue and White
Most capped player:
   Philippe Sella (111 caps for France)
Recent honours:
   None

More of an institution than a rugby club, the rugby bluebloods of Agen have long been a dominant force in French rugby both on and off the pitch. Their off-field domination comes from the patronage of the all-powerful Albert Ferrasse, a man who was for many years to French rugby what Rupert Murdoch still is to satellite television.

A former club captain who led Agen to victory in the 1945 Club Championship, Ferrasse ruled French rugby with a rod of iron for almost three decades until he voluntarily faded into the background in the early 1990s.

On the field, the power of this club from central southern France has been even more marked and has brought eight Club Championship wins at regular intervals between the first over Quillan in 1930 and the latest, over Tarbes in 1988, with a purple patch in the mid-1960s that yielded three Championships in five years.

The 1930 success was undoubtedly the sweetest for Agen, not just because it was their first Club Championship, but because on the way to the title, their 18 year-old winger, Michel Pradie, died from injuries received in an earlier round. It was his replacement, Marius Guirad, who dropped the winning goal in extra-time to give Agen an emotional win.

Agen have traditionally fielded well-balanced sides with tough packs and direct, hard-running backs. A name-check of Agen's past and present greats reveals a galaxy of gloriously talented players who have allowed the club to establish a versatile 15-man running game, which continues today.

Grizzled tight-forwards like Daniel Dubroca, Daniel Erbani and Francois Haget combined with back row legends such as Philippe Benetton, Pierre Biemouret, Abdelatif Benazzi and Guy Basquet to provide perfect ball for talented backs, of whom Philippe Sella — the legendary centre who remains the most-capped rugby player of all-time — and scrum-half Pierre Berbizier, the former French coach, remain the best known.

Auckland

New Zealand

Founded:
  1883
Stadium:
  Eden Park
Colours:
  Navy Blue and White
Most capped player:
  Sean Fitzpatrick (92 caps for New
  Zealand)
Recent honours:
  Winners of the Super 12 in 1996 and
  1997.

As befits the province which contains a capital city of one million people in a country of some 3,500,000 rugby-mad souls, Auckland have dominated New Zealand rugby since the game was first introduced in the 1870s. By whatever criteria Auckland are judged, the province has a record of success unrivalled in world rugby. Not only have they provided New Zealand with more All Blacks than any other province, but they have reigned supreme in both the Ranfurly Shield and the National Provincial Championship. As well as winning the NPC 11 times since its inception in 1976, Auckland also have a proud history in the Ranfurly Shield, in which the holders are subjected to constant challenges by would-be opponents.

Three periods of Auckland dominance stand out: the first after Auckland won the Shield from Wellington in 1905 and kept it for 23 challenges before losing to Taranaki in 1913; the second when the Fred Allen-coached side successfully defended their title a record 25 times between 1960 and 1963; and the third when John Hart's Auckland became the greatest provincial side in New Zealand history by retaining the Shield for an unprecedented 61 challenges over an eight-year period from 1985 until 1993.

That last stint of 61 defences was put together at a time when New Zealand rugby was at its most powerful. The core of the Auckland side that wrested the Shield from Canterbury in a contest of the highest drama were regulars in the All Blacks side which won the first World Cup in 1987, and five Aucklanders played in the 1995 World Cup final.

Although Auckland's grip on the Ranfurly Shield has been on and off since they relinquished it in 1993, they still won the 1996 and 1997 Super 12 competitions and have provided formidable opposition for touring teams. Australia have succumbed regularly, while Auckland claimed the Springbok head from the 1965 South Africans and have been putting British teams to the sword since the 1908 Lions were beaten 11–0.

Australian Capital Territories

Australia

Founded:
  1974
Stadium:
  Bruce Stadium, Canberra
Colours:
  White and Blue
Most capped player:
  David Campese (also NSW) 101
  caps for Australia
Recent honours:
  Runners-up in the 1997 Super 12.

After years of living in the shadows of New South Wales and Queensland, ACT were galvanised into action with an influx of Rupert Murdoch's cash that led to the setting up of what was essentially a Super 12 franchise in 1995.

Intent upon artificially strengthening a third province to boost Australia's representation in the Super 12 at the tournament's inauguration, the Australian Rugby Union chose ACT, a state centred around Canberra which was at the time vying with NSW Country for the position as the third state. In reality, ACT were a country mile behind the traditional powers of Queensland and New South Wales, but the ARU's financial largesse allowed a side to be constructed around the few home-grown players of genuine quality such as scrum-half George Gregan, hooker Marco Caputo and explosive utility three-quarter Joe Roff. A few grizzled veterans such as Troy Coker and Ewen McKenzie were thrown into the mix and, against all odds, the "new" province of ACT Brumbies (renamed after Australia's wild horses) performed outstandingly in its first Super 12 year, amazing the southern hemisphere with wins over Transvaal, eventual winners Auckland, and ending the season with a 70–26 thumping of Otago. The 13-9 win over former Super 10 champions Transvaal, whose owner Louis Luyt had derided ACT's prospects of avoiding humiliation, was particularly satisfying.

Despite the impact of the Super 12, the rugby history of ACT does not start and begin with the competition. As well as giving the world David Campese, who was born in the leafy Canberra suburb of Queanbeyan, ACT have notched up some famous wins over touring sides including a 21-20 victory over Wales in 1978 and a 35–9 win over Argentina in 1983. ACT also can boast the richest rugby club in the world, the Tuggeranong Vikings, a Canberra outfit whose wealth is built on the back of several hundred slot machines.

The Barbarians

Great Britain

Founded:
1890
Colours:
Black and White hoops

A unique club, the Barbarians have no home, no ground, no clubhouse and traditionally conduct all their business by post, yet an invitation to wear their broad black and white hoops remains one of the most sought-after honours in the game. The club originated in Bradford in 1890 by the famous Tottie Carpmael, a Blackheath forward on tour with a scratch London side who was so enamoured with the concept of an invitation-only touring side that he formed one at an after-match dinner. Carpmael's Corinthian founding principles have long been enshrined in the Barbarians code of honour, and the club's motto tells its own story: "Rugby football is a game for gentlemen in all classes, but never for a bad sportsman in any class." Accordingly, the Barbarians have played an adventurous and free-flowing brand of rugby that places endeavour and entertainment way above victory. Players are invited to play for the club on the basis that they adhere to those principles, and the result has been many outstanding games down the years. The most famous was the 1973 game against the All Blacks at Cardiff Arms Park in which, with the match only three minutes old, the great Welsh scrum-half Gareth Edwards rounded off one of the best tries ever scored on British soil to spark a contest of sublime skill and endeavour.

The Barbarians have tried to keep the fun in rugby and have always included at least one uncapped player while, in another quirky custom, players always wear their club socks. In the years after the Second World War, the nature of the Barbarians changed slightly, and as well as extending invitations to non-British players and touring some of rugby's far-flung corners like Canada and Namibia, any major touring side to the UK finish with a match against the Barbarians in one of the four national stadiums

It is a mark of the esteem in which the Barbarians concept is held that most other major rugby nations now have their own Barbarians side. The former Wellingtonian and All Black H.F. McLean set up a New Zealand equivalent in 1937, while Australia and South Africa followed suit two decades later. The most enthusiastic and the latest converts are the French, whose former captain Jean-Pierre formed a French Barbarians club in 1980.

Bath

England

Founded:
1865

Stadium:
Recreation Ground

Colours:
Blue, White and Black

Most capped player:
Jeremy Guscott (59 caps for England)

Recent honours:
English league and cup champions in 1995–96 and European Cup winners in 1998

It was the introduction of the Courage leagues into English rugby in the mid-Eighties that transformed Bath from an average side into all-conquering English champions. Having drifted aimlessly from one friendly match to another, the leagues now gave Bath the motivation they craved.

Bath adopted a professional attitude before the game even thought about jettisoning amateurism and amateur ways. A maelstrom of strong personalities constantly stirred by long-term coach Jack Rowell, Bath attracted players who wanted to push themselves and the club forged a self-sustaining ethos based around the ruthless pursuit of success.

Admittedly, they were helped by circumstances. A dedicated scouting duo in Tom Hudson and Dave Robson got the ball rolling by snapping up young talent from far and wide, while internal strife at traditional giants Bristol meant that players such as Gareth Chilcott, Nigel Redman and Richard Hill were driving through Bristol to play in the historic spa town of Bath.

Two immense local talents in Jeremy Guscott and flanker John Hall also added to the potent brew of talent and spiky temperaments, and from 1984, when they beat arch-rivals Bristol 10–9 to win the Knock-Out Cup for the first time, until the professionalism began to bite in 1996-7, Bath remained virtually unchallenged as the country's top side.

Since 1984 they have won the Cup ten times and the League six times since it was first contested in 1987 (including a run of four consecutive titles between 1990–94. Other players to feature heavily in the years of success include fly-half Stuart Barnes, full-back Jonathan Webb, flanker Andy Robinson, and centre Simon Halliday.

Bath became the first English club to win the European Cup when they beat Brive 19-18 in the 1998 final, but they have struggled to maintain that form in 1999, with clubs such as Leicester, Newcastle and Saracens catching them up.

Beziers

France

Founded:
1911
Stadium:
Stade De La Mediterrane
Colours:
Red, Blue and White
Most capped player:
Didier Camberabero (36 caps for France)
Recent honours:
None

Unlike Toulouse, Agen, Racing and Lourdes, those other giants of French rugby down the years, Beziers founded their period of dominance in the 1970s and early 1980s on an abrasive forward game supplemented with a percentage game behind the scrum.

Although neither popular nor pretty, it was a tactic that yielded spectacular results as Beziers' hardmen muscled their way to one adrenaline-fuelled Championship title after another. Taking over where Jean Prat's Lourdes had left off in 1960, Beziers won their first title in 1961, and have since gone on to lift the Bouclier de Brennus another ten times with a series of five back-to-back victories in 1971–72, 1974–75, 1977–78, 1980–81, 1983–84.

French rugby tends to be very parochial, and most players stick with their local club. In that sense, the small provincial town of Beziers was lucky in the 1970s that it threw up monster forwards such as Alain Esteve, Alain Paco, Michel Palmie and a prop from the lunatic fringe called Armand Vacquerin, who won 26 caps for France in the 1970s before killing himself in 1993 when he walked into a bar and played a (losing) game of Russian Roulette with himself after he failed to entice anyone else to play with!

The guiding light who transformed these desperadoes into one of the most formidable forward units European rugby has ever seen was a prop called Raoul Barriere, a man who saw more poetry in the blood and guts of a Kingsholm or Boet Erasmus than in the typical French virtues of guileful running and sleight of hand.

Barriere initiated, and for a long period sustained, Bezier's brutal assault on French sensibilities which lasted until the great pack finally began to fade in the late 1980s.

Blackrock College

Dublin, Ireland

Founded:
1882
Stadium:
Stradbrook Road
Colours:
Royal Blue and White
Most capped player:
Fergus Slattery (61 caps for Ireland)
Recent honours:
Runners up in the Irish league 1995

One of the foremost rugby nurseries in Ireland, Blackrock College nestles in a middle-class suburb of Dublin and, like virtually all of Ireland's top clubs, was originally conceived as an old boys club, although today all-comers are welcome.

Although many of today's players are no longer former Blackrock boys, the club still has a quiet and refined aura which belies the contribution that the club has made to Irish rugby since 1945.

Before the war, "The Rock" were overshadowed by fellow Dublin outfits Trinity, Bective Rangers, Old Belvedere, Wanderers and Lansdowne, yet in the last 25 years the sleepy club has made a profound contribution to Irish fortunes by supplying forwards of the quality of the uncompromising Willie Duggan, the toughest prop of them all in Ray McLoughlin and incomparable open-side Fergus Slattery, and backs such as Hugo MacNeill and the 55-times capped wing-cum-centre Brendan Mullin.

Since 1998, the Irish Rugby Union's efforts to entice Irish players back to play their rugby in the Emerald Isle has been a distinct blessing for Blackrock, with several recent internationals returning to boost their ranks while also turning out for the Dublin-based provincial side, Leinster, a boost for Irish rugby.

Bristol

England

Founded:
1888
Stadium:
Memorial Ground
Colours:
Navy Blue and White
Most capped player:
Robert Jones (54 caps for Wales)
Recent honours:
Division 2 champions in 1999

Schooled in the hard world of west country rugby and trips across "the bridge" to play the tough men from the Welsh valleys, it is perhaps surprising that Bristol has managed to keep up its reputation for enterprising and adventurous play throughout its illustrious history.

Nevertheless, from the early days when hooker Sam Tucker was a regular in Wavell Wakefield's outstanding England Grand Slam winning side of the 1920s, through to today, the west country club has consistently turned out exceptionally talented and competitive players. As well as forwards like Tucker, 42-times capped hooker John Pullin and teak tough flanker Tony Neary, Bristol have also produced a succession of fine backs such as prodigious wing Alan Morley, gifted fly-half Richard Sharp and L.J. Corbett, the "D'Artagnan of three-quarters" who mesmerised defences throughout the 1920s.

Bristol's greatest period was in the late 1950s, when the club scored 750 points in 42 games, conceding only 335, a huge differential in those days and proof that the all-action "Bristol Fashion" game was alive and well.

Bristol have not always had it their own way, however, and one of the most infamous days in the club's history remains the 41–0 thrashing administered by Dave Gallaher's All Black "Originals" in 1905.

More recently, the proud but somewhat hidebound club has seen a gradual decline in its fortunes, due in part to the emergence of local rivals Bath. The 28–22 cup win over Leicester in 1983 remains the Bristol's last major success, while the 10–9 loss to Bath in the following year's final signalled the start of a barren era from which the club has yet to emerge.

That, however, looks set to change in the near future. After the club suffered the indignity of bankruptcy in 1998, it was bought by local businessman Malcolm Pearce, who brought in a team including World Cup-winning Wallaby coach Bob Dwyer, who worked his magic to take Bristol back to the tp flight after only one season.

Canterbury

New Zealand

Founded:
1879

Stadium:
Jade Stadium, Christchurch

Colours:
Red and Black

Most capped player:
Richard Loe (48 caps for New
Zealand)

Recent honours:
None

The strongest side in New Zealand's
South Island, Canterbury have been the
most consistent challengers to Auckland
for the title of best province. Forward-
orientated Canterbury have presented
formidable opposition for touring sides
and domestic rivals alike since its formation in 1879 and retain a Ranfurly Shield
record that is second only to Auckland's.
The proudest of Canterbury's two major
Shield runs started in 1953 when
Wellington were dispatched 24–3, a win
which started a 23-challenge defence that
kept them at the top of the pile for most
of the 1950s. Arguably Canterbury
reached their zenith during that decade in
1956 when they beat the touring South
Africans 9–6, adding to their famous

defeat of the Springboks in 1921. The
men in red and black hoops also defeated
the Lions, Australia and the All Blacks in
the 1950s and have since gone on to
notch up wins against all the major touring sides. In doing so they have gained a
reputation as New Zealand's most brutal
province. Certainly 1971's 'Battle of
Canterbury' when British Lions' prop
Sandy Carmichael had his cheekbone
fractured five times, gives credence to
those who say Canterbury have trouble
differentiating between aggression and
downright violence.

Canterbury's second period of dominance started in 1982, when former All
Black and Canterbury skipper Grizz
Wyllie, a man who typified the harshly
physical, no-nonsense attitude of his
province, inspired Canterbury to win the
Shield from Wellington.

A record-equalling 25 defences later,
Canterbury were poised to win the record
for the most number of successful
defences when they met Auckland at Lan-
caster Park. But in a match of nail-biting
tension, Canterbury were defeated and the
power-base of New Zealand Provincial
rugby was transferred to the North Island
where it has remained ever since.

In the 1990s it must be said that Canterbury have found it hard to match the
pace set by Auckland, Waikato, Wellington and Otago in the Super 12 and in
1996 finished last in the competition.

Cardiff

Wales

Founded:
1876
Stadium:
Cardiff Arms Park
Colours:
Light Blue and Black
Most capped player:
Gareth Edwards (53 caps for Wales)
Recent honours:
Winners of the Welsh Cup 1996-97.

The self-styled "Greatest Club in the World", Cardiff have a playing pedigree and history that is unrivalled in the Northern Hemisphere. Originally a soccer club, Cardiff turned to rugby in 1876 four years before the formation of the Welsh Rugby Union, and started playing on a city centre site , the now famous Cardiff Arms Park. A continual conveyor belt of talent from Cardiff has kept Wales well supplied and the roll of honour at the club is impressive. Yet it says something about Cardiff that its players have not just been outstanding on the pitch, but have left an indelible mark on the game. Gwynn Nicholls is accepted as the founding father of Welsh rugby, while Frank Hancock, a gifted centre who played for Cardiff before the turn of the century, invented the modern three-quarters pattern that is standard today.

Percy Bush had a decisive impact in launching the game in France, while other Cardiff backs such as Wilf Wooller, Cliff Jones, Bleddyn Williams, Cliff Morgan, Rhys Gabe, Barry John and Gareth Edwards have become true greats of the game in their own right.

Blessed with such a wealth of talent down the years, Cardiif have claimed some notable scalps. The 1906 Springboks were beaten 17–0 in one of only two reverses on that tour (the other was against Scotland), while Australia have been beaten six times at the Arms Park, most memorably in 1947. But of all the wins in Cardiff's history, none is more sacred than the 1953 win over Bob Thomas's All Blacks, an event which is commemorated with a dinner each year.

So dominant were Cardiff in those years that they provided ten of the Wales' side which beat Scotland 14-0 in 1948, including captain Haydn Thomas and were able to field two first class XVs with identical fixture lists for many years.

Cardiff have struggled to retain their pre-eminence, but an appearance in the inaugural European Cup final and a spell out of the Welsh league, playing English clubs, have strengthened a very rich club – albeit one which has recently been at loggerheads with its Union – which also has the benefit of a huge following.

Cork Constitution

Ireland

Founded:

1892

Stadium:

Temple Hill

Colours:

White

Most capped player:

T.J. Kiernan (54 caps for Ireland)

Recent honours:

Irish Champions in 1990–91

One of the great sides of Ireland and the province of Munster, Cork Constitution have been enlivened by a century-long rivalry with the giants of Limerick rugby, Garryowen.

Formed in 1892 when the staff of the Cork Constitution, a local newspaper, joined forces with Cork Bankers, the genteel professional men of "Con" have been doing battle on Cork's behalf ever since..

The high point of Cork Constitu-tion's rugby came in the decade after 1963 which saw the club win six out of ten Munster Cup titles as the two greats of the club's history, flanker Noel Murphy and full-back Tom Kiernan, led a side which dominated the Limerick clubs and Con's Cork rivals, University College.

Noel Murphy, who won 41 caps for Ireland, eight for the British Lions and coached the 1980 British Lions to South Africa, is just one in a long line from the Murphy family who have seen service with the Cork club. Noel Murphy senior represented Cork and Ireland in the 1930s, and T.M. Murphy was a former chairman whose three sons all played for the club.

In recent years Cork Constitution have produced players of the calibre of second row Donal Lenihan, now Ireland manager, and scrum-half Michael Bradley, both of whom were Ireland cap-tains, but have struggled to remain com-petitive at the top level in the mid Nineties after a spate of player poaching by the newly professional English clubs and the Irish Rugby Union's decision to favour provinces over clubs as Ireland's representatives in the European Cup.

Coventry

England

Founded:
  1874
Stadium:
  Barker Butts Lane
Colours:
  Blue and White
Most capped player:
  David Duckham (36 caps for
  England)
Recent honours:
  None

Until the meritocracy of leagues foisted itself upon them in the 1980s, Coventry had enjoyed over a century of sustained excellence in which they had proved themselves one of the finest clubs in Britain. Formed in 1874, just three years after the RFU, Coventry soon established themselves as the dominant force in Midlands rugby and by 1908 had provided their first England cap in William Oldham. In the years that followed Coventry's status grew to the point where the club was seen as the main challenger to the Welsh "Big Three" of Cardiff, Swansea and Newport. The scintillating cross-border skirmishes of the late 1930s, in which Jimmy Giles and the Wheatley brothers took on the might of the top Welsh clubs, meant that the post-war clashes with Cardiff – the best club in Wales at that time – were eagerly awaited and drew sell-out crowds of over 40,000 whenever Coventry travelled to the Welsh capital. That period after the war was one of two halcyon periods for Coventry, with the Midlanders strutting their way through the 1950s in imperious style, often supplying two thirds or more of the Warwickshire side which won the County Championship seven times in eight years. Players like wing Peter Jackson typified the verve and elan of Coventry in those years, and it was no surprise when after a period of relative calm Coventry rose to prominence once again in the 1970s. As Coventry completed back-to-back Cup wins at Twickenham in 1973 and 1974, once again it was a stylish wing – this time called David Duckham – who captured the public imagination and came to symbolise the Coventry way.

The introduction of leagues in England in the 1980s, however, proved disastrous for Coventry as other clubs found the motivation and hunger previously lacking in their rugby and rapidly surpassed the once dominant Midlanders. Recently, however, post-professional Coventry have seen a large amount of cash come their way and have begun to knock on the door of big time rugby once again.

Eastern Province

South Africa

Founded:
1888

Stadium:
Boet Erasmus Stadium, Port
Elizabeth

Colours:
Red and Black

Most capped player:
Hannes Marais (35 caps for South
Africa)

Recent honours:
None

Eastern Province have a well-deserved reputation as one of the most intimidating and abrasive sides in world rugby and it is certainly true that some of the great rugby scraps of all time have taken place in Boet Erasmus.

Wilson Whineray's All Blacks gave as good as they got in the pitched battle of 1960, the 1974 Lions had to be at their punchiest to survive 80 torrid minutes, and in 1994 England back-rower Tim Rodber's international career took a major step in the wrong direction when he became only the second ever England player to be sent off following a punch-up in a bad-tempered clash with a Grizz Wyllie-coached Eastern Province. It is perhaps fitting that the most violent episode of the 1974 British Lions' tour, when the call of "99" went up and all-out mayhem ensued, was in the brutal Third Test at Port Elizabeth.

Yet, while Eastern Province's abrasiveness can cross the line, there is no doubt that the province has produced some fine forward packs in the past. The 35-times capped prop Hannes Marais is the best known Eastern Province forward, but by no means the only one.

Prop Amos du Plooy masterminded the defeat of Robin Thompson's 1955 Lions (Eastern Province also downed Ronald Cove-Smith's tourists in 1924); second row Gawie Carelse was enormously influential on the 1969 Springboks tour to Australia; and Willem Delport was the enormous hooker who combined so effectively with equally large tighthead Jaap Bekker to throttle the life out of Nic Shehadie as the Boks overwhelmed John Solomon's Wallaby tourists in 1953.

Eastern Province's favourite son remains centre Danie Gerber who, in a career ruined by the sporting boycott imposed on South Africa, still managed to accumulate 24 caps over 12 years.

Recently, however, the Super 12 reorganisation has meant that Eastern Province no longer exists in its old form.

Edinburgh Academicals

Scotland

Founded:
1857
Stadium:
Raeburn Place
Colours:
Sky Blue and White
Most capped player:
D.M.B. Sole (44 caps for Scotland)
Recent honours:
Scottish Division Two champions
1996-97

The oldest club in Scotland and argued by some Scots to be the oldest club in the world, Edinburgh Academicals was formed in 1857 to provide the old boys of Edinburgh Academy with sport and recreation. Since then, it has occupied a special place in rugby folklore, not least because its Raeburn Place ground was the venue for the first international ever played when England met Scotland in 1871.

That fixture was a result of the celebrated 'Letter' which appeared in The Scotsman newspaper on December 8th 1870, challenging the English clubs to an international match. The challenge

was accepted and on March 27th the game went ahead. Seven of the Scotland side were from the Academicals including the captain F.J. Moncrieff. The Academicals are also responsible for the oldest organised rugby game, that against Merchiston Castle School which was first played in 1859.

Immediately following their founding, however, matches for the Academicals were hard to come by, but gradually their fixture list increased, and by 1873-4 ten matches were played, all of which were won.

Since then, the club has gone on to supply Scotland with over 100 internationals, including the former captain of the national side Rob Wainwright, and one of his predecessors and arguably the greatest leader in Scotland's history, David Sole. It was Sole who led his country to the Grand Slam in 1990. He is now back at Academicals as coach and is determined to re-establish the club as one of Scotland's finest following the ignominy of being relegated from Division One at the end of the 1995-96 season.

With true Sole style the Academicals bounced straight back up again as 1996-97 Division Two champions, but have since struggled and have slipped out of Division One, threatening also to follow other august clubs such as Glasgow Accies into Scottish junior rugby.

Exiles

Great Britain
London Irish

Founded:
   1898
Stadium:
   The Avenue, Sunbury-on-Thames,
   Middlesex or The Stoop
Colours:
   Emerald Green
Most capped player:
   Brendan Mullin (55 caps for Ireland)
Recent honours:
   None

London Scottish

Founded:
   1878
Stadium:
   RAG or The Stoop
Colours:
   Blue
Most capped player:
   A.G. Hastings (61 caps for Scotland)
Recent honours:
   1991 Middlesex Sevens champions

London Welsh

Founded:
   1885

Stadium:
   Old Deer Park
Colours:
   Red
Most capped player:
   J.P.R. Williams (55 caps for Wales)
Recent honours:
   None

London has three main Exiles clubs, all based in the south-west of the capital. London Scottish, formed in 1878 and based in Richmond, are the oldest of the clubs and were the last to go "open" (in 1996). They have provided nearly 150 internationals, including Alistair McHarg, Gavin Hastings, past Lions captains Bill Maclagan and Darkie Bedell-Sivright, and ten who played in the Scotland team which beat the 1906 Springboks and won the Triple Crown.

London Welsh, formed in 1885, were at their zenith in 1971 when they were arguably the finest club side on earth. As well as providing the victorious 1971 Lions with captain John Dawes, they also supplied J.P.R. Williams, John Taylor, Gerald Davies and Mervyn Davies, quality players in the mould of earlier London Welsh greats Wilf Wooller, Claude Davey and Haydn Tanner.

London Irish, founded in 1898, were often regarded as the weakest Exile clubs, but in 1998-9 were strong enough to push for a European Cup place.

Gala

Galashiels, Scotland

Founded:
1875
Stadium:
Netherdale
Colours:
Maroon
Most capped player:
Derek White (41 caps for Scotland)
Recent honours:
Division 2 champions in 1999 and Tenents Velvet Cup winners, 1999

It is one of the enduring mysteries of rugby that the Borders of Scotland have managed to produce such a disproportionately large number of internationals for a rural region with only 100,000 inhabitants.

The Borders League, which was inaugurated in 1873, remains the oldest organised League in the world and is contested between the region's top seven clubs – Hawick, Melrose, Jed Forest, Kelso, Langholm, Gala and Selkirk. In an intense atmosphere permeated by ancient local rivalries, the Gala club has emerged as one of Scotland's finest outfits, supplying gritty players such as 27-times capped No. 8 Peter Brown, back

rowers David Leslie and Derek White and the hooker who captained Scotland's 1984 Grand Slam side, Jim Aitken.

Despite the fact that Gala's finest period in the 1970s came courtesy of some outstandingly combative packs with ferocious back rows, several of the club's most famous players have been backs of silky skills.

Current British Lions and Scotland fly-half Gregor Townsend, a local lad born in Galashiels within a mile of the club's ground Netherdale, won most of his early caps out of the Borders club, while Lions centre Jock Turner and his scrum-half partner Duncan Paterson were an enduring duo for Gala in the late 1960s. Gala provided six of the Scotland team which beat England twice in eight days in 1971, Peter Brown kicking a conversion at Twickenham to lay the Twickenham bogey to rest once and for all. Gala also stage an annual Sevens tournament, and as a club have traditionally been accomplished experts in the abbreviated code.

Although in danger of fading into obscurity at one stage in the mid nineties, when only a league reconstruction prevented relegation to Division Three, the club has found a new lease of life under new player-coach Gary Parker and in 1998-9 were not only promoted to Division One as champions, but also won the Cup, defeating neighbours Kelso 8-3.

Garryowen

Ireland

Founded:
  1884
Stadium:
  Dooradoyle, Limerick.
Colours:
  Light Blue
Most capped player:
  Gordon Wood (29 caps for Ireland)
Recent honours:
  Irish Champions 1994

Munster's premier club Garryowen play an adrenaline-pumping forward game that reflects the earthy nature of the club itself.

Coming from Limerick, the one place in Ireland where rugby has always been a game for all classes and all men, the players of Garryowen have an enthusiastic "up and at 'em" approach to the game that has spawned countless rumbustious forward charges over the 113 years since the club was formed. Indeed, the word "garryowen", which is now an accepted name for an up and under, has become a part of the game in itself.

First used in the 1890s when the men from Garryowen used the forward stampede forward in pursuit of a steepling up-and-under – all accompanied by the sound of the crowd's raucous baying – as a standard ploy, the tactic has remained synonymous with the Limerick club ever since.

A man from Cork, on seeing the "garryowen" in operation for the first time is alleged to have exclaimed: "Them Garryowen men are devils - they'd ate you without salt!"

It was certainly an effective tactic, with Garryowen winning the Muster Cup ten times in eleven years before the turn of the century, a proud record of success which has slowed but not died.

These days, Garryowen remain one of the finest clubs in Ireland, as befits a side which has boasted players of the calibre of 1950s prop Gordon Wood, his son Keith, 1980s fly-half Tony Ward and the Reid brothers, Paddy and Tom.

The origin of Garryowen's five pointed star sewn onto their jerseys dates from their early days. The star represents the five parishes of the city of Limerick and is considered a sign of good luck (although not necessarily for visiting sides).

Gloucester

England

Founded:
1873
Stadium:
Kingsholm
Colours:
Cherry and White
Most capped player:
Philippe Saint-Andre (69 caps for France)
Recent honours:
Cheltenhnam & Gloucester Cup winners, 1998 and 1999

Almost every major rugby country has a heartland in which rugby surpasses all other sports in popularity, and in England that heartland is the West Country in general, and the cathedral city of Gloucester in particular.

Nowhere in the country are townspeople as knowledgeable and passionate about the game as Gloucester, where the game crosses all social boundaries. Hard and remorseless, the Cherry & Whites of Gloucester are egged on at their Kingsholm ground by some of the most partisan and vociferous supporters in rugby.

A stoically forward-orientated club, Gloucester play a rugged ten-man game based around sheer power and a fly-half born to pump garryowens into the opposition 22 – a combination which has long made them the most formidable of opponents on their own patch.

That emphasis on forward play has resulted in a long tradition of supplying England with streetwise bruisers, men such as the flanker Tom Voyce who, along with Arthur Blakiston and Wavell Wakefield, made up the best back row in the world in the 1920s.

Other Gloucester men, such as 1981 Grand Slam tighthead prop Phil Blakeway, 1974 Lions loosehead prop Mike Burton and 1989 Lions Man of the Series, back rower Mike Teague, have typified the Gloucester approach.

Recently, the club has won plaudits by resisting the temptation to buy in the best players wholesale in the post-professional era, despite having the financial ability to do so. Sticking stoically to their network of traditional feeder clubs, the Kingsholm club have worked at developing their existing talent, hoping that the traditional fire, commitment and togetherness of Gloucester rugby would see them through.

Despite a disastrous inability to win away from home which cost coach Richard Hill his job in early 1999, the club has taken a conscious decision to retain its faith in bonding the innate talent of Gloucester players with a few talented imports.

Harlequins

England

Founded:
1866
Stadium:
Stoop Memorial Ground,
Twickenham.
Colours:
Light blue, magenta, chocolate,
French grey, black and light green
Most capped player:
Will Carling (72 caps for England)
Recent honours:
Pilkington Cup 1991

A founder-member club of the RFU, Harlequins have a famous tradition of elitism and a long and illustrious history. Well-heeled Londoners have always gravitated towards the club with the distinctive squares of blue, magenta, chocolate and grey, with sleeves of green and black.

Situated in Twickenham, Harlequins played their club games at the RFU Headquarters for many years (they played the first game there against Richmond in 1909) before moving to the nearby Stoop Memorial Ground, which was named after one of their finest early players, Adrian Stoop — who most to establish Quins as a side dedicated to producing brilliant running rugby, a tradition which is upheld to this very day.

Over the past 131 years, Harlequins have had a major effect upon the game in England, producing talented backs such as Ronald Poulton-Palmer, John Currie, Will Carling and Bob Hiller, as well as some outstanding forwards in Wavell Wakefield, Jason Leonard, Paul Ackford and Brian Moore.

Yet despite such rich resources Harlequins have long been seen as a club of wealthy dilletantes. It has not been an easy tag to shake in recent years, as Quins have shown an inability to reproduce their sparkling Cup form in the Leagues, a fact often blamed on their plundering of other London clubs for talent giving the impression that they are not a "club" in the traditional sense — more a home for a collection of economic migrants who are brilliant at rugby.

Nevertheless, with the arrival of professionalism, the London club have led the way in sponsorship by securing a five-year £4 million deal with Japanese electronics firm NEC. That money was used to buy in the cream of the current northern hemisphere crop, and to construct a magnificent new stand.

Despite still not challenging consistently at the top level, Quins have done enough to retain their Premiership status and qualify for Europe in the year 2000.

Hawick

Scotland

Founded:
1873
Stadium:
Mansfield Park
Colours:
Dark Green
Most capped player:
J.M. Renwick and C.T. Deans (Both
52 caps for Scotland)
Recent honours:
1996 Winners of the in augural
Tennents Cup

The most consistently powerful of the
Scottish clubs, Hawick is home to o ne of
the biggest population centres in the Borders and is a club with an enviable record
of success in Scotland. The club won the
first unofficial Scottish Championship in
1895 and since then have remained second to none north of the border.

Indeed, at one stage in the 1950s, so
outstanding was the general standard of
play at the club, particularly amongst the
forwards, that all 15 of the first team had
been approached by Rugby League
scouts from Yorkshire.

The first organised rugby matches in
Hawick, however, were far from out-

standing. It took the club a while before
goal posts were found, and for the first
couple of seasons matches were played
on a cricket pitch.

Despite these rather humble beginnings, Hawick can lay claim to being the
first Scottish club to host a floodlit
match. In 1879 they played a game under
electric light generated by two dynamos.
Unfortunately, the experiment was not a
success, with several players tackling
shadows in the general confusion.

Like all Borders clubs, Hawick's
game has traditionally been based on forward power and an intense rucking game
– as their nickname of the "Green
Machine" would indicate – yet the Mansfield Park men have also blended in
direct-running back play as part of a
wider game plan.

That has allowed backs such as slip-
pery 1970s' centre Jim Renwick and
wing Tony Stanger to play a full role
alongside a legion of forward greats such
as Colin Deans, Willie Kyle, Jock
Beattie, Hugh McLeod, Alan Tomes, and
Adam Robson.

Another local lad who looked set for
an illustrious career until injury intervened was Bill McLaren, the Hawick
Academy teacher who has gone on to
become the best-known and most highly
respected of rugby television commenta-
tor in Britain and probably the world.

Hawke's Bay

New Zealand

Founded:
1884
Stadium:
McLean Park, Napier
Colours:
Black and White
Most capped player:
Kel Tremain (38 caps for New Zealand)
Recent honours:
None

One of the giants of New Zealand's early rugby history, Hawke's Bay qualify as one of the Great Provinces largely because of two periods of dominance in the Ranfurly Shield that started in 1922 and ended in 1969, since when the rural province has gradually faded into the second tier.

Its first period of dominance began in 1922 when peerless full-back George Nepia and the famous Brownlie brothers – the "moving tree trunk" Maurice, plus Cyril and Jack – led Hawke's Bay in what was then a record of 24 defences of the Shield that lasted until 1927.

With coach Norman McKenzie at the helm, the side not only established a record of success, but also did it in style with some fine attacking rugby that was typified by Nepia's explosive running from deep.

Hawke's Bay's second period of success came thirty years ago when the great flanker Kel Tremain inspired his charges to first wrest the Shield from Waikato and then hold on to it for 21 defences in Fortress Napier until it was finally surrendered to Canterbury in 1969, having first being won in 1966.

As well as Ranfurly success in the Sixties, the decade was also notable for Hawke's Bay, not just because it produced the biggest ever attendance for one of its Provincial matches – 27,000 when Wellington came to play in 1967, but in 1963 the touring England side were thrashed 20-5.

Heriot's FP

Edinburgh, Scotland

Founded:
1890
Stadium:
Goldenacre, Edinburgh
Colours:
Blue and White
Most capped player:
A.R. Irvine (51 caps for Scotland)
Most capped player:
Winners of the Scottish Premiership, 1998-99

Heriot's FP, the old boys side for the famous George Heriot's College in Edinburgh, has a long and illustrious history in Scottish rugby, as do those other old boys sides in Edinburgh, Watsonians, Edinburgh Academicals and Stewart's Melville FP.

What makes Heriot's different is its ability down the years to produce truly talented full-backs as if they were coming off a conveyor belt. Ken Scotland is reckoned to be the greatest of them all, but 51-times capped 1970s legend Andy Irvine is not far behind and nor is the incomparable Dan Drysdale who played in all four Tests for the 1924 Lions in South Africa.

Other Heriot's full-backs worthy of a mention in the same breath are Jimmy Kerr, Tommy Gray, Ian Thomson, Colin Blaikie and Ian Smith.

Not to be outdone, however, the forwards have produced a mighty combination in recent years, with the Milne brothers Iain, Kenny and David all winning caps in Scotland's front row. Former hooker Kenny, who won 39 caps, became coach of Heriot's at the start of the 1996 season,but met with little success in his first year as the Edinburgh finished second from bottom.

Yet as the Scottish Rugby Union's Superdistricts policy removed many of the top players from club rugby, Heriot's underwent something of a resurgence in 1998-9, when Milne's young charges, superbly marshalled by captain and prop Jocky Bryce, brought the League trophy back to Goldenacre for the first time since the glory days of 1979.

Lansdowne

Dublin, Ireland

Founded:
 1872
Stadium:
 Lansdowne Road, Dublin
Colours:
 Red, Yellow and Black
Most capped player:
 Moss Keane (51 caps for Ireland)
Recent honours:
 Winners of the 1997 Leinster Cup.

A founder-member of the Irish Rugby Football Union, Dublin club Lansdowne are almost akin to England's Harlequins in that they play an adventurous brand of rugby and in that their long-term home is also that of the IRFU, Lansdowne Road.

Lansdowne have also managed to contribute a huge amount to Irish rugby, mainly through some of the outstanding players who have passed through their doors. In keeping with Lansdowne traditions, most of them are backs.

There were two star performers from the 1920s in full-back Ernie Crawford and talented scrum-half Eugene Davey, and at one stage in 1931 Lansdowne supplied the whole of the Ireland back line, with Ned Lightfoot, Morgan Crowe and Jack Arigho joining Davey in his country's colours.

Since then many other fine Lansdowne players have gone on to provide Ireland with distinguished service, including Des Fitzgerald, Alan Duggan, Michael Kiernan, Barry McGann and Eric Elwood.

Most of the club's original members were from Dublin University, Ireland's first rugby club, and Lansdowne's original name was in fact the Irish Champion Athletic Club. They became tenants of Lansdowne Road in 1872 and have been there ever since.

Although the first international match was played there as long ago as 1878 against England, it wasn't until 1880 that the Wanderers Football Club became co-tenants.

Another interesting aside concerning the Lansdowne club is that their colours of Red, Yellow and Black were adopted from the famous English cricket team, I Zingari.

Leicester

England

Founded:
1880

Stadium:
Welford Road

Colours:
Green, Red and White

Most capped player:
R. Underwood (England) 85 caps

Recent honours:
1997 Cup winners and European Cup runners-up. Premiership champions 1998-9

Leicester's growth into a giant of the English game started soon after the club's formation in 1880 when the organisational talents of a local merchant called Tom Crumbie helped transform the club into a slickly run operation. His cash also helped the Tigers travel far and wide and by 1909, when the Barbarians began their annual Christmas fixture at Welford Road, Leicester were firmly established in the top flight. After that, the club with letters on their backs instead of numbers – only Leicester and Bristol still retain this old tradition – went from strength to strength and in 1931 the club provided 12 of the players, including captain George Beamish and

playmaker Doug Prentice, who downed Benny Osler's touring Springboks by 30–21. Although Leicester continued to be a dominant force in English rugby, it was only in the 1970s that the club managed to pick up some silverware when the sides coached by Chalky White and containing players such as Dusty Hare, Les Cusworth, Clive Woodward, Paul Dodge and Peter Wheeler won 18 Cup matches in a row to take the Cup in the three consecutive years of 1979,80,81, thereby keeping the trophy forever. Since then the Tigers contested the Cup final six times, winning in 1993 and 1997.

Despite being one of England's top teams, Leicester have been unpopular among the country's rugby fans. A game-plan that involved keeping the ball in the forwards, only rarely letting the backs run with it, didn't endear them to the neutral spectator.

As conservative stalwarts such as Dean Richards and John Wells were phased out, however, Leicester returned to their trademark 15-man game, with backs like Austin Healey, Will Greenwood and Springbok No.10 Joel Stransky linking with forwards like martin Johnson and Neil Back. Although they lost in the final of the 1997 European Cup to Brive, they sent six players on the 1997 Lions tour to South Africa and now dominate the English premiership, winning the League in 1999.

Llanelli

Wales

Founded:
1872
Stadium:
Stradey Park
Colours:
Scarlet
Most capped player:
Ieuan Evans (72 caps for Wales)
Recent honours:
League champions, 1999
Welsh Cup and league winners 1993

When Llanelli scored their first victory over a major touring side with their defeat of Australia in 1908, it was seen as an event which warranted an extra verse to be added to the famous old club anthem "Sospan Fach". That song ("Little Saucepan", named after the end product of the nearby tin mines), was to be amended twice more in Llanelli's history: when Delme Thomas's men lowered the colours of the 1972 All Blacks and in 1992, when the Scarlets beat World Champions Australia 9–3.

Those are the proudest moments for the small-town club from the far West, where Welsh-speaking is the norm and rugby the religion. In the past thirty years, the club have been domestic champions on six occasions and have won the Welsh Cup nine times, including the three consecutive years from 1991.

Initially famed for tough packs which contained men such as Rhys Williams, the outstanding flanker for the 1930 Lions, Ivor Jones, Archie Skymm; 1966 Lion Delme Thomas and two great back-rowers of the 1970s: Derek Quinnell and Tom David, Llanelli are also widely famed for their spirit of adventure.

Llanelli have produced countless backs of immense talent down the years. Legends Rhys Gabe, Lewis Jones, Terry Davies, Wyn Brace, J.J. Williams, Ray Gravell, Phil Bennett, Ieuan Evans and Jonathan Davies have all worn the Scarlet colours with distinction, yet what few realise is that an adventurous game plan is no accident – Llanelli remain the only club in the world to have codified the running game so that it is part of their constitution. Every year John Maclean, who was Carwyn James's successor, sends out detailed instructions to every Llanelli player, of which the following forms a key part: "As in the past, the philosophy of Llanelli RFC is to try and provide entertainment and excitement for its supporters by playing effective and adventurous winning rugby which incorporates the belief that such an approach of justifiable risks, especially in running the ball from our own line and behind."

Lourdes

France

Founded:
1896

Stadium:
Antoine-Beguere

Colours:
Orange and Blue

Most capped player:
Michel Crauste (63 caps for France)

Recent honours:
None

When the Second World War finished and it became apparent that France were about to become a major force in the Five Nations, it was the great Lourdes side which formed the core of Europe's new power.

In particular, French captain and flanker Jean Prat was an inspiration and a seminal figure in the history of French rugby, yet he was by no means the only Lourdes player to play a key part in the coming of age of French rugby.

Before the war, Lourdes had just made it into double figures in terms of internationals to have played for the club, with 16-times capped 1920s star Christophe Dupont acknowledged as the best player to have represented the club.

After 1945, however, there was an explosion of talent in the small provincial town, with the Prat brothers Jean and Maurice to the fore.

Yet the Prats were by no means alone, and many of the true greats of French rugby played for Lourdes in the club's heyday between 1945 and 1970 when they won nine French Championships, including a run of six under Prat's inspired leadership.

The core of that side was formed by No. 8 Jean Barthe (who was once described by Danie Craven as the best forward in the world), Michel Crauste, Jean Gachassin, and many outstanding internationals whose names would not be out of place in France's Rugby Hall of Fame.

As a major power, Lourdes faded in the early 1970s as Beziers began to dominate, yet they have still managed to produce players of the quality of Louis Armary and Jean-Pierre Garuet as well as accomplished scrum-halves Pierre Berbizier and Alain Hueber.

Melrose

Scotland

Founded:
1877
Stadium:
The Greenyards
Colours:
Yellow and Black
Most capped player:
Craig Chalmers (59 caps for
Scotland)
Recent honours:
Scottish League and Cup Double
Champions 1996-97

For the last decade Melrose have been the Bath of Scottish rugby. Like their English counterparts, they have dominated the League Championship, winning the title five times in the first six seasons of the nineties.

Even in 1997, having suffered the loss of two of their stars to English clubs – Doddie Weir to Newcastle and Craig Joiner to Leicester – Melrose won another championship.

In recent years, Melrose have supplied a large number of players to Scotland, including scrum-half Bryan Redpath, fly-half Craig Chalmers, fullback Rowen Shepherd and hooker Steve Brotherstone.

But away from the high-pressured business of winning league titles, the small Border town of Melrose (population just 2,000) has become synonymous with the carnival atmosphere of Sevens. It was in Melrose that Ned Haig, a local butcher, founded Sevens at the end of the last century, and since then the Melrose Sevens have become one of the most endearing tournaments in the rugby calender.

As one of the founder-members of the Border League and as a club with a wide rural catchment area, Melrose have long produced quality players such as 1980s wing Keith Robertson, Scotland captain and hooker in the 1960s Charlie Laidlaw and Lions No. 8 Jim Telfer. Much of the credit for turning Melrose from an average side into the most professionally run club in Scotland goes to the coaching influence of Telfer, a hard taskmaster who played for Scotland and the Lions and expects nothing less than total commitment.

Ironically, it is also Telfer's new role as Director of Rugby at Murrayfield, where he has pushed the concept of district rugby at the expense of Scotland's top clubs, which has led to a decline in the club's fortunes.

Natal

South Africa

Founded:
1890
Stadium:
King's Park Stadium, Durban
Colours:
Black and White
Most capped player:
Mark Andrews (50 caps for South Africa)
Principal honours:
Currie Cup winners 1996

Known as the "Last Outpost of The British Empire", Natal is the most English-influenced province in South Africa, not that it helped them much when Bill Maclagan's British Lions side arrived in 1891 and administered a sound beating to a fledgling Natal side. Yet they improved quickly from those early days and by the time the Lions returned 33 years later under the leadership of Englishman Ronald Cove-Smith, the tourists were lucky to escape with a draw against a Natal side which included Alfred Walker and Walter Clarkson, two of the five Natal players who toured New Zealand with South Africa in 1921 (although only four won caps). In the years that followed, Natal's Springbok

representation became virtually continual, with the province's high point the selection of Greytown farmer Phil Nel as Springbok captain in 1933 – he even continued to captain South Africa in 1937 despite the fact that his Natal captain of the time, Ebo Bastard, was also in the Springbok side! By that time, Natal had become one of the mightiest provinces as the Big Six began to emerge, centred around the major cities.

Natal have also traditionally played with fast back rows and the ball moved wide at every attempt, a style helped by the tropical conditions in Durban, which tend to be wet under foot and extremely humid above ground.

Natal have scored many famous victories over visiting sides, including the Wallabies in 1953, 1963 and 1969, the English in 1972 and a 6–6 draw with the All Blacks in 1960. Past greats, such as back row men Tommy Bedford and Wynand Claasen, who were both Springbok captains, and outstanding 1960s fly-half Keith Oxlee, provided a benchmark for aggressive running rugby.

After winning the Currie Cup for the first time in 1990, Natal repeated the feat against Western Province in 1995, not only retaining the Currie Cup, but reaching the final of the Super 12 tournament. With Springbok captain Gary Teichman and fly-half Henry Honiball, Natal remain one of the strongest provinces.

Neath

Wales

Founded:
  1871

Stadium:
  The Gnoll

Colours:
  Black

Most capped player:
  Gareth Llewellyn (54 caps for
  Wales)

Recent honours:
  1996 Welsh Champions

In 1992 Wallaby coach Bob Dwyer memorably described playing Neath at The Gnoll, that tightly-packed and most intimidating of grounds, as "an ordeal". But then Dwyer also described the no-nonsense Welsh All Blacks of Neath as "the worst bagsnatchers [scrotum squeezers] in rugby," adding a salutary piece of advice: "anyone considering playing here should think about bringing a cricket box with them."

That is certainly advice that many players down the years would agree with, for Neath have proved themselves one of the most abrasive and aggressive of opponents, producing fearsome forwards such as Wales flankers Rees Stephens and Dai Morris, locks Roy John and Brian Thomas, and props Courtney Meredith and John Davies. Insular and tightly-knit with a "no one likes us we don't care" attitude, Neath have pursued success ruthlessly in the modern era winning the Welsh championship four times and the Cup twice in the late 1980s and early 1990s. But a steep decline set in when club coach Ron Waldron was given the job of national coach. He tried to get Wales to follow Neath's in-your-face, all-action, 15-man game and drafted in the majority of the Neath side to help him along.

However, what works at club level will not necessarily succeed at international level and Wales were humiliated in Australia in 1991, losing the Test 63–6, a dreadful state of affairs made worse by fighting between the pro and anti-Neath factions at the after-match dinner.

Nevertheless, despite no longer sweeping all before them after 1991, Neath's solidarity, self-belief and the consistency of players such as the Llewellyn brothers in the second row and full-back Paul Thorburn ensured that they remain competitive to the point that they won the League in 1995–96. With a large catchment area and a tremendous feeder school in the all-conquering Neath Tertiary College, Neath remains a fine nursery for young talent, but may have to look further afield in the future.

Newport

Wales

Founded:
1874

Stadium:
Rodney Parade

Colours:
Black and Amber

Most capped player:
Ken Jones (44 caps for Wales)

Recent honours:
None

Despite falling by the wayside in recent years, Newport were once regarded as one of strongest clubs in Britain. Much of their reputation was founded upon two of the best wins in Welsh rugby history: a 9–6 defeat of the 1912–13 Springboks and a 3–0 win over the otherwise undefeated 1963 All Blacks, courtesy of John Uzzell's famous dropped goal. (Uzzell was the son of Herbert Uzzell, another Newport forward who, as a member of the "Terrible Eight" played in what was reputed to have been one of the most violent games of rugby ever played when Wales met Ireland at Ravenhill in 1914.)

Other famous wins were over South Africa by 11–6 in 1969, and over Australia by 11–0 in 1957, while even the 1924 All Black "Invincibles", a side featuring legends such as the Brownlie brothers, George Nepia and Mark Nicholls, struggled to beat a determined Newport side by 13–10.

For all that, though, it is Newport's domestic record that really sets them apart. Formed in 1874 (three years before the Welsh Rugby Union was formed, which explains why the club was affiliated to the RFU in Twickenham as well), the Gwent club is the only first-class club in Britain to have gone through two full seasons undefeated.

Even more remarkably, Newport did this while also establishing a reputation for brilliant back play that is completely at variance with the preference of today's Gwent sides for 10-man rugby in the mould of England's West Country giants.

Chief among the players who established that reputation for adventure were Arthur Gould, who won 27 caps between 1885–97, and the 1904 Lions scrum-half and Newport tactical genius Major Tom Vile, who later went on to referee 12 Five Nations internationals between 1923–31.

Others followed in the same vein, most notably fly-half Roy Burnett who won only one cap thanks to the consistency of Cliff Morgan but who was idolised by the Rodney Parade faithful; and Keith Jarrett, who toured South Africa with the 1968 Lions.

New South Wales

Australia

Founded:
1874 (As Southern Rugby Union)

Stadium:
Sydney Football Stadium

Colours:
Light Blue

Most capped player:
David Campese (101 caps for
Australia)

Recent honours:
None

In the two decades after Dr Moran's first Wallaby side returned from Britain and defected to Rugby League en masse, rugby in Australia meant rugby in New South Wales (NSW). And although there were short periods of Queensland dominance after 1930, NSW remained the single most important source of international players until Queensland finally caught up in the 1970s.

Based around the intense Sydney competition, which has spurred clubs like Manley, Eastern Suburbs, Gordon and Randwick to produce a steady stream of outstanding players, NSW rugby has proved itself to be one of the most fertile hotbeds in the world. To give a list of the great players who have represented the Waratahs would take up the whole chapter, but a quick glance at the Greats chapter gives a fair indication of just how many outstanding players have come out of Sydney over the years .

Until 1955 NSW also encompassed areas which are now State sides in their own right, such as ACT and New South Wales Country. As that greater entity, NSW have a long and generally successful record of contact with non-Australian sides, starting with a tour to New Zealand in 1882, which was followed by a full "Test" series which New Zealand won 3–0. NSW eventually beat the All Blacks in 1907, and in 1922 defeated a full All Black side in a three-Test series.

The resurgence of Queensland in the 1970s and the recent rise of ACT means that NSW are not as dominant as they once were within Australia, yet that has to be seen within the context of Australia's enhanced standards. While NSW are not as successful within Australia, they have achieved some truly outstanding results, the most stunning of which remains the 71–8 humiliation of Wales in 1991. Most recently, NSW have had mixed results in the Super 12 competition, starting strongly but fading to the point where Queensland Reds have again become the most powerful State in Australian rugby.

NIFC

Ireland

Founded:
   1859
Stadium:
   Shaftesbury Avenue, Belfast
Colours:
   Red, Black and Blue
Most capped player:
   Mike Gibson (69 caps for Ireland)
Recent honours:
   None

One of the great clubs of Ireland, NIFC (North of Ireland Football Club) have provided over 70 international players since the first Ireland side played England at the Oval in 1875 containing six NIFC players.

In the first 100 years after its formation in 1874, the Northern stronghold won the Ulster Cup no less than 18 times in 77 starts, the best period coming in the decade between 1893 and 1902 when the club won the Cup nine times.

Although they have been gradually on the wane since the War, NIFC have still managed to keep up the tradition of turning out wonderful backs, a fact which has much to do with their proximity to the rugby nursery that is Queen's University.

It was through Queen's that Jack Kyle, that magical 46-times capped fly-half, came to join George Stephenson, Fred Gardiner and Noel Henderson at NIFC.

The last of the great backs to come out of NIFC was the incomparable Mike Gibson, whose international career spanned 15 years and 81 caps, including the British Lions between 1964–79. The gifted back was a Belfast man who did not come to NIFC via Queen's, but he remains virtually the last player of any note to have come out of the club.

Since his retirement only two players have represented Ireland: John Hewitt as a replacement twice in 1981 and Gordon Hamilton, the open-side flanker who scored Ireland's dramatic "winner that never was" against Australia in the 1991 World Cup quarter-final at Lansdowne Road. Since that date NIFC's failure to produce quality players has matched a general decline in the club's standing and it is slipping gently down the leagues.

Although the club's Ormagh ground in Belfast also houses one of the finest cricket wickets in Ireland, regularly used by the national side down the years, the change in population – where once the area was middle-class, but changing demographics now place it on the frontline – has persuaded the club's committee to sell up and look for a new site outside Belfast.

Northampton

England

Founded:

1880

Stadium:

Franklin's Gardens

Colours:

Black, Green and Gold

Most capped player:

Tim Rodber (40 caps for England)

Recent honours:

English Division Two Champions
1995-6; Runners-up Allied Dunbar
Premiership, 1999

One of the greatest of English clubs, Northampton have fought Coventry and Leicester for East Midlands supremacy for well over a century. In the process the Saints, as the club are universally known, have produced some of the most exciting backs ever to have played for England, including three greats in Dickie Jeeps, Jeff Butterfield and Lewis Cannell. Yet the emphasis in its early years was based more on forward power than three-quarter guile, with the first superstar of Saints rugby being Arthur Blakiston, the flanker who along with Wavell Wakefield and Tom Voyce formed a part of the best back row in the world in the 1920s. Most of the pre-War stars were forwards, with

the Westons and Ray Longland the most prominent, although of all Saints caps wing Edgar Mobbs probably remains the best known today because his name has been given to the annual Mobbs Memorial Match is contested between the Barbarians and the East Midlands. A popular player and local hero, Mobbs was too old for a commission in the First World War but raised a company of 268 local sportsmen, only for 183 of them to perish alongside him in the trenches.

Since 1945, Northampton have produced a wealth of internationals, and given the sort of total-rugby they have long attempted to play it is surprising that as many of them are backs as forwards. David Powell, Peter Larter, Bob Taylor, Martin Bayfield and Tim Rodber are all Saints forward who have gone on Lions tours, while props Ron Jacobs and Gary Pearce have represented England with much distinction. In recent years, the trend of producing internationals out of Franklin's Gardens has been accelerated by a new, more aggressive administration concerned at the club's low League ranking. First of all it brought in former All Black captain Buck Shelford, who has a catalytic effect on club aspirations and playing standards. His good work was built upon by coach Ian McGeechan, who has built a big squad of talented players, who finished second in the Allied Dunbar Premiership in 1999.

Northern Transvaal

South Africa

Founded:

1938

Stadium:

Loftus Versfeld, Pretoria

Colours:

Sky Blue

Most capped player:

Joost Van Der Westhuizen (50 caps
for South Africa)

Recent honours:

Currie Cup winners 1991 and 1998

The Blue Bulls of Northern Transvaal
have long been one of the formidable
units in South African rugby, and their
Loftus Versfeld fortress one of the most
impregnable.

Based in Pretoria on the oxygen-
depleted High Veldt, the rock hard conditions are perfect for the strength-sapping
forward-based game that Northerns have
played since the Union was formed in
1938.

This was allied to the phenomenal
kicking talents of Naas Botha from 1976
until his retirement in 1992, a period during which Northern Transvaal dominated
the Currie Cup with Botha contesting

eleven finals and winning nine of them.

But even without Botha's boot,
Northerns quickly managed to establish
themselves as one of the top Unions, losing to Sam Walker's 1938 Lions by only
eight points and soon claiming the scalps
of the Wallabies (1953), the Lions (1962),
the Welsh (1962), French (1967), England
(1972) and finally the All Blacks in a
game decided by a controversial piece of
refereeing by the home official (1976).

As Northerns have stacked up victories against the best in the world, so
their Springbok representation has bur-
geoned, with scrum-half Danie Craven
just one of five Blue Bulls to face the
1938 British Lions.

When South Africa toured Britain in
1951, their brilliant half-back pairing of
Hannes Brewis and Fonny du Toit came
from Northern Transvaal as did the key
forwards, Rhodesian Salty du Rand and
Jaap Bekker.

After the lifting of the boycott in
1992 Northerns have picked up where
they left off. In the first year of readmit-
tance, eleven Blue Bulls pulled on
Springbok colours.

That was the foundation for the
Northern Transvaal side which is today
still regarded as one of the leading
provinces in South African rugby and
which boasts in scrum-half Joost van der
Westhuizen one of the most dynamic and
exciting players in world rugby.

Orange Free State

South Africa

Founded:
1895

Stadium:
Springbok Park, Bloemfontein

Colours:
White and Orange

Most capped player:
Andre Joubert (30 caps for South Africa)

Recent honours:
None

With conditions very similar to those at Loftus Versfeld, Orange Free State (OFS) are a side in the same mould as Northerns, even if they have been conspicuously less successful.

Many of the reasons for this come down to force of circumstance: Bloemfontein may be a pretty town, but it has neither the population nor the wealth of Pretoria, and has consequently suffered from having its best players poached.

If anything, this trend has intensified in recent years as professionalism has become increasingly prevalent, resulting in a continual flow of players away from Vrystaat – and generally to Louis Luyt's Transvaal.

Nonetheless, OFS's local talent and sense of cohesion enabled the province to reach the semi-final of the Currie Cup in 1996, thus ensuring qualification for the Super 12 in 1997.

Although OFS had to wait until 1976 for its first Currie Cup success, the province has a long and distinguished history of putting the wind up touring sides.

Not only have they beaten the Lions twice in the space of two months (in 1924), but they also did the double to Australia in one year (28–3 and 23–13 in 1953) and have one of the best provincial records against the mighty All Blacks, following up a draw in 1949 with wins in 1960 and 1976.

Otago

New Zealand

Founded:
1881
Stadium:
Carisbrook, Dunedin
Colours:
Blue, Gold and Red
Most capped player:
Jeff Wilson (42 caps for New
Zealand)
Recent honours:
NPC champions in 1998

After the Second World War, Otago went virtually overnight from being a mediocre outfit to the dominant force in New Zealand. Not just that, but the fierce rucking game they developed changed the course of All Black rugby when it was adopted as a national style on the 1949 tour to South Africa. That style also went on to become the national style of Scotland, so struck was Jim Telfer by the efficiency and good sense it made when he encountered it as a Lion in 1966. It may be coincidental, but Otago was settled heavily by Scots, hence the province's nickname of "The Highlanders" and the fact that the streetplan of the Province's captial, Dunedin ("Edinburgh" in gaelic), is based on Edinburgh's.

Otago's no-nonsense style was based around forward might, so it is natural that the greatest Otago players of the post-war era would be hard, uncompromising but skillful forwards. Kevin Skinner, the hardman prop credited with single-handedly subduing the Springboks in the Second and Third Tests of 1956 to bring a victory the whole of New Zealand yearned for, is typical of the forwards Otago produced in those years and others to feature highly in this era include 1980s All Blacks Lester Harvey, Ray Dalton (father of Andy) and prop Mark Irwin. At that time backs like Ron Elvidge, the Haig brothers and Ernie Diack worked off bountiful possession and prospered.

Although Otago defeated the British Lions of 1950, '59 and '66, the province underwent a slump in the 1970s and early 1980s. Yet with a pool of talent from the famous rugby nursery, Dunedin University, it was always likely that Otago would rise again. Under coach Laurie Mains, himself a famous Otago captain capped four times by the All Blacks, and young captain Mike Brewer, Otago consolidated their status as one of New Zealand's top five provinces.

Recently, the Province have produced players of genuine quality in Jeff Wilson, Josh Kronfeld and Taine Randell, and their 1998 NPC triumph could well be a sign of the good time returning to the club.

Oxbridge

Great Britain
Cambridge
University

Founded:

1872

Stadium:

Grange Road

Colours:

Light Blue and White

Most capped Cambridge Blue:

Rob Andrew (71 caps for England)

Varsity Match record:

55 wins, 13 draws

Oxford University

Founded:

1869

Colours:

Dark Blue

Stadium:

Iffley Road

Most capped Oxford Blue:

Brendan Mullin (55 caps for Ireland)

Varsity Match record:

49 wins, 13 draws

The institutions of Oxford and Cambridge universities (known collectively as "Oxbridge") have had an almost unparalleled impact upon the game. As well as staging the third oldest continual fixture in the world in the Varsity Match (a 78,000 sell-out these days at Twickenham), both universities have contributed heavily to the development of the game.

It was at Oxford that the numbers in a team were first reduced from 20 to 15, while at Cambridge Wavell Wakefield decided to give each forwards a set position, rather than allowing them to pack down in the order at which they arrived at scrum or lineout, as was then the custom. Later, Wakefield's Cambridge were the first side to use the back row as a unit.

In 126 years of the Varsity match between the two universities, they have turned out more internationals than any other two "clubs" in the world. Drawn by the chance to gain a "Blue" (i.e. appear in the Varsity match) Oxbridge still attracts top players and until recently had a first class fixture list. For Cambridge, England's Rob Andrew, Wales's Wilf Wooller, Ireland's Mike Gibson and Scotland's Gavin Hastings are some of the most influential players; Oxford boast England's Harry Vassall (under whom Oxford won 70 matches in a row), Wales scrum-half Wyn Brace, Scotland's Ian Smith-led threequarter line of the mid 1920s, Ireland's Brendan Mullin, All Black captain David Kirk, and Springbok skipper Tommy Bedford (who reckoned his Varsity Match win in 1966 one of the highlights of his career).

Queensland

Australia

Founded:
1883 (As Northern Rugby Union)
Stadium:
Ballymore Oval, Brisbane
Colours:
Maroon
Most capped player:
Michael Lynagh (72 caps for
Australia)
Recent honours:
1995 Super 10 winners

The fact that the Union code has flourished in Queensland is nothing short of staggering. 80 years ago, after quarter of a century of success (between 1890 and 1900 Queensland beat New South Wales on 11 occasions and also savaged the Reverend Mullineaux's unofficial Lions in 1899), the game went out of existence in Queensland. Between 1908–29 there was no rugby union in Brisbane or the surrounding areas. Instead, with virtually the whole of the national side turning professional, League took over and Brisbane remains a League stronghold. Yet Union lived on in private schools such as the famous nursery Brisbane Grammar School and through the efforts of famous administrators such as Carter, Wesley

and Brown, union was restored to Brisbane, successfully persuading famous old clubs like Brothers and Southern Districts to revert to the 15-man code.

The pace at which Queensland then made up lost ground was truly staggering, and by the mid 1930s, the Reds (as Queensland are known) were back to their turn of the century strength, and contributing roughly a third of the Wallaby squads in those years.

Brisbane's weather promotes an outdoor life, while its hard grounds fostered adventurous running rugby, so the Union team soon became known for a "have-a-go" attitude. Queensland's strength built steadily, with the game also becoming well entrenched in outlying areas like the Darling Downs and Rockhampton, which have provided many outstanding players.

By the 1970s, they were the best provincial side in Australia. Since then Queensland have produced many of the best rugby players the world has ever seen, whether it is up front with players such as Jules Guerassimoff, John Eales, Stan Pilecki, Tony Shaw and Mark Loane, or in the backs with the likes of Michael Lynagh, Brendan Moon, Tim Horan and Roger Gould.

In very recent years, the form of Queensland has been generally outstanding. They won the Super 10 final against Transvaal in 1995 and are habitually Super 12 front-runners each season.

Racing Club de France

France

Founded:
1882
Stadium:
Stade Colombes
Colours:
Sky Blue and White
Most capped player:
Michel Crauste (63 caps for France)
Recent honours:
None

Often seen as the playboys of French rugby, Parisian giants Racing Club de France hold a central role in the history of French rugby.

It was in Paris that French rugby really began in the 1890s, and it was Racing and the club's Welsh international Percy Bush which acted as a powerful missionary force to establish the game in the north of the country.

The impact of the first French Championship, which Racing won by defeating the only other entrant, Stade Francais, fired the imagination of sportsmen in the South and created the southern-dominated game that France has today.

The French equivalent of London club Harlequins, Racing also play at the former national ground, Stade Colombes, and are regarded as the aristocrats of the game in France and play a similarly expansive game.

They also make sure not to take the game too seriously, as witnessed during the 1990 French Championship final, when the famous Racing three-quarters led by the charismatic Franck Mesnel and including Jean-Baptiste Lafond's "Le Showbiz" (a select group of Racing players) took the field wearing berets and pink bow ties.

As well as their choice of attire for the final, the Racing players ordered a bottle of champagne for half-time refreshment. Quite what their Agen opponents made of it all wasn't known, but the final scoreline in Racing's favour was a welcome fillip to all those who say rugby's Corinthian ethic is now dead and buried.

However, that was to be the last time Racing supped from the cup of success , and they have recently struggled against the burgeoning power of the Southern French clubs, which have taken virtually all France's European Cup places.

Swansea

Wales

Founded:
1873
Stadium:
St Helen's
Colours:
All White
Most capped player:
Robert Jones (54 caps for Wales)
Recent honours:
Welsh league Champions 1996-97
Welsh Cup winners 1999

"The Jacks", as Swansea are known, have never lost their place at the top of the game in Wales. Since the club's formation in 1874, Swansea have been based at the St. Helen's Ground. As well as being the ground where Wales regularly played rugby internationals before Cardiff Arms Park was built, St Helen's is also one of the principal venues for Glamorgan County Cricket Club, and has the distinction of housing the wicket where Sir Garfield Sobers once famously hit the hapless Malcolm Nash for six sixes in an over.

The ground has also witnessed some of Welsh rugby's greatest moments, most notably in 1935 when Claude Davey, Haydn Tanner and Willie Davies conspired to defeat Jack Manchester's All Blacks, making them the first British club to do so.

It was a famous day and completed the southern hemisphere "triple", coming after a 3–0 win over the 1912 Springboks and a 6–0 victory over the 1907–08 Australians (the Jacks were also to beat the Wallabies in 1966 and when they were world champion Wallabies in 1992).

The saddest moment in the club's history also came against a touring side in 1994 when the Springboks put 78 points past a devastated Swansea side which could only score eight in return.

Over the years Swansea have produced some of the finest rugby players of all time. Jack and Billy Bancroft together won over 50 caps between 1890 and the outbreak of the Great War in 1914, the same period in which scrum-half Dicky Owen won a record 35 caps and fly-half Billy Trew played 14 consecutive seasons for Wales starting in 1900.

More recently, players such as Robert Jones, Tony Clement and the Moriarty brothers have made sure Swansea remain at the very top of Welsh rugby, a point underlined when they won the league title in 1997.

However, since then, an ongoing dispute with the Welsh Rugby Union saw Swansea exiled from the Welsh League, although they took part in the cup in 1998-9 and beat Llanelli in the final.

Toulouse

France

Founded:
1899

Stadium:
Les Sept-Deniers

Colours:
Red and Black

Most capped player:
Rob Andrew (71 caps for England)

Recent honours:
French Champions and European
Champions in 1996

The greatest of all French sides, Toulouse have a record of sustained success that cannot be equalled even by Agen. They have won the French Championship 13 times since 1912, including five victories in the 1920s and, since 1985, they have added a further six titles to their roll of honour.

In 1996, the men from Toulouse were not only crowned champions of France, but when they defeated Cardiff in the inaugural European Cup competition, they earned the right to call themselves the unofficial club kings of Northern Hemisphere rugby.

Although the recent Toulouse record has owed much to a mean and mobile pack, the club has made it a priority to maintain a Barbarian philosophy which makes it the French equivalent of Llanelli.

That is why the club's favourite sons are, virtually to a man, backs. The one exception is Jean-Claude Skrela, a phenomenally talented flanker who established himself as one of France's all-time greats in the 1970s. Yet Skrela is so beloved of Toulouse precisely because he was able to play within the club's open game plan.

One man to benefit from Skrela's ball-winning abilities was the great Toulouse hero Jacques Villepreux, an unconventional genius who won 34 caps in the late 1960s and early 1970s and remains a key influence over not just Toulouse rugby, but also France now that he has become assistant coach to the national side, which is also coached by Jean-Claude Skrela.

Toulouse continue to produce backs of world class, in particular France's current fullback, Emile Ntamack, and gifted national fly-half Thomas Castaignede.

Transvaal

South Africa

Founded:
1889

Stadium:
Ellis park, Johannesburg

Colours:
Red and White

Most capped player:
James Small (36 caps for South Africa)

Recent honours:
Currie Cup winners 1993 and 1994

Although all the top provinces in South Africa present daunting opposition, Transvaal and Western Province have historically been the most feared outfits, with the "Blue Bulls" of Northern Transvaal lagging behind after they split from Transvaal in 1938.

Because of this, there is a long history of fierce rivalry between the two provinces, and it is fair to say that it is only in recent years that Transvaal have been in the ascendancy. Based around Johannesburg, Transvaal is the third of the major South African provinces which plays at altitude, currently at the imposing Ellis Park, a huge edifice capable of seating 80,000 people, as it did during the 1995 World Cup final when South Africa beat New Zealand to become world champions.

Transvaal have long been providers of Springboks from the earliest days of international competition when Bill Maclagan's British Isles side turned up in 1891, through to the World Cup final of 1995. In that latter game, the most historic in South African rugby history, the side was built around the strong mauling Transvaal side which had won the Currie Cup in the previous season and was led by inspirational captain Francois Pienaar.

That strength in depth and the forward-based game are both typical of Transvaal, and it is a combination that has sunk many touring sides. Although Maclagan's Lions returned from Johannesburg having won all their games, when Scotsman Mark Morrison took a party down in 1903, shortly after the Boer War, the reception was a might hotter, with Transvaal beating the British twice in a fortnight.

That was to become a familiar story with Tom Smyth's 1910 team also falling twice to Transvaal, while Maurice Brownlie's 1928 All Blacks and Alec Ross's 1933 Australians also succumbed to the might of Transvaal.

In recent years Transvaal have featured strongly in the Currie Cup, winning the title in 1993 and 1994 and losing to Natal in the 1996 final.

Waikato
New Zealand

Founded:

1909 as South Auckland (Changed
to Waikato in 1921)

Stadium:

Rugby Park, Hamilton

Colours:

Gold, Red and Black

Most capped player:

Ian Jones (76 caps for New Zealand)

Recent honours:

1992 National Provincial Champions

Without doubt the slow starters of the
massively competitive New Zealand
rugby scene, once Waikato finally managed to struggle out from under Auckland's umbrella in 1921 there was virtually no stopping them.

They had already served notice of
their intentions by the time they took and
held the Ranfurly Shield for almost two
years between 1951–53, but in 1956 they
really burst into the big league with a
stunning win over the touring Springboks on their first game on New Zealand
soil.

That match was played on a rain-
soaked pitch and because the whole of
New Zealand was frantic to remedy the
perceived wrongs heaped on Fred
Allen's 1949 All Blacks, who were
whitewashed in South Africa, the game
was one long brawl.

In between the fisticuffs, though,
Waikato showed that they were now a
force to be reckoned with. Up front prop
Ian Clarke and hooker Ron Hemi
emerged as players of real class, but it
was the eight points into the wind from
the boot of full-back Don Clarke which
really won the game, and it was around
Clarke that Waikato subsequently built
their game.

Waikato now have a reputation for
producing durable footballers in the
mould of All Black captain Wilson
Whineray and prop Richard Loe. In 1992
they scored a first when they overwhelmed Otago 40–5 to win the National
Provincial Championship, while in 1993
they went one better as they humiliated
the Lions 38–10.

Wellington

New Zealand

Founded:
 1879
Stadium:
 Athletic Park, Wellington.
Colours:
 Gold and Black
Most capped player:
 Stu Wilson and Murray Mexted (34
 caps for New Zealand)
Recent honours:
 None

When Charles John Monro returned to his native Nelson in 1870 after a spell at school in England and introduced rugby to New Zealand, his first step was to persuade the boys of his old school, Nelson College, to play the game. His second was to take the school on tour to Wellington and once there he formed New Zealand's oldest continuous rugby club, the Wellington Football Club.

The province has been at the heart of New Zealand rugby ever since, playing at the Athletic Park in a city dubbed "windy Wellington". Although Wellington have never been able to put together a lengthy spell of Ranfurly Shield defences in the style of Auckland, Hawke's Bay or Canterbury, it did manage to hold on to the Shield for 15 defences just after the First World War. Indeed it has won it often enough to have a record surpassed only by Auckland and Canterbury.

In the process Wellington have uncovered many fine players, including "Originals" back Billy Wallace, "Invincible" second five eighth Mark Nicholls, Ron Jarden (the man who the Springboks credit with single-handedly beating them during the first Test in 1956).

Also products of the Wellington "academy" are latter-day household names such as Grant Batty, Ken Gray, Murray Mexted, Stu Wilson, Bernie Fraser and John Gallagher.

With such an amazing list of truly great players, it is inevitable that the province has beaten all the major tourists over the years, its finest hour coming in 1965 when Avril Malan's poor Springbok side were well beaten at Athletic Park.

Although a competitor in the inaugural Super 12 series, Wellington have yet to excel in the tournament, although in full-back Christian Cullen they possess one of the most exciting players in world rugby.

Western Province

South Africa

Founded:
 1883
Stadium:
 Newlands, Cape Town
Colours:
 Blue and White
Most capped player:
 James Small (36 caps for South
 Africa)
Recent honours:
 None

Western Province have long been one of the two most powerful provinces in South Africa.

Much of the strength its rugby in the early years can be attributed to the influence of two remarkable rugby families: the Morkels and the Luyts. The Morkels were a 16-strong family in which all 16 played for Western Province and 10 went on to play for South Africa between 1903–28, including Duggie Morkel who captained the national side in two Tests.

The Luyt brothers of the same era were the same lines except there were only three of them. The Luyts, like many Western Province players, first played at

the top level while at South Africa's answer to Oxbridge, Stellenbosch University, and it is the existence of this centre of rugby learning that has helped keep Western Province at the top of the tree.

Stellenbosch has turned out hundreds of Springboks and was also home to the two gurus of South African rugby: A.F. Markotter and Danie Craven, whose perception and deep understanding of the game ensured that Western Province and the Springboks produced outstanding sides.

Although the 1997 Western Province side suffered the ignominy of failing to make the Super 12 series, down the years they have churned out some great players including a posse of Springbok captains in Paul Roos, Benny Osler, Danie Craven, Jannie Engelbrecht, Morne du Plessis and Boy Louw.

The two most significant Western Province players of the 1990s have been Joel Stransky, who kicked the winning drop-goal in extra-time of the 1995 World Cup final before heading off to English club Leicester, and Chester Williams, the extraordinary black wing who topped the try list at the same World Cup and made multi-racial rugby in South Africa seem a reality at last.

The new pin-up boy of Cape rugby, flanker Bobby Skinstad, is another in the mould of Morne du Plessis.

The Great International Competitions

Of all the sports in the world, Rugby Union is the one which has been the most reluctant to indulge in competitions. This was due in part to its administrators' genuine but misguided belief that quantifiable competition was too much of a temptation for ambitious clubs. This would lead to the poaching of players, monetary inducements and, ultimately, professionalism. History has proved they were right, for it was the biggest competition of them all, the Webb Ellis World Cup, that brought about the change from an amateur to openly professional game.

Rugby union was virtually the last major sport to have a world championship; the only sport not to possess a pan-European tournament and, until 20 years ago, the only team sport in which none of the major nations had any sort of league. Yet rugby is the most competitive of pursuits, and in such circumstances men always look for a marker to establish a pecking order. In rugby it has been cups that have done the trick. And rugby's cup really has runneth over, with even the smallest countries boasting some form of fiercely contested knock-out competition.

Now, after a century of ad hoc confrontations and cup clashes, rugby has caught the competition bug. International, club and provincial friendlies are out, silverware is in – and the resulting fusion of tradition and spectacle has created some of the best sporting action on the globe.

The World Cup

Given that the British Home Unions had so often taken a stand against the concept of expanding competition, it came as no surprise that England and Ireland were the last two nations to fall into line once the concept of a Rugby World Cup. As Dudley Wood, the then notoriously pro-amateur secretary of the RFU, was later to say: "We knew of course that once a World Cup competition got underway then the eventual outcome was always likely to be a professional game, and that is why we were so dubious about the concept.

Subsequent events have proved Wood's words prophetic. The World Cup has been a success on a scale that even its most ardent advocates could never have foreseen. The fourth tournament, to be held in Wales in 1999, will bring in receipts of well over £70m, and will be seen by three and a half billion television viewers in 150 countries, 70 of which will have teams competing in the tournament or its qualifying rounds.

Two million people will have attended games at which the most highly paid superstars in the history of the game will strut their stuff in front of 4,000 journalists. It will also return the fourth highest television ratings ever seen in sport, with only the Olympics, World Cup football and the International Athletics Championship pulling in more viewers.

Not bad for a tournament which was dragged kicking and screaming into the world and which many people doubted would ever break even.

But back in the mid–1980s those cynics and doubters certainly had a point as far as the early financial security of the tournament was concerned. Gates in 1987 varied from disappointing to downright poor, and even before co-hosts Australia were beaten by France in the semi-final, the modestly sized Concord Oval in Sydney was easily big enough to take the meagre crowds on the Aussie side of the Tasman.

Only the keen interest of the New Zealand public allowed the crowd figures to hit 600,000 and the tournament to return a profit of £1.5m. The Rugby World Cup, though, was always intended to be more than just facts and figures and, with hindsight, it's clear that what happened on the pitch in New Zealand and Australia in 1987 was enough to capture the imagination of the advertising and marketing men and set in train one of the greatest sporting tournaments anywhere in the world.

Much of the success of the 1987

World Cup was down to the fact that it was won by New Zealand on their own ground at Eden Park.

The All Blacks were by far the strongest side in the tournament, and opened the proceedings as they meant to carry on, with a record 70–6 win over hapless Italy. Crushing all before them, David Kirk's New Zealand wiped out Fiji 74–13 and Argentina 46–15, before powering through the quarter-finals with what many later considered their toughest match in the tournament, a 30–3 win against Scotland, and on to the semi-finals where they annihilated Wales 49–6, a score that sent shockwaves around the rugby world.

Even France, who had pipped Australia in one of the most exciting games of rugby ever played when they won the second semi-final 30–24 courtesy of an injury-time Serge Blanco try (see page 182), were no match for the Black steamroller. Two tries in two minutes in the second half finished off a game in which the plucky resistance of the French was always likely to prove insufficient to stop the best side in the world.

When Kirk lifted the Webb Ellis Trophy on 20th June 1987 in front of 48,000 screaming New Zealanders, it was the culmination of five years of planning since the sports entrepreneur Neil Durden-Smith had proposed just such a tournament in 1982 (even though a 1957

International Board regulation specifically forbade such a venture), and owed much to the tireless work of administrators such as John Kendall-Carpenter and Ces Blazey.

Yet it was a very conservative revolution, in the best traditions of rugby. There were no qualifying rounds, with the sixteen competing countries being invited to attend. This rather arbitrary system of selecting the teams led to much rancour, notably on the part of Korea and Western Samoans who failed to receive an invitation. Nonetheless, one of the most encouraging signs was that the tournament would help drag some of the smaller nations up by the bootlaces.

While sides such as Italy, Zimbabwe and Tonga received fearful beatings, the spirited contribution of the Canadians and Japanese was a powerful signal that the world of rugby was beginning to change.

That signal was reinforced as the preparations for the 1991 World Cup got underway. Qualifying rounds were held throughout the world, with 40 nations competing in regional pools. Financial support from the profits from 1987 was a vital component in allowing small unions to travel thousands of miles to compete in what quickly became a genuine worldwide competition.

The emerging nations were also engaged in a frantic round of Test matches to battle-harden their top players and by the time the second tournament kicked off in Europe, it was clear that the gap between the top sides and many of the more ambitious smaller nations had begun to narrow perceptibly.

This was proved in spectacular fashion when the tournament kicked off, with Wales the most high-profile casualties. Beaten 16–13 at Cardiff Arms Park by debutants and eventual quarter-finalists Western Samoa in their first game, Wales failed to advance beyond the pool stage.

They were the only actual casualties among the traditional powers, but other emerging sides such as Italy and Canada also proved that the status quo was changing rapidly, both of them pushing the All Blacks to the wire. Virtually every game was genuinely competitive and almost every match was played to a full house, making the tournament a resounding and highly profitable success.

The 1991 World Cup also reflected a shifting balance of power in world rugby, with Australia playing the most attractive and inventive rugby and thoroughly deserving to lift the trophy.

They confirmed their dominance of world rugby at the time by beating their two main rivals, England and the All Blacks, to win the tournament, the latter victory coming courtesy of a virtuoso performance by veteran wing David Campese.

Although the 12–6 final win over England was a dour event dominated by Australia's outstanding defence and England's tactical naiveté, the tournament included some of the most outstanding games of rugby ever played in Europe. The presence of hosts England in the final also ensured that the sport received the biggest single shot in the arm in its history – it was the event which catapulted rugby into the premier league of sport.

The decision to hold the 1995 World Cup in South Africa was controversial to say the least. The Springboks only rejoined the international rugby community in 1992 following the abolition of Apartheid, and many felt that the country's infrastructure was too flimsy for a sporting event of the magnitude of the World Cup.

But rugby is a religion in South Africa, and Nelson Mandela's government of national unity made it a priority to ensure that the tournament was a spectacular success. And it was, largely because South Africa crowned their return by beating the in-form favourites New Zealand in a try-less but nail-biting final encounter that the Springboks won with a Joel Stransky drop-goal late into extra-time.

The national outpouring of joy that

followed the famous win produced an amazing, spontaneous unity that transcended colour in a country in which colour played a central role. It was possibly rugby's greatest hour.

The 1995 World Cup was also the game's last as an amateur sport. The economic success and the huge television coverage of the event was too tempting for the satellite barons, and with All Black wing Jonah Lomu establishing himself as the game's first genuine world superstar after literally running over Wales, Scotland, Ireland and England, the game moved inevitably on to a new professional era.

Preparations for the next World Cup, the biggest yet, are now about to be put into action. Revenue is greater, the sport's profile is higher and the number of teams larger, with the old format of four pools of four teams being expanded to five pools of four teams. Even the qualifying rounds, which are now well advanced, are half as big again as they were in 1995, with 71 nations having competed.

With 1999 upon us, the thousands of fans guaranteed to descend on the Welsh capital will witness the final at a redeveloped Cardiff Arms Park, to be known as the Millenium Stadium, a fitting venue for one of the most glamourous and thrilling sporting events in the world.

The Five Nations Championship

The first instance of formalised contact sport between two British countries occurred on November 19, 1870, when England beat Scotland, at Association Football at the Kennington Oval. The match, played in front of a crowd of 4,000, was a heated affair eventually won by the English. But such was the rancour generated by the win that the Scots determined to have another go at the "Auld Enemy" the next year, and this time it would be on their own ground and on their own terms. Their own ground was Raeburn Place and their own terms was the 20-a-side game of Rugby Football, which was then making huge strides North of the Border.

When Edinburgh Academical FJ Moncrieff and a group of Scottish players issued a challenge to English rugby via the pages of a newspaper in 1871, and then won the ensuing match by a goal and a try to one try, they could have had no idea what they had set in train. One hundred and twenty-six years and nearly 1,000 fiercely contested international encounters later, however, the fruit of the seed they planted that day is the International Championship, commonly known as the Five Nations, the most prestigious and historic rugby tournament in the world.

Although a silver cup that bears an alarming resemblance to an oversized cafetiere was presented to the Five Nations organisers by Lord Burghersh in 1993, and a points system put in place in the same year to ensure that there was a winner to present the trophy to, the Five Nations existed for over a century without any level of formal organisation. Instead it has evolved gradually, and it is even impossible to discern a date when the phrase "Five Nations Championship" was first used. Nevertheless, the competition is the longest established international rugby competition in the world.

The inaugural England versus Scotland fixture of 1871 started the ball rolling, and has been played in every peacetime year since. From 1879 onwards, the fixture was played for the magnificent silver trophy called the Calcutta Cup which was presented by GAJ Rothney of the Calcutta Rugby Club after dwindling membership forced the club to close. The trophy, which takes the form of a tapered cup with three snake handles and an elephant as the lid, was actually made from melted down silver rupees withdrawn from the central bank of Calcutta from the club's funds when it was wound down.

It was not long before the two nations became the three, when Ireland (or, as with all early international matches, a club side – in this case Trinity College, Dublin – masquerading as the national side) played England at The Oval in 1875 and lost by the then handsome margin of one goal, one drop goal and one try to no score. Another five years passed and the three sides became four when Wales followed a well-worn path to The Oval and went home with a humiliating defeat by the enormous score of seven goals, one drop goal and six tries to no score (equivalent to a defeat of 82–0 on today's scoring system).

With the existing annual round of matches being gradually expanded on an ad hoc basis as Ireland first played Scotland in 1877 and Wales in 1882, while Scotland first locked horns with Ireland in 1877, a genuine Home Unions Championship was in full swing by 1890.

Although the intensity of those early clashes was every bit as severe as in Five Nations games of today, the laws that governed the game in those early days were very different indeed. There was no set points scoring system until the early 1890s and in the very early years the matches were declared drawn unless one of the two teams scored a converted try (a "goal"). Until 1877 matches were played with 20 players on each side and

with 13 of them as forwards, and it was those forwards which led the great dribbling rushes of the time. Only with the formation of the International Board after an Anglo-Scottish squabble over the laws in 1884 were the various practices and laws harmonised in the interests of fair international competition.

Although England, and to a lesser extent Scotland, held the whip hand in those early years due to their advanced experience and greater player base, by the late 1880s the four sides were playing off a relatively level playing field, with any one of the nations genuinely capable of winning all three of its matches. From the moment that England completed the first mythical "Triple Crown" in 1883 at only the second time of asking (and then added insult to injury by repeating the act the next year) the pursuit of a clean sweep has become the overriding aim of every British nation come the beginning of January. Just how much fortunes fluctuated between the four sides was obvious in the early 1890s when, in four consecutive years, each of the Home Unions won the Triple Crown in consecutive years: Scotland in 1891; England in 1892; Wales in 1893; and Ireland in 1894!

Although the Oxbridge connection was alive and well for England through players such as Harry Vassall and Alan Rotherham, the ultra-competitive club scene in the North of England in the 1880s and early 1990s provided the basis of England's strong international showing, while Wales were also beginning to prove themselves formidable adversaries in the annual round of increasingly less friendly internationals. The balance of power was to change radically in 1895, however, when England went into a spiral of decline after the heart of Northern rugby was ripped out by the decision of 20 top clubs and their players to form the Rugby League. Between 1895 and 1910, England were the whipping boys of British rugby with the Scots and Welsh only losing to them three times in 15 encounters, while the Irish lost only six times in the same period.

With a whole generation of outstanding players such as Gwyn Nicholls, Rhys Gabe and Percy Bush to call upon, it was the Welsh who took greatest advantage. Six times they won the Triple Crown between 1900–11, and with France joining the competition in 1906, Wales completed the first ever Grand Slam in 1908 and repeated the feat the next season. Not that the Welsh had it all their own way. Scotland were also a force to be reckoned with at the time, and with men like the rough tough forward "Darkie" Bedell-Sivright in their side they also boasted a formidable record, notching up three Triple Crowns between 1900–10.

But as England regained its strength following the 1895 debacle, Britain's most populous rugby nation reasserted itself once more and, with Wales' 1911 Grand Slammers the only nation to put up a serious challenge and War the only interruption, dominated the Championship from the time the 1910 season kicked off until Scotland's Grand Slam of 1925. Even today the names that led England to the greatest period of dominance in its history are still revered, names such as Ronnie Poulton-Palmer and Cherry Pilman, celebrated halfbacks Cyril Kershaw and "Dave" Davies, and the outstanding back row in English history, Wavell Wakefield, Tom Voyce and Arthur Blakiston. The all-white army marched to eight shared or outright Championships in ten seasons, winning three Grand Slams in four years along the way.

It was only the emergence of a truly great Scotland team that stopped England's triumphant procession. Led from the back by Dan Drysdale, and drawing on the cunning of fly-half Herbert Waddell and the famous Oxford University threequarter line of Wallace, Aitken, Smith and Macpherson, they dominated the 1925 season in which they won a Grand Slam. They were to remain one of the strongest forces in world rugby for the rest of the Twenties.

By now, France had begun to figure in the equation, although the figures tended to be in the "points conceded" column. France only beat England and Wales once between 1906 and the outbreak of war, and while they had better luck against Scotland (four wins) and Ireland (five wins), they were generally the whipping boys of the tournament. In 1931, however, they became more like the kicking boys – well, they were unceremoniously kicked out of the Championship when it became clear that their top clubs were openly paying their players.

France were not to reappear in the Championship until it restarted after the War. In the pre-war years, England and Scotland had been the two dominant forces, but as soon as post-war France took to the field it was clear that the balance of power had shifted dramatically. Although they only won two of their games, Jean Prat's France only lost to England by 6–3 and Wales by 3–0 and were clearly a force to be reckoned with. Although the Irish side led by mercurial Ulster genius Jack Kyle provided a flash of brilliance at the end of the Forties, collecting the only Grand Slam in Ireland's history in 1948 and a Triple Crown the next year, France, Wales and England dominated the Five Nations from the War to the present day.

For Scotland, a major pre-war power, the fall from grace was a heavy one. Seventeen matches were lost on the trot between 1951–55, including the famous 44–0 humiliation by Basil Kenyon's South Africa at Murrayfield in 1951, a thrashing akin to those endured by the Welsh at the hands of New Zealand in the 1987–8. Thankfully the late Fifties, Sixties and Seventies saw Scotland bumble along as also-rans, more often scoring a Wooden Spoon (ie: no wins) than a Championship win, but remaining competitive. That luck changed in the early Eighties when a crop of outstanding players spearheaded by halfbacks Roy Laidlaw and John Rutherford saw Scotland to a Grand Slam in 1984, its first since the glory days of 1925. Grand Slams in the modern era are uncannily like buses, and not only had one come along, but six years later Scotland were at it again. With inspirational prop David Sole and fullback Gavin Hastings as the main strike weapons, and with the back row of Finlay Calder, Derek White and John Jeffrey disrupting favourites England in the Grand Slam showdown at Murrayfield, Scotland scored the most famous victory in its entire history to complete a clean sweep in the 1990 Five Nations Championship.

Only in 1999, when an outstanding crop of young players – such as Gregor Townsend and Scott Murray – came to maturity, and Scotland won the last ever Five Nations, have Scotland looked capable of dominating for an extended period.

The main reason why Scotland invariably missed out on the privilege of occupying the Wooden Spoon berth in the post-war years was because it had already been taken by the Irish. Indeed, at times it looked as if the men in green had taken out a long lease on the position. Despite the efforts of giants of the game such as Willie John McBride, Mike Gibson and Fergus Slattery, the lack of strength in depth all too often extinguished the Irish fire. The only relief from the misery of mediocrity came from the hand of fly-half general Jack Kyle in the Forties and the boot of his Eighties counterpart Ollie Campbell, who kicked Ireland to Triple Crowns in 1982 and 1985. The Nineties, have been particularly unkind to Ireland, who almost seem to have discarded any lingering thoughts of sustaining a challenge for Five Nations honours.

Another country which has often seemed to have also fitted that bill during the Nineties is Wales, which is staggering for a country that has one of the proudest records in British rugby. After the War the Welsh carried on producing backs in the mould of Wooller, Tanner and Jones, with staggering talents like Cliff Morgan, Bleddyn Williams and Ken Jones dropping off the conveyor belt of talent in the late Forties and Fifties. Teak hard forwards such as Clem Thomas, Bryn Meredith and Rhys Williams were the backbone of sides which were among the most difficult to beat, and Wales were always formidable at the Arms Park. As the years wore on, so Wales became increasingly dominant, and after 1969, when Barry John and Gareth Edwards combined for their first full season together to bring Wales a Triple Crown, the men from West of Offa's Dyke became well nigh invincible.

Throughout the Seventies, it seemed that Wales was producing the best players in the world, certainly to judge from the evidence of the 1971 and '74 Lions tours. Greats such as JPR Williams, Gerald Davies and Mervyn Davies ruled the Five Nations and the world, and the prize was a hatful of honours, with the Grand Slams of 1971, 1976 and 1978 punctuating a run of Triple Crowns. Only as the Eighties dawned did Wales begin to decline, and even then it was a slow decline. England's Grand Slam of 1980 involved the narrowest of 10–9 wins against Wales, who were reduced to 14 men after dismissal of flanker Paul Ringer for a stiff arm tackle, and even in 1987 Wales were able to pull themselves up to a third-place showing in the first World Cup and winning the Triple Crown in 1988.

Yet the Five Nations is not a vacuum, and two huge defeats in New Zealand in 1988 led to numerous defections to League and crushed Welsh morale to the point where only now is a new generation coming through which genuinely believes itself capable of challenging for top honours on a regular basis.

England's post-War performances were in almost direct reverse to those of the Welsh. Despite possessing far and away the biggest playing constituency upon which to draw, England's most conspicuous talent until the late Eighties was underachievement. Despite producing backs of the class of Peter Jackson and forwards of the durability of Eric Evans, England's return was very meagre, with Triple Crowns in 1954, 1957 and 1960, and a solitary Grand Slam under Bill Beaumont in 1980. A lack of consistency in selection and the inability of the English club system to bring talent to the top meant that for the most part mid-table mediocrity was England's staple diet.

Only when manager Geoff Cooke combined with young captain Will Carling in the late Eighties did that situation change. That England 1988 vintage was certainly a quality one, although the continued decline in Welsh, Irish and Scottish fortunes, allied to the existence of a hard core of veterans in a pack centred around Wade Dooley, Dean Richards and Mike Teague, did suggest that England were to have the rub of the green at last. The results were amazing, with England winning back-to-back Grand Slams in 1991 and 1992, and then going on to win another in 1995 to rival the great England side of the Twenties.

Since then, however, results have been more moderate, with England being squeezed out first in 1997 and 1998 by France and then in 1999 by Scotland.

The final piece of the Five Nations puzzle is that most enigmatic of rugby countries, France. After expulsion in 1931 and rehabilitation in 1947, France prospered under the inspirational leadership of Lourdes legend Jean Prat. Far from being the perennial losers, France became the most vibrant force in the competition, invariably providing the main opposition to the top dogs if they were unable to assume that position.

France have long played the closest thing in Europe to total rugby, with backs like the Boniface brothers, Jo Maso and Serge Blanco combining with some gigantic forwards such as Jean Prat, Walter Spanghero and Jean-Pierre Bastiat to make France the most consistently entertaining side in the Championship. Grand Slams in 1968, '77, '81, '87 and '97 – the last one achieved when coming from 14 points behind after a ten-year losing streak at Twickenham – have underlined the strength of French rugby.

The year 2,000 also brings a new challenge – the Six Nations Championship, which has been created by the inclusion of Italy.

The Tri-Nations Series

When the Tri-Nations series was launched in 1996 as an integral part of the top Southern Hemisphere unions' deal with Rupert Murdoch's Sky satellite television channel, it promised the most exciting rugby ever played on an annual basis and the most ridiculously large Cup in any sport in any country in the world. The idea was a simple one: take the age-old rivalries between old adversaries New Zealand, South Africa and Australia (who also happen to be arguably the best three sides in the world) and create the equivalent of a Southern Hemisphere Five Nations, only with each of the three sides playing each other on a home and away basis every year.

Conceived in 1995 during the World Cup, the campaign pitted the world champions South Africa against the team that was generally regarded as the best in the competition but which had lost the final to the Springboks amid rumours of a poisoning scandal, the All Blacks. With Australia still smarting from a last-minute quarter-final exit at the hands of the dreaded Poms, the scene was set for a

blistering six-match series. Throw in the fact that the each of the countries' players knew each other intimately from the Super 12 series, and the fact that New Zealanders had also thrown in a three-Test tour to South Africa on top of their two home and away games against the Springboks and the series took on an even more rosy hue. New Zealand versus South Africa on five consecutive week-ends – the World Cup final may have said who was world champions on paper, but in both countries there was no doubt that this was seen as a real test of endurance, and that the winners would be de facto the best in the world.

Just for once, the hype was justified. An historic series featuring the three World Cup winners was worth every penny, or at least over half of the population of New Zealand thought so as they stayed up into the wee small hours to watch the Blacks bash the Boks in a choice of venues throughout South Africa. Hooker Sean Fitzpatrick's men were irresistible, and ended the most arduous season ever undertaken by any side as the undisputed champions of the world. For the first time ever, a New Zealand side had gone down to South Africa and won a series there. And they didn't just win it, they walked it in a series that never looked in doubt, even though the Boks pulled back the last Test at Ellis Park 32–22. By the end of the tour coach John Hart summed up the party's feelings as he reflected upon four wins over the Springboks, three of them on South African soil: "This is the greatest day in the history of New Zealand rugby. It is a record that can never be bettered and will probably never be equalled." The revenge for the '95 World Cup, the Cavaliers and Fred Allen's 1949 tour party that was whitewashed 4–0 amid what Kiwis saw as heavily biased refereeing, was at last complete.

With the All Blacks sweeping the board during the Tri-Nations and winning the payback tour to boot, that left the Wallabies and Springboks to fight it out for second place, a battle that saw honours even in their mini two-Test series. It was one of the greatest Test series ever played, but it was not, in many senses, "new", for the three countries have long histories of playing each other on a very regular basis, particular between the Antipodean duo. Although there has been no formal competition, so intense has the rivalry been between these three countries that it is recorded here as if it was.

That rivalry has also intensified over the past three years, with the changing fortunes of the three participants keeping interest very much alive.

In fact, so alive is interest in the series that when in 1997 the Australian Rugby Union decided to take two Tests outside the Aussie rugby heartland, the response was incredible. Within three days of going on sale in Melbourne, 80,000 tickets for the All Blacks game were sold. The final gate of 90,119 set a new record for a match involving the All Blacks.

Yet the New Zealanders went through the season undefeated to show why they were the main draw card in 1997. Not only did they put 55 points on the Springboks at Eden Park, but they also whitewashed the Wallabies, who also had the bad luck to be on the wrong end of a 61-22 pummelling by South Africa at Loftus Versfeld.

Yet the wonder of the Tri-Nations is that all three old adversaries are sufficiently strong to turn things around, and the 1998 season was a real eye-opener for the New Zealanders, who ended up on the wrong end of a whitewash as the Springboks went through the season unbeaten.

The 17-game record-equaling winning spell put together by Gary Teichmann's side showed just how quickly underdogs can become top dogs in Tri-Nations rugby. When all of the players are facing each other every week as part of a gruelling Super 12 programme, all weaknesses and dips in form are ruthlessly exposed – as All Black coach John Hart found out to his cost in the worst season of his career.

Bledisloe Cup

New Zealand v Australia

The symbol of trans-Tasman supremacy since 1931, when it was presented by the then Governor-General of New Zealand, Lord Bledisloe, the Bledisloe Cup was so often won by the New Zealand All Blacks that they thought of it as virtually their property.

Certainly that is the impression given, for after winning the Cup for the first time in 1932 when they defeated Australia 20–13, no mention of the Cup was made for almost half a century. That all changed after an historic afternoon in 1979 when the Wallabies defeated the All Blacks 12–6 in Sydney in one of the rare one-Test series between the two countries, thus claiming the Cup for the first time since 1949 (and that 2–0 series victory was regarded by most Kiwis as unimportant because it was achieved while the best 30 players in New Zealand were away in South Africa with Fred Allen – also getting whitewashed to make a unique double!).

Rare though it was, it wasn't the fact that the Wallabies had won the series that moved the goalposts (they had also won series in 1929, 1939 and 1949). No, it was the fact that, after having beaten the Blacks, they then proceeded to parade the huge and long-forgotten Cup around an ecstatic Sydney Cricket Ground.

The New Zealand rugby public, watching the match live in their sitting rooms, were mortified. Not only had the All Blacks been beaten, but here were the easybeats of world rugby – a side which had lost to Tonga on its own patch just six years before – lording it over the lords of rugby.

The occasion put a great deal of spice into the relationship and, with the Wallabies on an upward curve that led to a World Cup win in 1991 and competitiveness at the highest level ever since, the keenly anticipated Bledisloe Cup is now one of the highlights of the rugby year, with sell-out grounds whether games are played in the rugby heartland or in "development" areas such as Melbourne or Perth. After the Wallabies' 3-0 record against the Blacks in 1998, there will not be a spare seat for years to come.

No two Test sides have played each other more than New Zealand and Australia, who have now amassed over 100 Tests against each other since New Zealand first thrashed Australia 22–3 in Sydney in 1903, with more than half of those being for the Bledisloe Cup. New Zealand have, to date, won over 70.

New Zealand v South Africa

No Tests in world rugby, with the possible exception of a Lions tour, can create as much excitement and anticipation as the prospect of a meeting between the Springboks and All Blacks.

Since the two countries first shared the series in New Zealand in 1921, the rivalry between them has been the most intense and unremitting in world rugby. Numerous clashes between them could have made it into the Ten Greatest Games chapter, but the one chosen was the World Cup final for the added dimension the silverware gave to the whole match.

Of all the countries in the world, it was New Zealand which found it hardest to break with South Africa, when the country became a sporting pariah thanks to its adherence to the policy of Apartheid.

It seems all the more odd given that New Zealand is possibly the most racially harmonious countries in the world, with race hardly an issue for most Maoris.

Despite that, though, Maori players such as George Nepia were not allowed to play in South Africa before 1992. Even the first series was disrupted when row broke out after a member of the South African party, C.W.F. Blackett,

sent a cable to South Africa following the Springboks' ill-tempered 9–8 victory over the Maoris at Napier.

The offending passage read: "it was bad enough having to play a team officially designated New Zealand Natives, but the spectacle of thousands of Europeans frantically cheering on a band of coloured men to defeat members of their own race was too much for the Springboks who were, frankly, disgusted."

It says much for New Zealand's love of rugby that relations between the two nations continued until the 1980s, when matters reached a head.

The 1981 South African tour to New Zealand, for instance, was nicknamed the "Barbed Wire Tour" because all games had to be played behind barbed wire fencing to stop anti-Apartheid protesters invading the pitch.

That tour witnessed some of the most violent scenes of civil disobedience in New Zealand's history as the country was split in two over the issue, with rugby followers fighting in the streets with demonstrators.

The Third Test of that series saw a plane dropping bags of flour, carpet tacks and smoke canisters onto the pitch, while anarchy ruled outside the ground. Even then, only a legal decision that touring South Africa would violate New Zealand's constitution by denying Maoris the same rights as white New

Zealanders, stopped the tour, which then became an "unofficial" tour by the Cavaliers, who included virtually every All Black and were coached by All Black legend Colin Meads. That is how strongly New Zealand rugby people feel about South Africa, and it is an intensity that is reciprocated.

In the post-Apartheid era, that rivalry has, if anything, been intensified. The All Blacks rushed back in to play South Africa when isolation ended in 1992, and went through the tour undefeated but unimpressive. But it was the 1995 World Cup final, when favourites New Zealand were hustled by a formidably committed Springboks side, which really cemented and reinvigorated the rivalry.

A post-final jibe from SARFU supremo Louis Luyt that if the Springboks had been at the 1987 World Cup they would have won that too sent the whole of New Zealand into apoplexy, while All Blacks coach Laurie Mains' assertion that his players had been poisoned on the day of the final added extra edge to the rivalry.

That reinforced tradition of enmity with respect has played a part in producing some of the most outstanding games in rugby history in recent years.

It has also produced varying fortunes, with South Africa losing all four Tri-Nations games in 1997, a fate which was also to befall the All Blacks in their dark days of 1998.

Australia v South Africa

Before South Africa's international exile, Australia were not worthy of the intensity that Tests against the All Blacks generated.

Indeed, up until that time, the Springboks had won 21 of the 28 Tests between the two, with the Australians only winning the home two-Test series in 1965 despite some strong showings, most notably the 1963 tour to South Africa where the Wallabies won two of the first three Tests before drawing the fourth to square the series.

In South Africa's enforced absence, however, the Wallabies went from strength to strength, becoming world champions when they beat England to win the 1991 World Cup, and underlined that status by touring South Africa in 1992, where they humiliated the South Africans at Ellis Park, thrashing them 26–3, in the process showing the Springboks how far they had regressed during their years of sporting isolation.

Since then games between the two have assumed an added significance, especially after the Wallabies were beaten in the opening showpiece game of the 1995 World Cup by hosts South Africa, and especially because the Tri-Nations now pits the two sides against each other twice a year.

The Super 12 Trophy

Club or provincial rugby across countries or even continents is the latest and most exciting stage of rugby's development towards a truly global, professional game.

As with soccer, rugby first embraced the concept of a World Cup and then, after the game went open in 1995, sought to move towards a wholehearted acceptance of competitions based along the same lines as European soccer's UEFA Cup, where the best that each nation has to offer goes into a round robin stage followed by a knock-out competition.

Such regional competitions are now firmly established in both hemispheres, with the top Southern Hemisphere provinces competing for the Super 12 Trophy and a mixture of Northern Hemisphere clubs and provinces contesting the European Cup.

So successful has the innovation been in both cases that domestic competitions are now in real danger of becoming almost secondary to the real business of the Super 12 or European Cup competition.

Indeed, in the five countries where domestic performance is the key to entry into the Super 12 or European Cup – England, Wales, France, New Zealand and South Africa – the rush for inclusion at the higher level is a spur that has added extra spice to domestic competitions as clubs and provinces fight to reach a high enough position to gain entry.

So successful has the Super 12 been in every respect that in New Zealand, for instance, 56% of men said that they had seen the highlights of every game in the tournament, while over half a million New Zealanders went to see a Super 12 game live in 1998! That is a level of market penetration undreamt of in any game save for European soccer and American Football.

The Super 12 has also forced the professional provinces to market themselves in a way that would have been unthinkable a decade ago, and rugby is reaping the benefits. New names for each of the sides – Northern Transvaal are now the Blue Bulls, ACT are the Brumbies and Otago are the Highlanders – have widened the appeal, while a draft system in each country has ensured that the best players are always on show.

The competition is not perfect – it encourages player burnout and has had a seriously detrimental effect on club rugby in all three nations – yet as a means of making the transition to a truly global, truly professional game, it has proved priceless.

Super 12

The Super 12 series sprang into life in the wake of the 1995 World Cup when Union went professional. With the launch of the Rupert Murdoch-backed Super League and the Australian Rugby League's decision to target Union's top players by removing the salary cap only for players switching codes, it was clear that the status quo in Australia and New Zealand was no longer tenable. Something had to be done, and that something was a ten-year, £340m deal with Murdoch that built upon the existing infrastructure of Southern Hemisphere competition. The first element was the Tri Nations and the second was the the Super 12.

The concept is a simple one: the best 12 provinces from New Zealand, South Africa and Australia battle it out to find the best provincial outfit south of the equator. Each team plays every other team once in the group phase, with the top four teams progressing to the semi-finals. First-placed plays fourth-placed, while second takes on third, culminating in a showpiece final. Only Australia knows in advance which provinces it will enter into the competition, with its two established sides Queensland and New South Wales being joined by ACT, which was upgraded specifically so that it could push Australia's representation up to three. New Zealand enters five expanded provinces (usually Auckland, Wellington, Otago, Waikato and Canterbury), chosen on the basis of performances in the National Provincial Championship. South Africa enters the four semi-finalists from the Currie Cup (with Natal, Transvaal and Northern Transvaal being the ever-presents with Western Province recently giving way to Orange Free State).

Although the competition was rushed into life as a response to the looming threat of the expansionist tendencies of Australian Rugby League, the format had been a long time in the making and was based on two previous versions stretching back to 1986, the Super Six and the Super Ten. The Super Six, played between Queensland, New South Wales and the top four New Zealand provinces, was first contested the year before the first World Cup in 1987. Dominated by the two New Zealand provinces of Canterbury and Auckland until 1992, when Queensland at last emerged victorious, the tournament was a vital factor in the rise of the Wallabies and, more significantly, had put a framework in place for when South Africa's isolation ended in 1992.

As soon as South Africa were back in circulation, the Super Six format was radically extended to the Super Ten with the four New Zealand and two Australian provinces being joined by three South African provinces and, following the success of Samoa at the 1991 World Cup, the winner of the Pacific Championship played between Fiji, Tonga and Western Samoa. With two pools of five, the tournament was a huge success in almost every sense from its inception in 1993. Modest but steadily growing crowds ensured that the competition was financially viable, and Transvaal's stunning 20–17 win over Auckland in the inaugural final at Ellis Park ensured that the tournament got the kick-start it so badly needed. Sizzling competition and a willingness to run the ball characterised the tournament throughout its three-year lifespan, with Queensland's wins over Natal in 1994 and Transvaal in 1995 characteristic finales to this new level of provincial competition. The tournament also gave top players a taste of what professional rugby was like, which was to prove a decisive factor when events threatened to get out of control after the World Cup.

By the time the Super 12 came along in 1996, the groundwork had been done for what was quickly to become the greatest annual tournament in the rugby world. In terms of logistics, the number of matches, the size of crowds and the sheer pace of the rugby, the Super 12 has no equal in world rugby. Its crowds averaged almost 30,000 at each of the 69 matches last year, and the standard of rugby is unquestionably the highest and most entertaining in the world, not least because in the professional age every side seems to have taken it upon themselves to play open, running rugby. The "draft pick" system in place in Australia and New Zealand also ensured that the best players available were on show, while the decision not to poach players from one country to another and the decision to award bonus points to sides that score four tries in a match, as well as teams which stayed within seven points of the winning side, means that all sides are relatively strong. Every Super 12 side is capable of beating any other, either home or away.

The commitment to attack has produced some of the finest matches ever seen, and although the mistake rate is high, so is the endeavour, the player fitness and the try count.

Auckland, in particular, played some outstanding rugby in 1996, when they beat Natal 45–21 in a spectacular final at Eden Park, and in 1997, when they retained the trophy in a 23–7 victory over surprise package ACT.

Auckland's grip, however, appears to be fading. In 1998, they were beaten 20-13 in the final by the Canterbury Crusaders, while in 1999, they performed so dismally that they were never in with a real chance of making the play-off stages.

European Cup

Although it was the go-ahead Unions from Australia and New Zealand who got the show on the road, it was actually in Europe that the first faltering attempt at getting a pan-national club competition underway were taken. That was in the early Sixties when the French-controlled FIRA organisation (see page 26) tried to inaugurate a European competition. Inevitably the British unions declined to participate, although it was wider financial problems which put paid to the idea after three years.

Europe had to wait until the 1995–96 season to develop the real McCoy for itself. Even then, the failure of the English clubs to commit themselves in the first year made the competition something of a Franco-Welsh affair, although the whole tenor was raised by a hugely entertaining final between Toulouse and Cardiff at the Arms Park, which the Frenchmen won 21–18 in extra-time.

Having seen the enormous potential of a European Cup, the following season saw England enter four clubs and Scotland put forward three districts to join representatives from Ireland (3), France (4), Wales (4) and Italy (2). The 20 teams competing were split into four pools of five, from which the top two sides went into the quarter-finals.

Despite pooling all their top players into provinces for the event, the Irish and Scottish fared little better than the Italians, and the quarter-finals were dominated by the English, Welsh and French big guns. Although not open running rugby in the Super 12 style, the matches were nevertheless gripping enough to ensure that the European Cup ties have taken on a mystique and aura that the domestic competitions still lack. In particular, games at winners Brive's packed ground and the seething atmosphere of Wasps' Loftus Road when Cardiff came to town were a level of intensity up from domestic fare. The final, a contest between Leicester's strong-mauling pack and Brive's free-running backs was a classic encounter, with French passion overcoming English determination as Brive took a grip on the match late on, winning 28–9 at the Cardiff Arms Park.

Although Brive failed to retain their trophy, losing out to Bath in a heroic final the following season, the European Cup was then plunged into a period of political turmoil when the English clubs pulled out for during 1998-9.

That, though, didn't stop Ulster from surprising the whole of French rugby by beating highly-fancied Stade Francais in an emotional final in front of a packed Lansdowne Road. It truly was one of European rugby's most memorable days.

Asian Championship

The struggle for supremacy in Asia began in 1969 when Japan won the first Asian Championship in Tokyo, hardly a shock outcome given that with a playing population in excess of 100,000, Japan have almost as many players to call upon as the rest of of the Asian Championship countries put together.

Moreover, rugby has been established in Japan far longer than in any of the other countries, and Japan boasts a unique system where clubs are run by companies, making most of the country's top players virtual professionals in all but name.

Nevertheless, Japan have not had it all their own way in the bi-annual tournament, not by a long chalk. Hong Kong put up a strong challenge early doors, but the first nation to break Japanese hegemony was Korea, which won the 1982 tournament by beating Japan 12–9 at the eighth time of asking.

That win was achieved after the scores were level 9–9 at full-time, with Korean fly-half Moon Yuang Chan kicking the winning drop-goal quarter of an hour into extra-time.

From there on in the competition has been a two-horse race between the speedy Japanese and the larger Koreans – who are almost all soldiers – a rivalry which has been spiced up by the historical and vicious history between the two countries (Korea was a Japanese colony for almost half a century, and the Seoul government is still in the process of dynamiting buildings constructed to spell "Long Live Japan" when viewed from above!).

The most bittersweet moment in the many clashes between the two came in the Asian Championship which doubled as a qualifying round for the 1995 Rugby World Cup, when Japan recovered from a half-time deficit of over 20 points to sneak a win at the wire. Korea's best run was three wins on the trot between 1986–90.

Japan and Korea may have completely dominated the competition, but in conjunction with the Hong Kong Sevens it still provides an arena of meaningful international competition where the small frames of the Asian races will not be a factor.

As well as the two habitual winners, the Championship is also contested by Hong Kong, Sri Lanka, Malaysia, Thailand, Singapore and Taiwan, although quite what impact the adoption of the game by the two million soldiers of China's Red Army will have upon the involvement is unclear.

Pacific Championship

Although the qualifying rounds for the 1995 World Cup showed that rugby is alive and well on Pacific Islands such as the Cook Islands, Tahiti, Papua New Guinea and Soloman Islands, the long-established Pacific Championship is restricted to a three-way tournament between the three regional giants, Fiji, Tonga and Western Samoa.

The Championship kicked off in 1924 when Fiji travelled to Tonga and drew the three-Test series, and consolidated its position as a three-way affair the next year when Fiji visited to Samoa and beat the hosts 6–0 on a field which had a large tree between the goal line and the 25-yard line! Since then finances and the difficulty of travel have often disrupted the tournament, which is played on an ad hoc basis.

At one stage before the last World Cup, the winners of the Pacific Championship were granted entry into the Super 10 provincial series, but the tournament's evolution into a Super 12 tournament.

Another feature of the Pacific Championship has been the fierce rivalry between the island races, which has sometimes threatened to get out of hand. When Fiji played in Apia in 1993, for example, the Samoans had to cancel police leave and put the army on standby!

The Pacific Championship has now, however, been absorbed into the Pacific Rim Championship, an annual six-team event which pits Fiji, Tonga and Western Samoa against three interlopers – Japan, Canada and the USA.

Conceived in 1997, the tournament finally got underway on May 1st 1999, helped largely by cash from the game's governing body, the International Rugby Board. In a shock result, Japan – featuring five former New Zealanders, including two ex-All Blacks – pipped Canada 23-21 in Tokyo.

FIRA

Once a powerful administrative body encompassing most of the world's unions outside the Big Eight, the Federation Internationale de Rugby Amateur – FIRA – is now essentially a European competition for all those countries not in the Five Nations (except France, which competes in both although it invariably plays an "A" team in the FIRA competition).

The organisation was initially started in 1932, the year after France were thrown out of the Five Nations Championship. Desperate for alternative international fixtures, France approached Germany, and the two countries formed an organisation which also had Romania, Italy, Holland, Catalonia, Portugal, Czechoslovakia and Sweden as fellow founder-members.

After the war, when France were readmitted to the Five Nations, FIRA had grown in stature as it widened its net in Europe and took on associate members from outside the continent, and it sought wider aims such as regaining rugby's Olympic status, lost after the 1924 Games, and establishing a European clubs competition (which it did briefly in the early Sixties before financial considerations finished the tournament).

Although FIRA's days as a direct alternative to the International Board are over, thanks to the IB's decision to embrace the concept of a World Cup and to extend membership to every rugby-playing country in the world, the FIRA Championship which was first played in 1974 still provides Europe with a valuable outlet for national competition.

Played in three divisions containing virtually every country in mainland Europe and Francophone North Africa, France have invariably headed the First Division, although Romania have also won it five times and the USSR once.

In the 1997 match between Italy and France, the Italians caused a major upset when they defeated a near full-strength French side shortly after they had won the Grand Slam for the first time in a decade.

The FIRA tournament has also been augmented by the Latin Cup, a gong that was first played for in 1995. Contested between France, Italy, Argentina and Romania, the event is expected to be contested on a bi-annual basis.

It is also expected that France will come to dominate the competition as it dominates FIRA. That was certainly the case in the first two Latin Cups, the first held in Buenos Aires in 1995 and dominated by France, and the second held in Paris in 1997, and dominated by the hosts, although don't rule out Argentina.

North America

The Americans and Canadians have markedly different rugby traditions, but share two common bonds: huge geographical and financial problems in attempting to devise any national competitions and the Can-Am Series.

The problem of finances and geography has infiltrated both the national and the domestic level, with the Can-Am Series, which has been played between the US national side, the Eagles, and Canada every year since 1977, only going ahead most years after players paid their own air fare. Perhaps because most of its players come from the same province, British Columbia, the Canadians have dominated the series, winning on all but six occasions.

The USA's inaugural club championship was played in 1979, but with the country's two strongest rugby communities 3,000 miles apart in California and on the East Coast, only with the recent injection of $10 million from Sky has a genuine national championship been financial or logistically feasible.

Much the same goes for Canada, where the Carling Bowl has long been the measure of domestic success. Inter-Provincial competition has been a recent innovation, but the climatic problems that exist in many areas (New Foundland, for example, only play rugby in the summer), the huge distances involved, a lack of serious funding and the dominance of the British Columbians limits its usefulness.

However, the professional era has been kind to both nations. The USA has managed to get several of its top players placed with British clubs – most notably No.8 Dan Lyle at Bath – while the Canadians have been even more successful at blooding their players at the very top level, with players like Dan Lougheed at Leicester typifying the progress being made by the Canucks.

Professionalism could also be the making of the Eagles, however. With the Murdoch money behind them, they have already been able to make inroads in the universities and colleges, but the ASARFU has also been working with Fox to produce a professional game in America in much the same way as Gridiron's NFL has tried to transplant its game in Europe.

The plan involves six professional franchises, costing £50m over ten years, and playing top level rugby in the USA's major population centres. As John Hart once said: "god help us if the Americans really ever take to rugby." It may just be time to start saying a prayer or two!

Sevens Tournament

Sevens first poked its head out into the rugby world in 1883 in the tiny market town of Melrose, centre of Scotland's rugby heartland in the Borders. At the time Melrose were on the verge of bankruptcy and were desperately looking for a way to bring in some paying punters to fill up their empty coffers. The halfbacks of the side, two butchers from the town called David Sanderson and his apprentice Ned Haig, hit upon the idea of using the forthcoming sports day as a way of raising money.

The passion for rugby is etched deep into the psyche of the tightly-knit Borders community, and the pair knew that if they could harness this spirit and enthusiasm they could have a potential money-spinner on their hands.

As Haig said many years later, when reflecting on the Sevens: "Want of money made us rack our brains as to what was to be done to keep the club from going to the wall, and the idea struck me that a football tournament might prove attractive. But it was a hopeless task to have several games in one afternoon with 15 on both sides so the teams were reduced to seven men."

In fact, although Haig has always received the praise for being the founding father of sevens, the birth of the game was as much down to Sanderson, who came up with the idea after playing an abbreviated code of the game while working south of the border. Posterity has denied him his rightful place in the history of the game however, mainly because of a argument he had with the Melrose club years later which led to his role being downplayed (and often even deleted) from official histories of the sevens.

But whoever came up with the idea, the important thing is that it stuck. Even more importantly, the innovation was an instant success at the Melrose Sports day, as this extract from the Border Telegraph of May 2, 1883, shows: "By the time of the event, an enormous crowd of spectators had assembled, special trains having been run from Galashiels and Hawick and about 1,600 tickets being taken at Melrose during the day.

The competition had been looked forward to with great interest, as most of the clubs of the district were expected to compete for the prize – a silver cup presented by the ladies of Melrose."

The success of the day was sealed when Melrose beat neighbours and great rivals Gala in a tense and exciting final. With the scores level at full-time, a period of extra-time was decided upon, at which stage captain Sanderson scored a cheeky blind-side try.

As skipper, he immediately led his side off the pitch and claimed the Ladies Cup to howls of protest from the Gala players who thought that extra-time should be another 15 minutes. This is where the precedent for the first score in extra-time being the winning score comes from.

The tournament saved the Melrose club from bankruptcy, and established a tradition that was to flourish and, as Scots travelled the rugby world, spread until sevens became a respected code in its own right. Although the accompanying festivities, including foot races, dribbling races, drop-goal and place–kicking competitions, were later dropped, it was otherwise a format that was widely copied.

A Borders sevens circuit soon sprang up and by the end of the century there were tournaments at Gala, Hawick, Jed-Forest, Langholm, Selkirk and Kelso. Yet Melrose still remains the biggest and most prestigious competition to this day, with a Melrose winner's medal second only to a Scotland cap in the honours list north of the Border.

Perhaps, explains Walter Allan in the Official History of the Melrose Sevens, that is why an episode in 1983 when several of the victorious French Barbarians, the first non-British winners of the tournament, handed over their medals to local beauties caused such deep offence in the town.

Far from spreading quickly from those ancient beginnings in the Scottish Borders, for the best part of a century sevens remained a minority pursuit generally played for a bit of fun and to keep fit at the end of the season.

Even without Sanderson's recollections of having played the game south of the Border there is a good deal of evidence that an abbreviated rugby game was played in England on an informal basis in rugby's early years.

Despite this, though, relatively few sevens tournaments raised their heads in England. Places like Caldy, in Lancashire, and the Snelling Sevens in Wales, still have tournaments that were started just after the turn of the century, but by and large sevens has never been big in Britain outside the Borders. Indeed, for many years it was known as "The Borders Game".

The one major exception was the Middlesex Sevens, which has been held annually at Twickenham since 1926 and which has regularly played to full houses of 60,000. Yet that tournament is as much a social occasion as a serious sporting day out, with beer and sunshine the priority on the last day of the season. Until recently, it was restricted to clubs from the London area, but in recent years it has issued invitations to guest sides and recent winners include sevens specialists Fiji and Western Samoa.

It was not until the launch of the Hong Kong Sevens in 1976 that sevens spread outside Britain and became a truly global game. The Hong Kong tournament was the brainchild of a number of ex-pat Scots working in the Colony, chief among them was "Tokkie" Smith, now regarded as the father of modern sevens. From its first tournament, won by the Cantabrians side from Christchurch, New Zealand, it was abundantly clear that the Hong Kong event was something out of the ordinary.

In particular, the chance to compete on a more even playing field with the bigger sides in world rugby was welcomed by the people of Asia and the numerically smaller nations of world rugby. Sides such as Korea, Taiwan, Sri Lanka, Papua New Guinea, Holland and Germany all came to prominence at the sevens alongside the giants of the abbreviated code, New Zealand, Australia and Fiji, with the unique system of having three competitions – a bowl, plate and cup – making the competition especially "minnow friendly".

From the early Eighties, it was national sides only at Hong Kong, with the exception of the Home Unions who are in the middle of heavy domestic competitions when the sevens are held in late March. Instead, specialist sevens touring sides like the Barbarians (Britain), the Co-Optimists (Scotland), the Wolfhounds (Ireland), Crawshay's (Wales) and the Penguins (England) came out from Britain to try their luck at Hong Kong, although the only northern hemisphere side to win at Hong Kong so far was the Barbarians in 1981.

These days Hong Kong is a glittering event which essentially doubles as a world championship of sevens, although quite how the Chinese takeover will impact upon the fun-loving aspects that have done so much to popularise the tournament is anyone's guess. In many ways, though, Hong Kong has already fulfiled its important mission by establishing sevens as a missionary force in the game, a quick and easy introduction to the essentials of rugby without many of the technicalities that baffle newcomers.

If nothing else, the success of Hong Kong as a tourist magnet has set off a trail of sevens tournaments in exotic locations around the world that has established an unofficial sevens circuit. Sevens specialists Fiji and a raft of invitation teams compete for cash prizes up to £25,000 in places as beautiful as Dubai, Singapore, Paris, Benidorm, Punta del Este in Uruguay, Lisbon, Barbados, Catania in Sicily, Tokyo, Suva in Fiji, Stellenbosch, Madrid, Denver and

Victoria Falls in Zimbabwe.

Sevens has become so popular that it even featured as the demonstration sport at the 1998 Commonwealth Games in Kuala Lumpur, Malaysia (which is the birthplace of the increasingly popular game of tens and the venue for the famous Cobra Tens).

Although it has yet to achieve anywhere near the popularity of the World Cup or even the Hong Kong Sevens itself, the rise of sevens has led to the introduction of a World Cup Sevens tournament every four years under the auspices of the International Board's commercial arm, RWC Ltd. Contested for the Melrose Cup, the first tournament was a low-key affair staged at Murray-field in Edinburgh.

Despite the southern hemisphere sides being firm favourites at the outset of the tournament, England upset the form book beating Australia in the final.

Logic and form reasserted themselves four years later, however, as Fiji beat South Africa in a closely-fought final in Hong Kong. Indeed, not one of the northern hemisphere sides managed to reach the semi-final stage.

Unlike the 1993 World Cup Sevens, the 1997 tournament was played in the warm, to packed crowds amid a cacophony of raucous singing and a deluge of warm beer.

The British Lions

Before the advent of the first World Cup in 1987, British Lions tours represented the apex of a player's career. To play for the Lions or against the Lions was the highest honour the game could bestow, and the coming of a Lions tour would dominate the sporting agenda in in the host nations for months before the tourists' arrival. There have been many great players to have played for their individual countries, but until 1987 it was virtually impossible for a player to achieve legendary status unless he had tested himself in the furnace of a Lions Test.

Although universally known as the British Lions since 1924, when the side gained the nickname due to the logo on their tour ties, the tours are in fact undertaken by the British Isles Rugby Union Team.

The tour party is chosen from the geographical entity of the British Isles, which for these purposes include England, Wales, Scotland and Ireland (both North and South), and tours to either New Zealand or South Africa on average every four years.

Only in 1989, when South Africa were still isolated after the 1980 tour and the Wallabies were emerging as a genuine third force in the Southern Hemisphere, did Australia feature as a destination in its own right rather than as a staging point on the way to the real challenge in New Zealand.

It was on a joint trip to Australia and New Zealand that the concept of the Lions was first born. The trip in question was James Lillywhite's 1876–7 cricket tour. Marvelling at the hunger of the Australians and New Zealanders for sporting competition, the English cricketers Alfred Shaw and Arthur Shrewsbury (the former was the first man to bowl a ball in Test cricket) eventually hit upon the idea of filling their winter with a rugby tour and promptly cabled the RFU.

Typically, the game's English administrators had no interest in sending a representative party, but had no problem with a side travelling southwards. An agent was appointed and within six months a 21-strong tour party sailed for New Zealand and Australia under the leadership of Swinton's Bob Seddon. In fact, virtually all of the tour party came from either the Northern clubs or from the Scottish cotton mill town of Hawick, which had very strong ties with Yorkshire rugby.

Only Welshman William Thomas and the Isle of Man's AP Penketh were drawn from other areas and only three of the squad were established internationals, the rest being club players.

Before the tour had even left it hit controversy when it was discovered that at least two players had received "expenses" of around £15 each, yet on March 8, 1888 the party left for New Zealand, where it met up with England cricket captain Andrew Stoddart. He was later to assume captaincy of the rugby side as well after Seddon was drowned in Australia's Hunter River during a boating accident (making him the last man to captain England at both rugby and cricket).

In Australasia, the clash of rugby cultures was intriguing, with the British introducing the concept of heeling back and passing from the scrum, while also playing several games under Australian Rules in Victoria. In all the side played 35 games and lost just two of them, to Taranaki and Auckland, scoring 292 points, conceding 98 and finding the going significantly harder in New Zealand than in Australia.

It has been one of the RFU's enduring characteristics that if a venture succeeds, it inevitably annexes it, and so it was three years later when Cecil Rhodes, then governor of the Cape Colony, requested that a British tour party be sent to Southern Africa.

This time the tour party was to play Test matches and was accordingly placed under the leadership of experienced Scottish cap Bill Maclagan and made up of experienced English and Scottish players, of whom half were internationals.

The result was a victorious trek around Southern Africa in which 19 unbeaten games were played and 221 points scored, with only one conceded. Bustling Blackheath centre Randolph Aston, who scored 30 tries, including two in the 3–0 Test whitewash, to be acclaimed the star of the tour, typified the outstanding back play of the British.

Although their first two tours were triumphant romps punctuated by glittering social occasions, it was not long before the British headstart had begun to be eroded. When Johnny Hammond returned to South Africa in 1896 with a team made up of English and Irish players, for instance, he was amazed to find how far the colonials had come on. Strong forwards and a better tactical appreciation meant there were less easy matches and for the first time the British lost a Test when they were defeated 5–0 by South Africa in the Fourth Test at Newlands.

It was the same story in 1899 when the Rev Matthew Mullineux's party lost three of its 21 games in Australia, including the First Test 13–3. The 1891 tour to South Africa remains the only Lions tour where the tourists have completed a whitewash. By the time the new century dawned, the process of catch-up had been completed and British visits to the Southern Hemisphere began to take on a pattern that still exists today – the British provide weak forwards and inventive backs, a combination which is reversed in their opponents.

Mark Morrison's 1903 side were the get a taste of the things to come when they lost the Third Test 8–0 and with it the series 1–0 in South Africa after the first two Tests were drawn. It was a similar situation the following year when Darkie Bevell-Sivright's hugely talented Welsh threequarters Percy Bush, Teddy Morgan and Rhys Gabe inspired the British side to a won 14, lost none record in Australia.

In a foretaste of the future, however, the same side won only two of its five games in New Zealand, and lost the Test 9–3. Worse was to come in 1908 when Scotland and Ireland refused to contribute players for the tour to New Zealand after an argument over All Black expenses on the 1905 "Originals" tour. Squabbles about money occured even in those days!

The weakened Anglo-Welsh tour party lost one of its three major matches in Australia, was beaten by five New Zealand provincial Unions and despite managing to draw the Second Test 3–3 after the All Black selectors rested seven of its best players, lost the other two Tests by the unprecedented scorelines of 32–5 and 29–0.

Even when Tom Smyth's 1910 party contained the cream of all four Home Unions, the result was depressingly familiar; only 13 of 24 games won and a 2–1 series defeat. The status quo had changed forever.

The shift in power was confirmed in dramatic fashion during the two tours to South Africa and one tour to Australasia between the wars. In twelve Tests, the Lions only managed to win two, scoring 90 points but conceding almost double that number.

Yet if the tours were not successes in terms of playing results, they did at least consolidate the Lions reputation as a side which played some of the most attractive, open, running rugby in the world as men such as Haydn Tanner, Iain Smith, Carl Aarvold, Harry Bowcott and Vivian Jenkins cut a swathe through the Southern Hemisphere. Had the British tight forwards been able to live with their Southern Hemisphere counterparts, the roles may well have been reversed.

Indeed, had the British sides been able to draw fully from the talent available, they would undoubtedly have proved far more competitive, but the long duration of tours undertaken by cruise liner, which could last up to six months, meant that many top players declined the invitation to tour.

After the war, the growing prestige of the Lions meant that virtually every top player was available to tour New Zealand, and in 1950 only two of Britan's leading players were unable to make the four-month tour.

That tour, although unsuccessful, remains famous for the flair and inventiveness of Lions backs such as Irish fly-half Jack Kyle and Welsh centre Bleddyn Williams. Once again, forward deficiencies – in particular the inability to cope with the hard rucking percentage game pioneered by Viv Cavanagh and Otago – meant that the Lions lost three of the four Tests in New Zealand, winning both in Australia. But Karl Mullen's men played an attacking game of such fervour and in such stark contrast to the home sides that they were feted wherever they went.

The 1950 Lions were also the first side to wear the now famous kit incorporating the colours of the four Home Unions: the red of Wales on the shirt; the white of England on the shorts, cuffs and collar; the navy blue of Scotland and the green of Ireland on the socks.

The 1950 tour set the standard for the remaining two tours of the Fifties. As with the 1950 tourists, Robin Thompson's 1955 side left an indelible mark on the history of South African rugby. Travelling by air for the first time, the tour was also covered extensively by newspapers and the new medium of television, with the result that the party became stars.

As in New Zealand, the South African public were desperate to see talented backs given free rein, and they were not to be disappointed by the Lions. With a streetwise pack that was at last able to hold the Springboks at bay, backs like Irish wing Tony O'Reilly, English centres Butterfield and Davies, and half-backs Dickie Jeeps and Cliff Morgan ran rings around Stephen Fry's Springboks.

The First Test in Johannesburg, which the Lions won 23–22 in front of 95,000 spectators after playing the whole second half with only seven forwards was reckoned one of the greatest games ever played and set the tenor for a series of high excitement which the Springboks counted themselves fortunate to eventually share.

1959 witnessed another spectacular series in Australia and New Zealand, with the Lions throwing caution to the wind in a run-at-all-costs strategy. And it almost paid off. After convincingly winning the two Tests in Australia, the forward frailty re-emerged and the Lions lost the New Zealand leg 3–1, yet it was a far from discreditable performance. Indeed, many New Zealanders conceded that the 18–17 First Test defeat, which came when All Black fullback Don

Clarke kicked six penalties to the Lions four tries, was at the very least a moral victory (which would now be a 25–18 win that would have tied the series).

The Sixties were an unmitigated disaster for British rugby as the forwards continued to be battered by the Southern Hemisphere, while the conveyor belt of inventive threequarters which had sustained the Lions up to 1959 dried up almost completely. The '62 Lions in South Africa lost three Tests and drew one, but were at least competitive. The '66 Lions looked business like in Australia, but were humiliated so completely in New Zealand that captain Mike Campbell-Lamerton dropped himself amid a four-Test whitewash. South Africa in '68 was little better, with Tom Kiernan's charges avoiding defeat in just one of the Tests, a 6–6 draw in in Port Elizabeth.

If the Sixties was the Lions' dismal decade, then the Seventies was to emerge as its golden era. The major obstacle to success for the Lions had always been a lack of possession, but by the time of the 1971 tour to New Zealand, Britain had a set of outrageously talented backs and a pack able to dominate the best in the world. And that's exactly what the Lions did for the duration of the tour.

Revitalised by the evidence of the 1969–70 Springbok tour of Britain, which showed the gap between Southern and Northern Hemispheres closing, the Lions played 26 games on that tour, losing just two against Queensland and the Second Test in Christchurch. With coaching genius Carwyn James in the background directing operations and Welsh fly-half Barry John providing peerless on-field tactical acumen, the Lions inflicted the first series defeat on New Zealand soil since the 1937 Springboks.

The bedrock of the challenge was the forward power provided by men like Willie John McBride, Mervyn Davies and Ian McLauchlan. The decisive factor was the best set of backs ever dispatched from Britain – JPR Williams, Gerald Davies, John Dawes, Mike Gibson, John Bevan, David Duckham, Barry John and Gareth Edwards are all as revered now, quarter of a century later, as they were then.

Barry John's '71 Lions were the finest all-round side ever to have pulled on Lions' shirts, but there is equally little doubt as to which is the best set of Lions forwards ever to have represented Britain.

The pack that toured South Africa in 1974 destroyed the Springbok eight and any provincial forwards who had the gall to go head to head with one of the hardest packs ever to play the game. McBride had toured South Africa as a Lion in '62 and '68 and had come to fully understand the role intimidation played in top level rugby there. His reaction was, as he put it, "to get our retaliation in first." The Lions refused to take a step back as they brawled their way round The Republic, using the now notorious "99" call – where every forward punches the nearest Springbok on the basis that the referee has to send them all off or none of them off – and ending the tour unbeaten.

With hefty wins in the first three Tests, only a controversial 13–13 draw (controversial because a perfectly good Fergus Slattery try was disallowed on the stroke of full-time) marring the perfect record.

However, while the Lions of '74 had outstanding forwards, the back play had declined somewhat from its peak in New Zealand three years before. By the time Phil Bennett led the Lions back to New Zealand in 1977, the backs had become the Achilles heel of the side. The forwards were again outstanding, but with poor back play and a curious lack of spirit in the squad which many ascribed to the very high number of players (18) from one country (Wales), the Lions lost the series 3–1.

It was again a similar scenario in 1980 when poor back play and injuries meant Billy Beaumont's fiercely competitive pack managed only one win over the Springboks from four Tests that could have swung either way. By 1983,

when Ciaran Fitzgerald's Lions were destroyed by the All Blacks, who won the series 4–0, it was clear that the forward dominance of the Seventies had completely dissipated.

By the time coaches Ian McGeechan and Roger Uttley led the Lions to Australia in 1989, the whole balance of power had shifted once more. The Wallabies had been building impressively since their unexpected failure to make the World Cup final, and the Lions arrived with a formidable pack based on an experienced English eight which was completely dominating European rugby. Only Welsh lock Bob Norster had been capped by the Lions before, and he only played in the First Test defeat.

It was obvious after that First Test defeat that the quick, rucking game favoured by the Celts was not going to beat an ultra-fit Australian side, so the decision to draft in two more Englishmen in Wade Dooley and Mike Teague and base the gameplan around the strong-mauling English forwards was taken.

It worked like a dream, with Teague taking the Man of the Series and the Lions totally outmuscling the Wallabies to win the Second Test 19–12, a win wrapped up by a virtuoso Jeremy Guscott try in the last few minutes of a pulsating match.

Unfortunately the Test series was played against a backdrop of lurid Aussie press headlines brought on by the Lions' aggressive but legitimate style of play. The deciding Test was settled by a Ieuan Evans try after a David Campese blunder behing his own try – line. The Lions 2–1 series win may not have been pretty, but it was certainly effective as the tourists came back from 1–0 down to win the series for only the second time.

Outmuscling the Wallabies with teak hard forwards in their prime is one thing, but trying to do the same to the New Zealanders when the core of your pack is clearly past its sell-by date is a different proposition altogether.

Yet that is what the Lions attempted to do in 1993, and it almost worked. With tyro twin tower locks Martin Johnson and Martin Bayfield dominating the line-out and with captain Gavin Hastings, centres Guscott and Gibbs, and wing Ieuan Evans in outstanding form, the Lions stormed back from a 20–18 First Test loss to take Second Test 20–7.

Even though the midweek side performed woefully throughout the tour, the Lions had high hopes for the Third Test, but despite being 10–0 up at half-time, they were crushed 30–13 in an awesomely efficient second-half display by the All Blacks.

With the advent of professionalism many people erroneously assumed the Lions' future would become increasingly parlous as club sides refused to release their prized assets for gruelling and demanding tours that could well bring their players back to them injured and therefore unable to play for them in September when the domestic season started.

But the 1997 tour to South Africa, the first time the Lions had visited the country since 1980, generated a massive amount of media hype.

Given no chance of winning the three–Test series when they arrived in South Africa, the Lions stunned the Springboks, winning the first two Tests by the skin of their teeth – the second by a Jeremy Guscott dropped-goal five minutes from time – to take the series 2–1.

It was a victory which was founded on the superb technical genius of Scots coaches Jim Telfer and Ian McGeechan, who used their outstanding backs to full effect while also working out various tactical ruses to keep their outmuscled forwards from being completely swamped.

A superb goal–kicking display by full–back Neil Jenkins throughout, and some robust defending in the first two Tests gave the Lions a series victory that only the most ardent Lions' supporter would have predicted at the outset. More importantly, the success of the tour guarantees the future of the Lions into the next century. Next on the agenda is Australia in 2001.

The Great Matches

Every so often, a match of true greatness comes along. A contest so intense and satisfying that everyone it touches has their faith in the sport restored forever; so gripping that it begs the uninitiated to begin a lifelong love affair with the game; so heart-stopping that huge passages of play remain indelibly etched in the memory. It is rugby's ability to rise above the mundane and throw up contests of spectacular endeavour and unsurpassable drama that makes it the most compulsive sport in the world.

But rugby's splendour can take many forms. First there is the grandstand finish: who can forget Gareth Edward's early charge for the Barbarians against the All Blacks in 1973? Or Serge Blanco's heroic last-ditch try to snatch the 1987 World Cup final place from under the Wallabies' noses?

Not all matches need one defining moment to be forever memorable, though. Nothing is more satisfying than the sight of a triumphant underdog. And which underdogs could have faced greater odds than the Jaguars side that faced South Africa 5,000 miles from home and with only a week to erase the memory of a 50-point Test savaging back in 1982.

The greatest theatre can come when old rivals lock horns. Grand Slam showdowns, that involve rivalries going back well over 100 years and which inevitably have added spice because of the historical connotations: England vs. Scotland or the perpetually bruising France vs. England encounters.

Lions's tours also bring out the best in the opposition; witness the 1997 tour of South Africa. Clashes between the All Blacks and the Springboks also provide utterly compelling spectacles; witness Joel Stransky's injury-time drop-goal to win an absorbing World Cup final. High drama, high entertainment.

Wales black out New Zealand

Wales 13
New Zealand 8

19 December 1953
Cardiff Arms Park

For many of the early years of rugby, one of the fiercest rivalries was between Wales and New Zealand. Of all the rugby-playing countries, only South Africa can come close to matching the passion which these two rugby-mad nations bring to the game.

Although it may seem like a quirk of history today, when New Zealand played Wales at Cardiff Arms Park in 1953, it was the All Blacks who were the underdogs.

They had only previously managed to beat Wales once, in 1924, they had already been defeated by Cardiff a month earlier, as well as being held to a 6–6 draw the previous week by Swansea.

Moreover, Wales had completed a Grand Slam in 1952, and only a shock 8–3 loss against England in Cardiff had prevented them winning a second successive Slam in 1953.

Wounded All Black pride is a dangerous enemy, however, and as soon as the match got underway it was clear that the New Zealanders were a far more effective unit than the one that had struggled against Swansea and Cardiff.

The tourists dominated the early forward exchanges and looked to be controlling the pattern of the game as the first quarter passed without a score. But against the run of play it was the beleaguered Welsh who drew first blood when fly-half Cliff Morgan hoofed the ball downfield from a collapsed maul in Wales's 22.

Full-back Bob Scott fielded the ball, but had no time to work with it as the ultra-fast wing Ken Jones arrived and piled in to Scott. Isolated and running out of options, Scott tried to find wing Ron Jarden, only to spill the ball into the path of the oncoming flanker Clem Thomas who hacked ahead to create an easy try for Sid Judd.

The New Zealanders hurled themselves at the desperate Welsh defenders, redoubling their efforts in attempt to get points on the board. Cracks began to appear in the Welsh defensive wall and after Jarden had kicked a touch-line penalty, the All Black forwards took over, applying every ounce of muscle at their disposal.

It was a tactic which began to work as the Welsh defence flagged. Finally, with half-time looming, Jarden put up a steepling garryowen which Wales failed to deal with and the first man to the ball was the flanker Clark.

The conversion made it 8–5 to the All Blacks at half-time, but this score, which made it appear as if the match was a pretty close contest between two evenly matched sides, completely failed to show quite how dominant the visitors had become.

In a frenetic second half, the All Blacks laid siege to the Welsh try-line, yet it was the home side who were to break out and score next to level the match at eight points each. For the All Blacks it was more of the same as they launched attack after attack at the Welsh line. Once again, though, Wales held firm before scoring a try against the run of play.

With five minutes to go, New Zealand lock Alan Elsom failed to control a line-out ball and Thomas pounced on it, swinging his foot in the same instant to send the ball spiralling downfield. Winger Ken Jones, a famous sprinter and by far the fastest man on the pitch, raced up as much as in hope as in expectation, but the ball took a wicked sideways bounce to wrong-foot the hapless Jarden and Jones gratefully accepted his slice of luck, scoring the decisive try that gave Wales a famous victory against the odds.

WALES: *G. Williams; K. Jones, G. Griffiths, B. Williams (capt), G. Rowlands; C. Morgan, R. Willis; W. Williams, D. Davies, C. Meredith, R. John, J. Gwilliam, S. Judd, J. Stephens, C. Thomas.*

NEW ZEALAND: *B. Scott; A. Elsom, Tanner, R. Jarden, B. Fitzpatrick; L. Haig, K. Davis; K. Skinner, R. Hemi, I. Clarke, G. Dalzell, R. White, R. Stuart (capt), W. Clark, W. McCaw.*

Courageous Lions come roaring back

South Africa 22
British Lions 23

First Test. 6 August 1955
Ellis Park, Johannesburg

When Robin Thompson's 1955 Lions arrived in South Africa, they soon established themselves as the best touring side to visit the Republic since the turn of the century, winning ten of the 12 matches in the lead-up to the First Test.

It was a gloriously talented side in general, but six players in particular stood out: the England centre pairing of Phil Davies and Jeff Butterfield, the Welsh outside half Cliff Morgan, the Irish winger Tony O'Reilly, English scrum-half Dickie Jeeps and the formidable Welsh hooker Bryn Meredith.

The Lions' success in the opening games and the controversial appointment of veteran flanker Stephen Fry to lead the Springboks, ensured that interest in the First Test was at fever pitch, with 95,000 spectators cramming into Johannes-burg's Ellis Park stadium. What unfolded over the next 80 minutes was a contest that the great South African Danie Craven reckoned was the best he had witnessed in all his years of playing and watching the game.

The Lions drew first blood when Davies made a break in midfield and delivered a wayward pass to the feet of the onrushing Butterfield. Without breaking stride, the Northampton man picked the ball off his bootlaces with one hand and, as he took out two tacklers, flung the ball to flying Irish wing Cecil Pedlow for the opening three points (the value of a try in 1955). Despite being under the cosh, the Springboks staged a mini rally with two penalties from full-back Jack van der Schyff being followed by a Briers try after a storming run by Fry. With the score at 11–3 and the home side in danger of pulling away, the Lions clawed their way back into the game. Morgan was the catalyst, spearing through a gap in the South African three-quarters before off-loading to Davies, who put the smooth-running Butterfield over for a try which bought the Lions back to 11–8 as the half-time whistle blew.

By the time the two teams resumed battle in the second half the atmosphere was alive with anticipation that grew even more intense three minutes into the second half when outstanding English flanker Reg Higgins was carried off, leaving the Lions with only seven forwards (there were no replacements in 1955).

Yet rather than be overwhelmed by the size of the task facing them, the Lions staged one of the most dramatic comebacks in the history of Test rugby. It was again Morgan who made the breakthrough, rounding the flat-footed Basie van Wyk for one of the greatest individual tries in Lions' history. But rather than shut up shop, the 14-man Lions began to run riot. Morgan was again the prime mover, this time through two garryowens he put up to test the nerve of fullback Van der Schyff. The Springbok failed to cope, and with the ball taking a wicked bounce on both occasions, first Jim Greenwood and then O'Reilly charged over for tries which gave the Lions a 23–11 lead.

Gradually however, the disadvantage of playing with one man fewer than their opponents began took its toll and, as the Lions' forwards tired, the home side came storming back with a try of their own from scrum-half Tommy Gentles. When the bulky figure of Chris Koch weaved over for a another try, the crowd erupted. Sensing a famous victory, Fry led the charge deep into the Lions' half. Piercing through the visitors' defence, he fed the ball to wing Theuns Briers for the try that brought South Africa to within a

point of the Lions. The conversion, which was to be the last kick of the game, was half way between the posts and touch-line. Ninety-five thousand supporters held their breath as Van der Schyff ran up, kicked and missed by a whisker. The whistle blew, the Lions jumped for joy and Ellis Park knew it had witnessed the greatest of matches.

SOUTH AFRICA: *J. van der Schyff; J. Swart, D. Sinclair, T. van Vollenhoven, T. Briers; C. Ulyate, T. Gentles; A. du Plooy, C. Kroon, C. Koch, Salty du Rand, J. Claasen, C. van Wyk, S. Fry (capt), D. Retief.*

BRITISH LIONS: *A. Cameron; T. O'Reilly, J. Butterfield, P. Davies, C. Pedlow; C. Morgan, D. Jeeps; W. Williams, B. Meredith, C. Meredith, R. Williams, R. Thompson, R. Higgins, R. Robins, J. Greenwood.*

A game to end all Games

Barbarians 21
New Zealand 13

27 January 1973
Cardiff Arms Park

Of all the rugby games staged on British soil, the 1973 Barbarians game against the All Blacks has gone down in history as the most thrilling ever played. A joyous celebration of the Barbarians' ethic of throwing caution to the wind, the match started with a try by Gareth Edwards, a sublime moment unequalled in British rugby.

The try started with an innocuous kick-ahead by the New Zealand's Bryan Williams four minutes into the game. Phil Bennett fielded the ball in front of his own posts and prepared to kick right. Just as the cover closed down on him he changed his mind, throwing two outrageous side-steps to flat foot the oncoming All Blacks. Bennett headed left and, as the third would-be tackler closed in, the Llanelli man off-loaded to J.P.R. Williams, who was half caught around the neck but managed to ship the ball on to and English hooker John Pullin.

Pullin took a couple of steps before handing on to captain John Dawes, who stepped inside a tackler and stormed up the pitch. The move was now in full flow, with the ball nearing half-way and the crowd on its feet. Flanker Tom David was the next to field a pass, taking it at such pace that he looked as if his own momentum was about to make him fall over. As he stumbled, David flung the ball single-handedly, and fellow back-rower Derek Quinnell stooped to pick the ball off his bootlaces. Realising he did not possess the pace to make the line, Quinnell looked for wing John Bevan and floated a pass towards the Welshman. It never made it to Bevan. At exactly that moment, scrum-half Gareth Edwards hit the accelerator and picked off the pass from Quinnell. Pinning back his ears he dashed straight for the line, flinging himself into the corner before the pursuing Grant Batty could get across in cover. The audacious move had covered the length of the pitch and passed through seven pairs of hands to produce the most memorable start ever to a major international.

Rather than an end in itself, the try sparked a game the like of which has not been seen on British soil since.

With David Duckham in supreme form, the Barbarians played enterprising, all-action rugby which the All Blacks did their best to match, but by half-time the visitors trailed 17–0. Through the whole of the second half the All Blacks rallied themselves for a supreme effort, and scrum-half Grant Batty's virtuoso individual try brought them back to 17–11 down with 15 minutes to go. Yet a weaving run by Duckham, leading to a try by J.P.R. Williams, finished off the All Blacks with five minutes remaining. It was a remarkable way to round off the most extraordinary of games.

For British rugby supporters it was a victory of supreme importance. An outrageously talented Lions party spearheaded by Barry John and Gareth Edwards had gone to New Zealand in 1971 and returned with the prize of a series win. A major event, the confidence from that unprecedented run of success had been gradually eroded throughout the All Blacks' 1972–73 tour to the British Isles.

BARBARIANS: *J.P.R. Williams; J. Bevan, J. Dawes (capt), M. Gibson, D. Duckham; P. Bennett, G. Edwards; S. Carmichael, J. Pullin, R. McLoughlin, W.J. McBride, R. Wilkinson, T. David, F. Slattery, D. Quinnell.*

NEW ZEALAND: *J. Karam; G. Batty, B. Robertson, I. Hurst, B. Williams; R. Burgess, S. Going; G. Whiting, R. Ulrich, K. Lambert, P. Whiting, H. McDonald, I. Kirkpatrick (capt), A. Scown, A. Wyllie.*

Mauled by the Jaguars

South Africa 12
South American Jaguars 21

Second Test; 3 April 1982
Bloemfontein, South Africa

This extraordinary game was remarkable for providing one the biggest upsets ever recorded in international rugby. For the Jaguars, an Argentinian touring side in all but name, to beat the mighty Springboks was virtually unthinkable at that time. It was like the British Lions losing to the Cook Islands, or the All Blacks being put to the sword by Hong Kong. Argentina were not a force in world rugby and defeat for the South Africans just wasn't an option that had been seriously considered.

The two-Test tour had been organised by Danie Craven and the SARB, who by 1982 were feeling the anti-Apartheid pressure and were increasingly desperate for as much overseas contact as possible.

As no South American country would have countenanced sending a representative side to play in South Africa, a composite Jaguars side that contained 30 Argentinians, five Uruguayans, five Chileans and two Paraguayans was put together specifically for the 14-match tour. Out-gunned in the provincial games, the Jaguars came a spectacular cropper in the First Test at Loftus Versfeld when the Springbok three-quarters cut them to pieces. Danie Gerber, Carel du Plessis, Willie du Plessis and Ray Mordt scored eight tries between them as the Jaguars were crushed 50 points to 18. After that loss, nobody expected the Jaguars to attain anything other than doormat status in a Second Test that was reckoned a home banker by the rest of the world. Even the Jaguars' captain, the legendary Argentine fly-half Hugo Porta could not conceive that his side might turn the tables. "Morale was at rock-bottom after Pretoria," Porta said later, "and although I have never in my life started a game thinking that I might lose, before the game in Bloemfontein I told the players that our objective must be to make sure we did not lose by 50 points again."

Arriving at the Free State Stadium in Bloemfontein, the Jaguars were well aware that their only realistic hope of success was over-confidence on the part of the Springboks. The tourists were not to be disappointed.

The Jaguars' well-deserved win was founded on some huge tackles from the back-row of Branca, Allen and Megri, and some stonewall midfield defence from Loffreda and Madero. Knocked back time and time again, the Springboks found that when they lost the ball the Jaguars pack, in which Dengra and Ure were heroic, were capable of shielding the ball as they advanced slowly upfield. What had been expected to turn into a romp turned into a war of attrition in which victory would go to the side with the most desire – and that battle was won by the Jaguars.

By half-time the realisation that the South Americans could win began to dawn on Porta and his players. "I just said to the players 'Yes, we can win, just carry on as you did in the first half.'" And carry on they did. Porta continued to pin back the Springboks with searching kicks into the corners, while the Jaguars pack amazed both the Boks and themselves by gradually shading the battle up front. Halfway through the second half they were winning the forward tussle convincingly, deploying the eight-man shove of the "bajada" scrum to devastating effect. So dominant were the Jaguars that the first score came from a strike against the head, from which lock Ernesto Ure fed Porta, who dummied his way over for a richly deserved try.

The Springbok ill-tempers which had been bubbling under for much of the match now came to the fore as time and again brawls broke out, with four penalties from Porta's boot the end result. Five minutes from time, Porta put the result beyond doubt with a drop-goal to bring his points total to a match-winning 21. This victory did much to raise the profile of rugby not only in Argentina but throughout South America.

SOUTH AFRICA: *J. Heunis, C. du Plessis, W. du Plessis, D. Gerber, R. Mordt; N. Botha, D. Serfontein; P. du Toit, W. Kahts, O. Oosthuizen, B. Geldenhuys, T. Stofberg, L. Moolman, R. Louw, W. Claasen (capt).*

SOUTH AMERICA: *Sanguinetti; Varone, Loffreda, Madero, A. Puccio; H. Porta (capt), Soares-Gache; S. Dengra, Courreges, Devoto, E. Ure, Bottarini, E. Branca, Allen, M. Negri.*

French cockerel crows

France 30, Australia 24

World Cup Semi-Final
13 June 1987
Concord Oval, Sydney

Australia had eased their way through the opening pool of the inaugural 1987 World Cup, dispatching England, the USA and Japan. In just three games they had scored 108 points, but conceded 43. Yet all that was forgotten after Australia overwhelmed Ireland 33–15 to book a place in the semi-final against France. As far as the home media was concerned, the "dream ticket" final of co-hosts Australia playing New Zealand was a virtual certainty.

In many ways, the home confidence was not too surprising. France had stuttered all the way into their semi-finalists berth. They had been held by Scotland and had laboured to beat weak Romanian and Zimbabwean opposition, while in the quarter-final they had only overcome unseeded Fiji by applying forward muscle. More to the point, the Wallabies had totally outplayed the French just a year before at the same venue, and so Australia expected to win at a canter once again.

At no stage of the semi-final was the result ever assured, with the lead changing hands six times in a see-saw game of startling intensity. It was as much a meeting of styles and of cultures as a rugby game, and it provided a fascinating contest. On the one hand were the French, all panache and pace behind the scrum, but with lock Alain Lorieux inspiring an awesome effort from his strong-mauling forwards. By contrast, the huge Wallaby machine, with the faultless tactical play of half-backs Michael Lynagh and Nick Farr-Jones working off a set-piece platform that gave them an immense amount of ball to work with.

Lynagh started the scoring, with a drop-goal after five minutes and then added three more points when the French collapsed a maul. Despite France playing the more attractive rugby, it was again Lynagh who stretched Australia's lead to nine points ten minutes before half-time. This time France's response was instantaneous, with Laurent Rodriguez setting up a number of driving mauls which tore through the heart of the massive Wallaby pack. It was dynamic, pragmatic and it worked, Lorieux driving over the Australian try-line from a line-out for a vital score just before half-time.

When Philippe Sella carved his way through for a try just after the break to make it 12–9 to France, the 17,000 crowd began to stir. Australia hit back through a David Campese try, but the French responded through the long-striding French full-back Serge Blanco who sent winger Patrice Lagisquet over for a try that made it 21–15. The match was reaching boiling point when replacement flanker David Codey latched on to a knock-on and stormed over unopposed for a try that made it 21–21 with five minutes remaining. Such was the tension that when Blanco fielded a ball on his own line, he fumbled and put his centres in trouble before Lynagh was awarded a penalty which he duly kicked, only to see Didier Camberabero slot over a penalty of his own to make it 24–24. Then came a passage of play which will be forever remembered as one of the most inspirational and memorable moments in the game's long history.

The French forwards began a rolling maul deep in their own half, before flanker Eric Champ burst into open space linking with Lagisquet. Suddenly the move gained momentum as first Berbizier, then Mesnel, Charvet, Berbizier again and Lorieux poured deep into Wallaby territory. Just as the move appeared to be breaking down, with injured and exhausted players lying prostrate, Rodriguez fed the hamstrung Blanco. Outstripping the cover defence over 20 metres, the full-back dived past the despairing hooker Tom Lawton, knocking over the corner flag a split second after he had touched down to seal a Final place in the most dramatic fashion.

AUSTRALIA: *P. Grigg; M. Burke, A. Slack (capt), B. Papworth, D. Campese; M. Lynagh, N. Farr-Jones; A. McIntyre, T. Lawton, C. Lillicrap, S. Cutler, B. Campbell, J. Miller, S. Poidevin, T. Coker.*

FRANCE: *S. Blanco; D. Camberabero, P. Sella, D. Charvet, P. Lagisquet; F. Mesnel, P. Berbizier; P. Ondarts, D. Dubroca, J-P. Garuet, A. Lorieux, J. Condom, D. Erbani, E. Champ, L. Rodriguez.*

English rose wilts under power of Scotland

Scotland 13 England 7

Five Nations; 17 March 1990
Murrayfield, Scotland

When the unbeaten English visited Edinburgh on the final Saturday of the 1990 Five Nations championship to contest the Calcutta Cup, Triple Crown and Grand Slam with unbeaten Scotland, there was more at stake than just mere trophies. This was a meeting of two proud nations determined to show to the other that they were the stronger. It was a match which was to bring the drama and exhilaration of the Five Nations to a whole new audience, so keen had become the e interest throughout both England and Scotland.

England arrived seeking their first Grand Slam since Bill Beaumont's unbeaten season in 1980, and they had every justification in making themselves hot favourites to walk away with the

prizes on offer. Their monster pack had steamrollered the French by 20 points in Paris, while their rapier backs had put 30 points on the hapless Welsh at Twickenham, and produced a performance of sublime confidence to beat Ireland 23–0 on their home ground. While England were hitting their most purple of patches, Scotland had stuttered to one unconvincing win after another, eking out victories through sheer willpower and stubbornness.

It looked for all the world like a game between two unequals, yet the joy of the Five Nations is that status is as nothing next to the passions that "local derbies" can bring. Scotland used the tag of underdog to work themselves into a frenzy which they unleashed on overconfident England to devastating effect. In a gesture that is now legendary, captain David Sole led his side out onto the pitch at a slow, almost funeral march. As a statement of intent it was a masterstroke. It said to the watching England players that here was a deliberate, focused side ready to do battle in the next 80 minutes.

As soon as the match got underway, the Scottish game-plan became crystal clear. England's big pack had yet to be shifted around all over the paddock, so the Scots back-row got on the case, disrupting possession wherever possible, switching play wide whenever the chance arose. All the while the Scottish centres were stepping up to the gain-line and making huge tackles that stopped the English in their strides. For an England side used to controlling proceedings the whole effect was profoundly disorientating, and despite scoring the only try of the first half through the skills of centre Jeremy Guscott, it was the home side which went into half-time in front. Better still, Scotland fly-half Craig Chalmers had managed to kick three penalties, and the Scots had withstood the one extended period of pressure the English pack had been able to exert through a punishing series of scrums on their try-line in the minutes leading up to half-time.

In the first few minutes of the second-half, a mistake by Mike Teague, the England No.8, when he fumbled the ball as he tried to pick up from a scrum, led to a Scottish scrum from which Scotland scored what was to be the decisive try of the match. Veteran blind-side John Jeffrey picked up and fed the ball to Gary Armstrong. The scrum-half took out his marker before firing a pass to full-back Gavin Hastings. Heading towards the touch-line, Hastings managed to put up a perfectly weighted kick ahead. At that moment it became a simple race between the two wingers, Scotland's Tony Stanger and England's Rory Underwood. The Scot was first to the touchdown, and although England clawed their way back to within six points, the defence and sheer resilience of the Scots proved too much for England. When the final whistle went, the whole of Scotland celebrated a famous victory.

SCOTLAND: *G. Hastings; I. Tukalo, S. Hastings, S. Lineen, T. Stanger; C. Chalmers, G. Armstrong; D. Sole (capt), K. Milne, P. Burnell, D. Cronin, A. Gray, F. Calder, J. Jeffrey, D. White.*

ENGLAND: *S. Hodgkinson; R. Underwood, J. Guscott, W. Carling (capt), S. Halliday; R. Andrew, R. Hill; P. Rendall, B. Moore, J. Probyn, W. Dooley, P. Ackford, P. Winterbottom, M. Skinner, M. Teague.*

A war of attrition

France 10
England 19

World Cup Quarter-Final
19 October 1991
Parc des Princes, Paris

The intense rivalry that developed between Europe's top two powers, England and France, during the late 1980s and early 1990s exploded in an autumn afternoon in 1991 when the two sides met in a charged World Cup quarter-final at the Parc des Princes. The match was a culmination of a three-year struggle for domination of Europe which England were winning hands down. In that time, Will Carling's side had won every match between the two sides, although they had only won one game in Paris.

The quarter-final came just six months after England had won their first Grand Slam since 1980 by beating France at Twickenham. Yet that victory over the French was by no means a comfortable one: a youthful France had lost 21–19, but Philippe Saint Andre had scored one of the greatest tries ever seen at Twickenham and the French had generally felt they had the measure of the English at last. In Paris, they reasoned, it would all be different. They didn't just hope to win, they expected to win.

When France and England walked out on to the Parc des Princes turf on a sunny Saturday in October, nothing could have prepared them for the atmosphere that awaited them.

The stadium was a intimidating riot of colour and noise unprecedented in European rugby, and the potential for an explosive game of rugby was there for all to see and feel in those tense moments before the game kicked off.

England hooker Brian Moore, who has played in every major Test venue in world rugby, reckoned that atmosphere by far the most intimidating he had ever come across, anywhere. "The French were psyched up beyond belief," said Moore. "All I can remember now is the whistle going and the whole place going crazy. It was 80 minutes of sheer guts that brought us through."

The pent-up tensions and emotions of the French players became clear as soon as the whistle was blown. The blue pack tore into the English and private battles quickly developed in the heat of the forward exchanges. Within five minutes the pattern for the rest of the game had been set when England wing Nigel Heslop put up a garryowen which French full-back Serge Blanco gathered.

Heslop, arriving fractionally late, clattered into Blanco and all hell broke loose as the Englishman was punched to the floor in an uncharacteristic assault by Blanco.

From that moment on, the two sides indulged in an epic confrontation in which one side never truly gained control. The match threatened to descend into violence at several stages, with Philippe Sella laying out England fly-half Rob Andrew, English fists leaving Laurent Cabannes with a bloodied nose and English flanker Peter Winterbottom lucky to escape censure for a flinging his boot at Laurent Cabannes' head.

With the score locked at 10–10 and extra-time looming, French prop Pascal Ondarts was penalised for handling in a ruck and fullback Jonathan Webb kicked a penalty that took his side into the slenderest of leads.

The French, who had become increasingly ragged as the game reached its heady climax, were finally beaten in the last minute when Carling put up a garryowen and, chasing up, caught Blanco in the act of fielding the ball, dispossessing him in the process and diving over for a try that finally put England out of sight. It had been a nerve-jangling match of relentless effort and hostility. It had been a war of attrition, and powerful England emerged triumphant and on their way to the 1991 World Cup final.

FRANCE: *S. Blanco (capt); J-B. Lafond, F. Mesnel, P. Sella, P. Saint-Andre; T. Lacroix, F. Galthie; G. Lascube, P. Marocco, P. Ondarts, J-M. Cadieu, O. Roumat, E. Champ, L. Cabannes, M. Cecillon.*

ENGLAND: *J. Webb; N. Heslop, W. Carling (capt), J. Guscott, R. Underwood; R. Andrew, R. Hill; J. Leonard, B. Moore, J. Probyn, P. Ackford, W. Dooley, M. Skinner, P. Winterbottom, M. Teague.*

Last-gasp Lynagh breaks Irish hearts

Ireland 18
Australia 19

World Cup Quarter-Final
20 October 1991
Lansdowne Road, Dublin

If the definition of a great match is one that is packed full of drama, then the 1991 World Cup quarter-final between Ireland and Australia must surely qualify as one of the greatest matches ever played. The match was all the more dramatic because its course was so unexpected. Australia had been going like a steam train all year, beating England 40–15, annihilating Wales 63–3, winning the Bledisloe Cup at a canter and coming unbeaten through a difficult pool which included Argentina, Western Samoa and Wales. Ireland, on the other hand, had come in to the tournament on the back of a humiliating series loss in Namibia and a Five Nations in which they failed to win a match. They only managed to make the quarter-finals because they

were in the same pool as Zimbabwe and Japan, the two weakest sides in the competition. As far as the world was concerned, they were mere canon fodder for the most exciting Wallaby side since the Grand Slam team of 1984.

Yet as all Ireland's Five Nations opponents could have predicted, nothing is ever straightforward at Lansdowne Road in front of a capacity crowd of 50,000 when the Irish are in their favourite position of complete underdogs. Irish passion is a dangerous emotion when let loose, and even on a beautiful autumn day, perfect for the running rugby so beloved of the Wallabies, Ireland came within a whisker of derailing the side which was to go on and claim the title of world champions within a fortnight.

Not that the game plan which so rattled the Wallabies emerged by chance. If Ireland have one strength, it is their willingness to "have a go"; to get in under the opposition's skin and disrupt everything at source. It was a strength they were determined to deploy. Buoyed by the ball won at the set-piece, Ireland's forwards were in rampant form, matching their illustrious Wallaby counterparts in virtually every sphere and completely outperforming them in the area of sheer effort. Ireland were like terriers, snapping at the heels of the Australians every time they moved in an adrenaline-fuelled performance that never allowed the Wallabies the time to settle.

It was certainly the right way to play the game, because as they demonstrated all too graphically when they managed to move the ball wide, Australia's backs were just too slick for the Irish. David Campese rammed home the point with two outstanding scores, the first coming when he scythed through the Irish midfield for a try under the posts. But with their pack applying pressure up front, Ireland managed to doggedly stay in touch through the boot of fly-half Ralph Keyes. Yet with five minutes remaining and the score at 15–12 to Australia, it seemed as if the Irish had shot their bolt.

But that was when the old stadium witnessed the most amazing scenes in its history. As time ebbed away, the ball ran loose on the left side of the stadium, and wing Jack Clarke picked up and fed flanker Gordon Hamilton. The Ulsterman tore through one tackle and headed toward the Australian line 40 yards away. As the Lansdowne roar grew, Hamilton pinned back his ears as Wallabies Roebuck and Campese gave chase. Campese just managed to get to the flying Irishman, but could not stop him grounding the ball in the corner for a try which bought a mini crowd invasion amidst jubilant scenes. Keyes' touch-line conversion made it 18–15 to Ireland.

The Wallabies had three minutes to make amends. With the match three minutes into injury time and with Ireland winning a line-out just outside their own 22 they looked to have blown their chance. But then Irish scrum-half Rob Saunders missed touch with his kick,and Australia, knowing that his was their very last chance to snatch the win, moved the ball infield. Lynagh shipped it on to Horan, and looped behind his centres taking the pass from Campese and going over for a try which shocked Lansdowne Road into silence. Australia had won, leaving the Irish to cry into their Guinness.

IRELAND: *J. Staples; S. Geoghegan, B. Mullin, D. Curtis, J. Clarke; R. Keyes, R. Saunders; N. Popplewell, S. Smith, D. Fitzgerald, D. Lenihan, N. Francis, P. Matthews (capt), G. Hamilton, B. Robinson.*

AUSTRALIA: *M. Roebuck; R. Egerton, J. Little, T. Horan, D. Campese; M. Lynagh, N. Farr-Jones (capt); A. Daly, P. Kearns, E. McKenzie, R. McCall, J. Eales, W. Ofahengaue, J. Miller, S. Poidevin.*

The try from the end of the world

New Zealand 20
France 23

Second Test
3 July 1994
Eden Park, Auckland

France had arrived in New Zealand in 1994 via North America, where they had been beaten for the first time by Canada in a full Test match. Team talisman Philippe Sella had been sent off and the French, who were touring on the back of a Five Nations in which they had won only two of their four matches, looked to be in disarray. As if to further prove the tourists' weakness, they had been edged out 27–23 when they played North Harbour, the only first class New Zealand province they were scheduled to meet before the First Test in Christchurch.

By the time the First Test dawned in late June, the Kiwi prophets of doom had already written the French off. Yet in an authoritative display the All Blacks were outclassed, out-gunned and plain outplayed by a French side which showed much of the verve and flair that had been missing throughout their poor season. Loose-head prop Laurent Benezech and flanker Philippe Benetton led the charge against a curiously listless home pack while full-back Jean-Luc Sadourny, wing Emile Ntamack and centre Philippe Sella carved holes through the New Zealand backs almost at will. After 80 minutes France comfortably deserved a 22–8 win for only their second Test victory on New Zealand soil.

Amid a great deal of soul searching, the All Blacks prepared grimly for the Second Test to be held a week later in Auckland. The New Zealand public, already in a froth over the inexplicably dull display by the All Blacks in Christchurch, was whipped up into a frenzy when the French lost 30–25 in midweek to an average Hawke's Bay side. Media comment and a wave of public discontent made it clear that New Zealand expected nothing less than complete crushing of the tourists.

As soon as the first whistle blew at Eden Park, the All Blacks tore into the French. With hooker and captain Sean Fitzpatrick in no mood to take prisoners, and the home forwards completely dominant, wave upon wave of All Black attacks smashed into Sella and Thierry Lacroix in the French midfield. But while the French bent, they did not break and just before half-time wing Emile Ntamack ran the length of the field to claim an interception try which gave France an unexpected lead at the interval.

That insult, however, only seemed to spur the bullocking All Black forwards on to greater heights and shortly after the interval hooker Fitzpatrick rounded off an irresistible drive by his forwards with a try. Five penalties from Matthew Cooper meant that with normal time about to run out France were trailing 20–16.

Into injury time, the French threw caution to the wind when All Black fly-half Stephen Bachop kicked long towards the French corner flag and failed to find touch. Saint-Andre knew there was time for one last counter-attack. Setting off on a mazy run from behind his own posts, the French captain brushed past three would-be tacklers before linking with scrum-half Accoceberry who, in turn, passed to the charging prop Benezech. Ntamack took it on next, injecting pace as he surged into the All Black half. Next in on the act was Laurent Cabannes who made a crucial change of direction, allowing Jean-Luc Sadourny to sprint for the line for the greatest try ever seen at Eden Park.

The ball passed through nine pairs of hands for a series-winning try which French captain Philippe Saint Andre rightfully called: "a counter-attack from the end of the world – a true image of French rugby."

NEW ZEALAND: *J. Timu; J. Kirwan, F. Bunce, M. Cooper, J. Lomu; S. Bachop, S. Forster; R. Loe, S. Fitzpatrick (capt), O. Brown, I. Jones, M. Cooksley, B. Larsen, M. Brewer, Z. Brooke.*

FRANCE: *J-L. Sadourny; E. Ntamack, P. Sella, T. Lacroix, P. Saint-Andre (capt); C. Deylaud, G. Accoceberry; L. Benezech, J-M. Gonzalez, C. Califano, O. Merle, O. Roumat, A. Benazzi, L. Cabannes, P. Benetton.*

The rainbow nation rises to the challenge

South Africa 15
New Zealand 12

World Cup Final
24 June 1995
Ellis Park, Johannesburg

As a feast of open running rugby, the 1995 World Cup final doesn't even get a mention in dispatches. But if you are looking for drama, intrigue, scandal and a game of unparalleled passion, then look no further. This was a gladiatorial contest that pitted two ancient and fierce rivals against each other.

For rugby-mad South Africa, the All Blacks playing the Springboks was a dream final. New Zealand had swept aside all opposition with contemptuous ease, putting 43 points on Ireland, 34 on Wales and setting a new record when they beat Japan 145–17. Scotland were comfortably beaten in the quarter-final. To cap the run-in to the final, in a riotous semi-final, Jonah Lomu scored four tries as England were utterly annihilated

45–29 in the most outrageous display of running rugby ever seen at the famous Newlands Stadium.

South Africa had beaten world champions Australia in the opening match of the tournament, but looked unconvincing after that. What the South Africans did have was unity and a whole country behind them. President Nelson Mandela embraced the Springbok cause, and for the first time both blacks and whites saw the team as theirs, a process helped by the fact that their top try-scorer was a black wing named Chester Williams.

When the day of the World Cup final dawned, the whole of South Africa had thrown itself behind Francois Pienaar's underdogs, and domestic politics were put on hold as for the first time all South Africans united together in a common cause. It was difficult for the new nation to keep at bay the feeling that winning the 1995 Webb Ellis Trophy was South Africa's rugby destiny.

Into this highly charged atmosphere came the All Blacks. Yet as the match began it became clear that South Africa would present a far tougher proposition than England had in the semi-final. Every time giant wing Jonah Lomu received the ball, he was gang-mugged, with the gritty scrum-half Joost van der Westhuizen to the fore. It was no surprise to hear after the match that the Springboks had been on a bonus for every time they brought down the huge New Zealander.

Not as sharp as they had been in previous matches, the All Blacks allowed themselves to be harried, put off their stride and disrupted at every turn (it transpired later that a stomach bug had laid low many of the side, giving rise to the allegation that the side had been poisoned – see Scandals).

The South Africans smashed into the All Blacks, allowing them no time to dwell on the ball and stopping the supply line to Lomu. For the first time in the World Cup, the New Zealand team began to look vulnerable.

As the match progressed, so close were the two sides that neither managed to get more than three points in front as the lead see-sawed. A match of unrelenting tension and drama was not to see any tries, however, and at full-time, despite the impression that the All Blacks were gradually getting on top through the line-out work of Ian Jones, the frantic Springbok defences had held tight and nine points from the boot of All Black fly-half had been matched by a similar total from Joel Stransky. A missed drop goal attempt from Mehrtens on the stroke of full-time meant that the scores were 9–9 at the close.

In that charged atmosphere of extra-time, Mehrtens and Stransky again swapped penalties before Stransky knocked over a drop goal with two minutes remaining to give South Africa a 15–12 lead that they never lost. South Africa had fulfiled their destiny.

SOUTH AFRICA: *A. Joubert; J. Small, J. Mulder, H. le Roux, C. Williams; J. Stransky, J. van der Westhuizen; P. du Randt, C. Rossouw, B. Swart, K. Weise, H. Strydom, F. Pienaar (capt), R. Kruger, M. Andrews.*

NEW ZEALAND: *G. Osborne; J. Wilson, F. Bunce, W. Little, J. Lomu; A. Mehrtens, G. Bachop; C. Dowd, S. Fitzpatrick (capt), O. Brown, I. Jones, R. Brooke, M. Brewer, J. Kronfeld, Z. Brooke.*

England scorched by the Dragons' Fire

Wales 32
England 31

Five Nations
11 April 1999
Wembley, London

It was never supposed to be this way. England had crushed Ireland at Lansdowne Road, squeaked past a nervous but innovative Scotland at Twickenham and kicked the French to death on their own turf. It hadn't always been pretty – in fact, it definitely hadn't been pretty – but it had been winning rugby.

After years in the wilderness watching France claim back-to-back Grand Slams, England were about to reclaim their rightful place in European rugby's pecking order. To make matters even better, while they were technically away from home, the reconstruction of the Welsh national stadium meant that the match took place less than 20 miles from

Twickenham. And all of this on the final Sunday of the last Five Nations tournament, on the day after Scotland had humiliated France in Paris to ensure that England had to win their final game to win the last Five Nations Championship outright.

Scotland's win had given the game an extra edge which Welsh captain Robert Howley later admitted had buoyed his side. They had already beaten France 34-33 in Paris, in one of the epic encounters in Five Nations history, and crucially believed that England were eminently beatable if their powerful forwards could be kept in check.

That gut instinct turned out to be spot on. In 80 gruelling minutes, England totally dominated possession without ever quite managing to turn that territorial or possessional dominance into enough points to make Wels heads drop.

The Welsh Rugby Union had done their best to make Wembley a part of Wales for the day. Max Boyce had come on to sing "Hymns and Arias" and the 76,000 crowd were treated to Tom Jones' famous rendition of Delilah.

But after less than three minutes, England had claimed the opening try. Good work by fullback Matt Perry breached the Welsh defence and set wing Dan Luger up for an outstanding try.

Although England had claimed first blood, the match had always been billed as a battle between two peerless goal-kickers in Wales's Neil Jenkins and young Englishman Jonny Wilkinson. Jenkins soon showed how right the pundits were with two quick penalties, before Wilkinson responded to give England a 10-6 lead.

The game followed that pattern from there on: England stretching away while their indiscipline and Jenkins' boot kept Wales in touch. It was an absolutely enthralling contest, but one that England always looked destined to win.

That feeling was strengthened when young 6ft 3in wing Steve Hanley crashed over for a debut try after Wilkinson had seared through the Welsh back line. Mike Catt should have stretched England's lead still further, yet an infringement from Neil Back instead gave Jenkins the chance to kick Wales back on level terms. he didn't disappoint.

Just before the break, flanker Richard Hill scored England's third try when Wales's Thomas and Shane Howarth both tried to claim the same high ball, but within minutes of the second half restarting, Jenkins put fullback Howarth in for Wales' first try.

Frustrated at their inability to pull away from the Welsh, continual England infringements kept Jenkins busy. But as full-time approached, England were still holding onto a 31-25 lead, a margin which looked all but unassailable. That, though, is where England got it all wrong.

As England waited for the final whistle, Wales launched a final, desperate offensive, winning a lineout on the England 22. As the clock showed two minutes of extra-time played, lock Chris Wyatt soared to claim the ball, which was quickly fed through skipper Howley to fly-half Jenkins. No.8 Scott Quinnell had popped up in midfield and slipped the ball to centre Scott Gibbs, who came onto the ball at full pace, evading the otherwise outstanding Tim Rodber to skip over for a try which left Jenkins with a conversion to break English hearts.

Jenkins' aim was never in doubt, and as the ball went over to complete the No.10's 22-point haul, Wales had secured one of the most famous victories in the 118-year history of their fiercely contested internationals against England.

WALES: S Howarth; G Thomas, M Taylor, S Gibbs, D James; N Jenkins, R Howley (captain); P Rogers, G Jenkins, B Evans, C Quinnell, C Wyatt, C Charvis, B Sinkinson, S Quinnell.

ENGLAND: M Perry; D Luger, J Wilkinson, B-J Mather, S Hanley; M Catt, M Dawson; J Leonard, R Cockerill, D Garforth, M Johnson, T Rodber, R Hill, N Back, L Dallaglio (captain).

The Great
Stadiums

**Great sport is great drama, and to be fully savoured every moment of
theatre needs to be played out on a fitting stage. Of all the sports in the
world, none can boast better stages than the world of Rugby Union. The
game is a wide church and its places of worship around the world reflect
that tradition marvellously. Which other sport can offer a range of venues
as diverse as Billy Williams' stately "Old Cabbage Patch" in suburban
London, through to the gleaming splendour of downtown Johannesburg's
Ellis Park, and on to Hong Kong's So Kun Po Stadium, Asia's high-tech
monument to the game of Sevens.**

The great rugby stadia of the world aren't just piles of bricks and mortar where people
happen to play the game. And they are more than mere symbols of the game for the
wider world. Grounds such as Twickenham, Eden Park and Murrayfield represent the
living soul of a game which places a premium on tradition. The great grounds of world
rugby provide an element of continuity that provides a bridge between today's professional era and the Corinthian days of the early pioneers. So when the Lions stepped out
onto the Newlands turf in the summer of 1997, they knew they were following in the
footsteps of Bill Maclagan's first Lions side over a century before. Or when a Welshman strikes up a chorus of "Land of My Fathers" before a game against England in
Cardiff, he knows he is not just one but one of millions standing on the same spot to
have done so. Rugby now has the biggest and the best stadia in the world – but tradition
means that the game's great grounds will always be measured by more than just their
seating capacity.

Ballymore

Brisbane, Australia

Capacity:
30,000

Opened:
1968

Hosted:
1987 World Cup semi-final

There are conflicting theories as to how Ballymore was given its name. One suggests the origins are Irish, the word "Bally" meaning "village" in Ireland. While there is actually a town outside Dublin called "Ballymore", in Brisbane the origins of the name are generally reckoned to be of Scottish origin.

Ballymore Park was at one time a munitions dumping ground. It became headquarters of the Queensland Rugby Union in 1966, when the first game a club match between Teachers and Wests was played.

The home of Australian Super 12 giants the Queensland Reds, Ballymore is one of the most impressive stadiums in the southern hemisphere. Its development and eventual opening in its present form in 1968 also coincided with the dramatic rise of "The Reds" and of Queensland rugby in general.

A bold venture at the time, particularly as Queensland were suffering once again from the incursion of Brisbane's powerful Rugby League clubs (or more specifically from their powerful cheque books), the financial outlay has been more than recouped in the intervening years. Not only do Queensland play at Ballymore, but the ground has become a regular Test venue for the Wallabies.

Ballymore was a radical departure for Australian rugby. Until its conception and construction in the late 1960s, provincial and national level Rugby Union had been played at cricket grounds, whether in Sydney or Brisbane. Tests in Queensland had been played at either the famous Gabba, Brisbane Exhibition Ground or, latterly, the Brisbane Cricket Ground. All very good for cricket spectators, but in a land where Rugby League was king, the viewing problems presented by playing at cricket grounds did not help Union's meagre crowds.

As a vehicle for expanding rugby in Queensland, Ballymore has fulfilled its role perfectly. As it has grown steadily, so have the crowds. Interest has received a spur since the launch of the Super Ten, and then the Super 12 tournaments, with crowds averaging almost 30,000 – which is a full house at Ballymore and a huge support at Australia's provincial level.

It is a level of interest that owes

something to Rugby League's internal disputes, but even more to the sparkling play from Queensland which culminated in winning the 1995 Super Ten when they beat the much-fancied South African side, Transvaal, 30-16 at Ellis Park.

The Reds treated their fans to more of the same the next year when they thrashed Auckland, the eventual winners, 51–13 in the finest Queensland display Ballymore has ever witnessed. Since then, with Queensland rugby going from strength to strength, there have been some outstanding Super 12 clashes at Ballymore.

Not that there is a shortage of candidates for the prize of greatest match ever seen at Ballymore: how about Wales's 63–6 annihilation at the hands of Australia in 1991; or Queensland's defeat of the 1971 Lions (one of only two defeats for the Lions during their 26-match tour); or even the tumultuous 19–17 Second Test win over the All Blacks in 1992 which clinched the Bledisloe Cup for Australia ?

Whichever one of those matches is chosen, one thing is for sure – there is no better place to watch rugby than in the warm, temperate climate of Brisbane. Situated in a leafy, middle-class suburb of Brisbane, Ballymore's main pitch (it also has practice areas and a gym) is now flanked by two grandstands, each with the capacity to hold around 10,000 seated spectators.

The balance of the 30,000 capacity is made up from two grassy banks where spectators can come and eat food in a relaxed atmosphere. It is from these grassy banks, in particular, that the fierce parochialism of Queensland's supporters is the most vocal.

Millennium Stadium

Cardiff, Wales

Capacity:
72,500

Opened:
1884 & 1999

Hosted:
1991 World Cup final third-place play-off. (as Cardiff Arms Park)

When Wales kick off the World Cup against Argentina on October 1st 1999, they will do so in the new, state-of-the-art Millennium Stadium. It will undoubtedly be one of the best sports stadia in the world.

With government grants worth almost £100 million, the Arms Park has risen once more in the centre of Cardiff in its new guise as the Millennium Stadium. Wales's most famous landmark has been completely remodelled.

The new-age bowl design includes a roof which can be moved into place and seating for 72,500 supporters. The stadium has also been pivoted through ninety degrees to ensure sufficient space to develop even further.

With bridges over the river Taff to increase access and a new high-tech turfing system – turf can be stored in batches under the stands and then laid on a game-by-game basis – the standard of facilities has been massively increased both on and off the pitch itself.

It's a new stadium for a new century, hence the reason for the ground being renamed The Millennium Stadium.

Yet tradition is an enduring thing and it already seems certain that the ground will continue to be known locally as the Cardiff Arms Park.

There is a good precedent for believing so, as after the last time the ground was completely rebuilt between 1968 and 1980 it was renamed the National Stadium, only for everyone to continue referring to it as the Arms Park.

(The Arms Park is, technically, the 20,000 capacity ground of the club Cardiff, which currently backs on to the Millennium Stadium where the national side play, a quirk of history left over from the days before 1962 when Wales played on Cardiff's pitch.)

Before the turn of the century Wales played at a variety of venues, including Newport's Rodney Parade and Llanelli's Stradey Park, before finally alternating between Swansea's St Helen's ground and Cardiff's Arms Park (so called because it was built on the site of a pub of that name).

That arrangement continued until

1937, and since then, with the exception of an enforced move during the building work in 1997-99 Cardiff has been the venue for all internationals unless bad weather has intervened.

The first match at Cardiff took place on 12 April 1884, when Wales beat Ireland by a drop goal and two tries to no score, although the most memorable feature of the match was that Ireland had to borrow two Welsh players as two of their number failed to turn up!

Since that day there have been many truly memorable matches on the famous pitch. One epic battle was the controversial 1905 match when Dave Gallaher's New Zealand "Originals" lost the international 3–0, the only defeat of a tour that included 32 matches in Britain and Ireland, after young Kiwi centre Bob Deans was dragged back over the line after grounding the ball in the final minutes of the game.

Another game played at the Arms Park was the 1973 Barbarians game against New Zealand which started with Gareth Edwards' amazing try and ended with a 23–11 Barbarians win in one of the most spectacular games of rugby ever played.

Yet whether or not the ground is called the Arms Park, the National Stadium or the Millennium Stadium, the city centre ground has an aura all of its own. With a current capacity of 55,000, it nestles on land that once belonged to the Marquis of Bute and now stands in the middle of a bustling shopping centre.

The last match ever staged at the Arms Park was the 1997 Welsh Cup final when Cardiff beat Swansea in a suitably thrilling contest that included a try from Cardiff wing Nigel Walker.

The following day, some of the stadium's memorabilia was auctioned off; among those items that fetched a tidy sum was the seat reserved when the Princess of Wales was a guest (£1,600), while a square yard of the famous old turf was going for £1.50.

Carisbrook

Dunedin, New Zealand

Capacity:
33,000
Opened:
1908
Hosted:
1993 Bledisloe Cup v Australia

The Test venue in Dunedin in New Zealand's South Island, Carisbrook has the distinction of being perhaps the only major sports ground in the world to be named in memory of a honeymoon.

An early colonial administrator in the Otago province, James Macandrew, had honeymooned at Carisbrooke Castle on the Isle of Wight and had perpetuated his happy memories of the event by naming his Dunedin home Carisbrook (without the final 'e').

The home overlooked a swamp that was part of land owned by the Presbyterian Church and when cricketers in the 1870s developed the area for their own use, they took the name of Macandrew's home.

The name was retained when rugby men became residents more than 20 years later, continuing to lease it from the Presbyterian Church until buying the freehold in in the Otago Rugby Union's Centenary year, 1981.

Cricket continues to be the main summer user of Carisbrook and much other sport has been played there, including international soccer, hockey and even a trotting meeting, to which the Presbyterian trustees fervently objected until they learned that the totaliser at the meeting would ensure the canny Scots got their rent.

But it is for rugby which Carisbrook is most noted, from the first international in 1908, when the All Blacks thrashed a forerunner of the Lions, the Anglo-Welsh, 32-5.

The Lions in fact have inflicted the All Blacks' only defeat at Carisbrook – in 1930 when Doug Prentice's side beat New Zealand 6-3 in a game that began when Carisbrook was carpeted with snow, and in the memorable match in 1971 that set the Lions on the road towards winning a series in New Zealand for the only time.

John Dawes' team won 9-3, Ian McLauchlan scoring the only try when he charged down an attempted clearing kick by All Black No.8 Alan Sutherland and flopped on the ball inches from the dead ball line.

The All Blacks' only other loss at Carisbrook was in 1973 when they were beaten by a national Under-23 team, the

New Zealand Juniors, who were coached by a future All Black coach, Eric Watson, who still lives just around the corner from Carisbrook.

In the opinion of many, one of the All Blacks' most talked-about wins should, in all justice, have been a loss. That was in 1959 when Ronnie Dawson's Lions scored four tries to none but still lost the Test 18-17 thanks to the prodigious kicking of the All Black fullback Don Clarke, who landed six penalties.

Carisbrook is the home to the Otago provincial side, renowned for its free-flowing approach to the game, even when they're losing, and revered by the Otago University students ("the Scarfies") who pack the terraces.

Like any sporting team, Otago's for-tunes have waxed and waned and their high point was either side of the Second World War when they and neighbours Southland shared the premier domestic rugby trophy, the Ranfurly Shield, for the best part of a decade.

In the 1990s, when Otago regained their reputation for being long on spirit and attitude if sometimes short on raw talent, Carisbrook became known fondly as the "House of Pain", a phrase coined by an Otago No.8 Brent Pope, after a particularly gruelling training session under Laurie Mains, the Otago coach who was in charge of the All Black's from 1992 to 1995.

Of New Zealand's major rugby grounds, Carisbrook is generally regarded as the one with the most distinctive atmosphere.

Eden Park

Auckland, New Zealand

Capacity:

47,000

Opened:

1921

Hosted:

Inaugural World Cup in 1987

Such has been the strength of Auckland and All Black sides down the years that playing at Eden Park has become the ultimate challenge, whether domestically or in a Test match. Most major sides have now triumphed in the stadium's 76-year history, but none has ever found it easy.

South Africa were the first to try and succeed when the 1921 Springboks, led by "Boy" Morkel beat the All Blacks in one of the most memorable matches of all time.

With the scores level early in the second half, Springbok full-back Gerhard Morkel (yet another scion of the famous rugby family from which ten boys from the same generation represented Western Province) picked up the ball well inside his own half, ran in-field a few steps and smacked a drop goal between the uprights for the winning score.

Pandemonium ensued, and several of the 40,000 supporters on hand rushed on to the pitch to offer Morkel a drink, which he duly took after toasting the crowd. Matters got even more out of hand in the second half when wing South African Bill Zeller broke clear and was heading towards the line when he found himself surrounded by a pitch invasion!

The Springboks won that match 9–5, and managed to triumph the next time they were in New Zealand in 1937, when they were rated the best 'Boks ever. Since then, however, the All Blacks have triumphed every time at Eden Park, and even the top South African provincial sides have had precious little joy in recent seasons against Auckland in the Super Ten and then Super-12 competitions.

Eden Park itself is a very open ground which has only been used for Test rugby since 1921 and only regularly since the late 1930s. The lushness of its turf means that it has also been put to other uses, and as well as being the venue for the Empire Games of 1950, it has also staged Test cricket matches and one-day Eventing.

The ground has also hosted many of rugby's biggest events, with the 1987 World Cup final, in which David Kirk's New Zealand beat Pierre Berbizier's gritty France by 29–9 foremost amongst these.

As well as some big Tests, Eden Park has played host to some outstanding internationals. The Second Test against France in 1994, for instance, rates as one of the ten greatest games of all time, while the Tests played against the British Lions at Eden Park comprise one of the most thrilling series of rugby matches ever played, with five of the eight Tests played there won or lost by three points or less.

Perhaps the most bizarre match to have been staged at Eden Park was the 1975 Test against Scotland when a pre-match downpour made conditions treacherous. The pitch was so wet that many considered it extremely dangerous to play on, but the match went ahead and it was the Scots who failed to come to terms with the conditions as they lost 24-0. Afterwards, Andy Leslie, the All Black captain, was heard to say, "This was one of the greatest moments in New Zealand swimming."

While Eden Park does not have the claustrophobic intensity of an enclosed arena such as Murrayfield or the Parc des Princes, the passionate and vociferous crowd do their best to make up for it. Since starting their record Ranfurly Shield run in 1985, Auckland have become the strongest provincial side in the world.

The Auckland Blues for so dominated New Zealand domestic rugby and swept through Southern Hemisphere provincial rugby, winning the 1996 and 1997 Super 12s at a canter.

In the process they made Eden Park the single most forbidding rugby ground to visit in the world, and although the Auckland Blues no longer have a stranglehold on Super 12 rugby, it is still one of the last places most sides would choose to visit needing a win.

Ellis Park

Johannesburg, South Africa

Capacity:
  80,000
Opened:
  1928
Hosted:
  1995 World Cup final

When new Ellis Park was reopened in 1982, it was undoubtedly the most impressive monument to the game of rugby the world had ever seen. Indeed, it was the most hi-tech stadium in the world in any sport – even the top American Football venues were not on the same level.

Although the capacity had been reduced from 95,000 to 70,000, the ground had been improved immeasurably. All-covered and all-seated, the home of the powerful Transvaal Union looked to all the world like a potent symbol of the strength of Rugby Union in South Africa and a testament to the financial clout of the Johannesburg rugby community.

However, things are rarely what they seem and the reconstruction of Ellis Park brought with it almost as many problems as it solved.

So far-reaching were the problems associated with the rebuilding that many of the profound changes that have shaped the game in recent years stem directly or indirectly from that renovation.

Turning the ramshackle and extremely dangerous scaffolds of pre-1970 Ellis Park into the gleaming monument to rugby that had been built by 1982 was an expensive business. The final bill, which included factors such as lost gate revenue during rebuilding, is estimated to have been the equivalent of £60 million.

Twenty years ago, it was more than the union could sustain, and by the mid-Eighties, Transvaal's finances were in crisis as debts of £25 million became public knowledge. The upshot was that the architects of the rebuilding, veteran administrator Jannie le Roux and his committee, were forced to resign and replaced by irascible multi-millionaire Louis Luyt.

Luyt is a formidable man. As well as getting Transvaal's finances in check, he invested heavily in playing personnel, which in turn ensured success on the pitch and full houses at Ellis Park.

As Transvaal became more successful and worked their way into the black, Luyt also became head of the South African Rugby Football Union, and from that position he was able to strengthen the already strong voices calling for the 1995 World Cup to be held in South Africa. More than that, Luyt was also able to ensure that Ellis Park was the venue for the major showpiece events in rugby in South Africa.

When, for instance, isolation ended in 1992 and South Africa re-entered the international fray, it was at Ellis Park where the Springboks met the All Blacks. In 1995, when South Africa was awarded the World Cup, Ellis Park, which had undergone further work to expand the capacity to 80,000, was the venue for the final between South Africa and New Zealand.

With international rugby and the Super 12 now regular features of the South African season, Ellis Park is better used than ever before, even though Luyt has now been ousted from rugby at the behest of the government.

As well as the lush grass of its pitch, the stadium is also noted for the large video screen which replays tries. Yet even before it was redeveloped after 1972, Ellis Park was one of South Africa's premier venues.

Built on the site of a disused brick factory in 1928, Ellis Park has played host to some of the greatest games of all time. The All Blacks have always played a Test at Ellis Park, including the 7–6 victory the year the stadium was built, while the First Test between the Lions and Springboks in 1955, a game which the Lions won 23–22 and which the then coach Danie Craven considered the most exciting ever played, was played in front of a record 95,000 spectators.

Hong Kong Stadium

Hong Kong, China

Capacity:
40,000
Opened:
1994
Hosted:
World's premier Sevens tournament

The main sports stadium in the tiny former British colony of Hong Kong, the Government Stadium is not one of the biggest venues in world rugby; it has not staged any of the world's most dramatic Test series and it cannot boast a history to rival the game's undisputed shrines such as Twickenham, Ellis Park or Eden Park.

Yet for all that, Hong Kong's significance as a rugby missionary centre which has spread the gospel of the game through its annual Sevens tournament, and which has almost single-handedly popularised the abbreviated code outside the Scottish Borders cannot be underestimated.

For many years rugby was alive and well in Hong Kong. There is evidence of rugby being played on the Island almost as soon as it had been wrested from China by the British in the early 1840s, but the game remained the domain of expats and visiting servicemen for over a century.

However, with the post-1946 commercial explosion of the Pacific Rim, Hong Kong became a major financial and trading centre and there was a massive influx of professionals from Britain. Many of these found their way into the rugby clubs and a great number were Scots.

Hong Kong had joined the Asian Championships in 1969 and played occasional matches against touring nations in the 1960s and 1970s, but the HKRFU felt there was a need for a more regular form of international contact.

The idea of Sevens raised its head at the behest of a Scot called "Tokkie" Smith, who suggested a Sevens tournament on the lines of those held at Borders clubs in his native land and the idea was accepted, not least because it would give the physically smaller Asian nations a chance to compete on a more level playing field (not to mention the indigenous Chinese, who the HKRFU were keen to spread the game to).

When the invitations went out in 1975 and the Cantabrians, an invitation side from Canterbury, won the inaugural 1976 tournament, few could have really understood what was underway.

The invitation-only competition grew steadily in size and status, with more and more national sides attending, and by the mid-1980s, the All Blacks, Wallabies, Fijians, Tongans, Argentinians and Samoans were all regular participants, and stars such as Jonah Lomu, Christian Cullen and Waisale Serevi all gained wider recognition through playing in Hong Kong.

But it was the inclusion of up and coming nations like Taiwan, Japan, Germany, Holland, Papua New Guinea which made the world take notice.

For many of these smaller nations, the Hong Kong Sevens was a lifeline to the big time and a valuable source of kudos for the game in their country.

But if the rugby at Hong Kong was important, so were the environs. Played in the scenic 30,000-seater Government Stadium overlooking Kowloon Bay, the tournament is as much a social as a sporting occasion; one in which spectators are as likely to return with as many memories of the famous Joe Bananas bar as they are of events on the pitch.

For Asian participants and spectators, the social side of the tournament and the general bonhomie are eye-openers which go some way to showing that rugby can be more than a pursuit restricted to the elite.

Although in 1994 the tournament was switched to the sparkling new stadium of the same name, the ethos of sporting excellence allied to drunken excess has continued unabated to this day.

It is a combination that started a new rugby era in the Government Stadium in Hong Kong. With China now in charge – albeit a China which has now taken rugby up on an industrial scale – one can only hope that the festivities are allowed to continue.

Lansdowne Road

Dublin, Ireland

Capacity:
49,600
Opened:
1878
Hosted:
1991 World Cup quarter-final

Lansdowne Road remains one of the most atmospheric of rugby grounds. With Ireland having played all of their games there since the thumping loss to England by one try and two goals to no score in 1878, it is also the oldest Test ground in the world.

Originally bought by Henry William Dunlop, a Trinity College graduate, the site of the ground is on seven acres between the River Dodder and the Lansdowne Road railway station. Initially purchased so that the old boys of Trinity College who were playing for Lansdowne Rugby Club would have a home (the club, which was at one stage nicknamed the "Second Trinity", still play in the Irish first division next door to the national ground), Dunlop also allowed Dublin Wanderers to use the site.

When Ireland played England in 1878, they handed over the princely sum of £5 to Dunlop for the privilege of using the Lansdowne Road ground.

For the next three-quarters of a century, Ireland internationals were staged at either Lansdowne Road or at one of three Belfast venues, North of Ireland FC's Ormeau ground (which also doubles as the finest cricket ground in Ireland), the Royal Ulster Agricultural Society's Balmoral Exhibition Ground or, after 1924, Ravenshill.

The building of the latter venue in the early 1920s coincided with the end of work to upgrade Lansdowne Road, a project into which the bulk of the IRFU's resources had been poured. The Dublin stadium was given a West Stand in February 1908, which was eventually finished in 1955, and work on the East Stand started in 1923, to be finished in 1927.

The basic layout of the ground has remained pretty much unchanged ever since, with the East Stand rebuilt in 1982, and the West Stand undergoing major work in 1955 and 1978. The capacity today stands at just under 50,000.

The IRFU planned more work at Lansdowne Road, including North and South Stands, but political considerations were to take a front seat in the early 1920s – the Republic of Ireland and

Ulster split in 1922 – and in order to ensure that the IRFU continued to be made up of all four provinces, it was decided to invest heavily into building Ravenhill and to play internationals there.

That state of affairs continued until crowds begin to dwindle, with Scotland and Wales in particular playing many of their games in Belfast until 1956, when a terminal lack of interest in Ulster meant that all major games were transferred to Dublin.

Lansdowne Road is now the only major ground in the Home Unions to have terracing. That makes for interesting times at key Five Nations matches when visiting fans turn up ticketless and fall prey to the counterfeiters.

The end result is a crowd which can often swell to almost twice the recommended size. It is this, plus the restrictions of a site that at seven acres is just too small for a major rugby stadium, that has prompted thoughts of moving the home of Irish rugby away from Lansdowne Road.

Certainly, further development of the ground is problematic: the rail route which runs under one of the two stands presents one insoluble problem, while the dogged resistance of the genteel residents of Ballsbridge to further building work provides another.

With the IRFU's administrative offices housed in an old town house across the railway tracks, the thinking now is that the home of Irish rugby will soon have to be moved, with Pheonix Park, an old horse racing venue on a greenbelt site on the outskirts of the city the favoured venue at the moment.

The Great Stadiums

Loftus Versfeld

Pretoria, South Africa

Capacity:
60,000
Opened:
1906
Hosted:
1995 World Cup final third place play-off

In these days of intense rivalry between provinces, it is interesting to note that the man who gave his name to the home of Northern Transvaal's Blue Bulls was in fact a dyed-in-the-wool Western Province man.

One of four rugby-playing brothers, Loftus Versfeld was probably the least successful of the quartet. All four played against Bill Maclagan's British touring side in 1891, with Marthinus playing in all three Tests and the family's other cap, Hasie, scoring the only try conceded by the British in three gruelling months of touring.

The third brother, Charles, also represented Western Province (or Cape Town as it was then known) against the

British.

But for all his relative under-achievement on the field of play, Loftus Versfeld's impact as a rugby missionary will live for many years longer than any memories of his brothers' on-field heroics.

As one of the men responsible for bringing rugby to Pretoria, and to the Transvaal in general, Versfeld ensured his posthumous fame by giving his name to Loftus Versfeld stadium in Pretoria and in starting up the Pretoria University Rugby Club, which remains the largest in the world with 60 teams playing every week.

Situated just four miles from the city centre, the ground which was to become the Loftus Versfeld stadium was originally erected in 1906 to house the University rugby club. Two years later it also began to serve as the headquarters of the Pretoria sub-union of the Transvaal Rugby Union, and by 1910 two wooden stands had been erected.

However, the stadium stayed relatively undeveloped until Northern Transvaal finally pulled away from neighbours Transvaal in 1937, at which stage work began in earnest. In 1938 the ground was finished and the new stadium was officially named the Loftus Versfeld Stadium.

The first major match in the stadium was in 1938, when Sam Walker's British

Lions beat the new Northern Transvaal union 20–12 in a match that was a lot closer than the scoreline suggests. Walker's men found out early what the rest of the world's Test sides were soon to discover for themselves, that at 1,000 ft. above sea level and with a rock hard, grassless pitch Loftus Versfeld presents one of the most inhospitable environments in international rugby.

The 1953 Wallabies were the first to be beaten at Loftus Versfeld, but Northern Transvaal soon claimed the scalps of the Lions, French, Welsh, English and All Blacks, the latter in a controversial match played in front of a crowd of almost 60,000 in 1976.

When Loftus Versfeld started to stage Test matches regularly after 1963, it became clear that the ramshackle stands fringing the ground had to be modernised. In the 1970s, a major reno-vation of the stadium was began. Each stand was replaced and by 1976 a brand new all-seater stadium with a capacity of 60,000 supporters was unveiled, making Loftus Versfeld one of the four Test venues in South Africa alongside Ellis Park (Johannesburg), Newlands (Cape Town) and King's Park (Durban).

Such is its importance that at the 1995 World Cup it was the venue for the third-place play-off between England and France, and the New Zealand versus Scotland quarter-final.

The rebuilding of Loftus Versfeld also coincided with a period of immense strength for the Northern Transvaal side.

In the late 1970s, men such as Frik du Preez kept Northerns at the top of the pile, while the emergence of the great fly-half Naas Botha led to an unprecedented run of Currie Cup success in the 1980s and early 1990s.

Murrayfield

Edinburgh, Scotland

Capacity:
    67,500
Opened:
    1925
Hosted:
    1993 World Cup Sevens

Situated three miles from the city centre in the western suburbs of Edinburgh, Murrayfield was originally the site of the Edinburgh Polo Club at Murray's Field until the ground was purchased by the Scottish Rugby Union in 1922 to provide a permanent home for Scottish rugby.

The national side had first played at Edinburgh Academicals' Raeburn Place before making Inverleith the regular venue, but by end of the First World War it was clear that Inverleith was no longer suitable, and so the decision to move west was taken.

The youngest of the Five Nations grounds, Murrayfield was first used to stage international rugby in March 1925, when Scotland reclaimed the Calcutta Cup after a seven-year losing streak beating England 14–11 in front of a crowd of some 30,000.

From that date, Murrayfield developed into a Caledonian fortress, helped no doubt by the fact that in the 1920s Scotland possessed an outstanding side in which the famous four Oxford three-quarters were peerless.

The success of that era and the crowds it drew gave the SRU the funds to develop Murrayfield and in 1935 the West Stand was built, to be followed a year later by the North and East Stands. Since then, the ground has staged many memorable games in front of some huge crowds.

The biggest of them all was in 1975, when 104,000 crammed into Murrayfield to see Andy Irvine's Scotland defeat a Welsh side including such greats as Phil Bennett, Gareth Edwards and JPR Williams 12–10 in a match of breathtaking endeavour. So dangerous was that crush, however, that the following season major matches were made all-ticket, a restriction that is still in force.

There have been many other great games to have been played at Murrayfield, not least the Grand Slam contest between England and Scotland in 1990, which Scotland famously won 13–7 against a powerful English side that was considered overwhelming favourites.

That English side was to have its revenge at Murrayfield 18 months later, however, when England beat Scotland 9–6 in the 1991 World Cup semi-final.

Since then the ground has undergone a complete rebuilding programme that cost almost £50 million. In 1993 the North, West and South Stands were completely rebuilt to add to the work completed on the East Stand in 1983, the final effect being to produce a stadium in the modern method – a bowl shape with all the stands completely covered.

Despite being constructed in record time (certainly compared to Twickenham), with seats relatively distant from the field of play and a reduced all-seated capacity of 67,500, the "new" Murrayfield seems to have managed to retain far more of its old character than its soulless southern counterpart.

Indeed, Murrayfield has the same intimidating atmosphere that made it such a difficult place to conquer (the French, for example, failed to win there between 1978 and 1994 despite producing some immensely powerful sides during that era). It was that which gave the ground its sobriquet, "Fortress Murrayfield".

Just as importantly, perhaps, Murrayfield matches remain the same powerful social occasions that they have always been. No matter what the weather, the back pitch car park is still always full, the pubs are bulging at the seams and the city centre revelry goes on late into the night.

There has also been a new departure of late with the regular use of the stadium by the American Football team, the Scottish Claymores. Their average gates have been over 10,000 for their six "home" games at Murrayfield.

There are also further development plans afoot, with a railway station planned on Murrayfield ground and building works proposed on the site of the ice rink adjoining the stadium.

Newlands

Cape Town, South Africa

Capacity:
    51,000
Opened:
    1888
Hosted:
    1995 World Cup semi-final

Rugby in South Africa started in the Cape and to this day Western Province have remained arguably the single most dominant force in South Africa.

Cape Town was the base for the British Isles side in 1891 after an invitation from the then governor of the province, Cecil Rhodes, led to South Africa's first incoming tour.

Although the British toured the whole of southern Africa and played three Tests, they concentrated their efforts in Cape Town, where they played more than half their 20 games during their four-month tour, including the final Test at the Newlands ground, which was then three years old.

In that Test, the British had to fight for a 4–0 win against a South African side which indulged in "fast and furious play" according to the Cape Times (this

was hardly surprising as 11 of the side, including captain Alf Richards and H.H. Castens, were from Cape Town).

Although already an excellent playing surface, after winning the Cape Town Test British vice-captain Johnny Hammond suggested that playing at Newlands was bound to cause problems for later sides, partly because of its "hard ground" but even more because of the "overwhelming hospitality" of the Cape Town rugby authorities.

Needless to say, Hammond's words have proved prophetic. When the British next came back in 1896 with Hammond as captain, the 5–0 fourth Test defeat at Newlands was their only loss. In 1903, Cape Town was once again the only Test loss for the British tourists and in 1910 Irishman Tom Smyth's Lions lost their final Test by the unprecedented score of 21–5.

Yet for all the South Africans' early successes at Newlands, the ground is considered unlucky by followers of the national side because of the high number of Test defeats suffered at the venue. The reason for the run of losses is put down to the un-South African conditions that exist at the Cape Town stadium.

Not only is the ground not at altitude (as are the "Veld grounds" of Pretoria's Loftus Versfeld and Johannesburg's Ellis Park, Test venues where tourists have traditionally struggled) but Cape Town's temperate weather means that the ground is softer than almost anywhere else in South Africa, with lush grass and a cool breeze.

In short, conditions that are far closer to what New Zealanders and British players are used to than anywhere else in South Africa.

But whether or not Newlands is a place where the Springboks have the best chance of success, it is certainly the most beautiful ground in South Africa, and possibly the world. Nestling at the foot of Table Mountain, Newlands is a beautiful ground in a quiet residential area less than a kilometre from the equally famous Newlands Cricket Stadium, also the finest in South Africa.

Both stadiums have been renovated extensively over the past decade, with Newlands now a gleaming testament to the financial power of Western Province rugby.

Although capacity has been reduced by 5,000 to 51,000, the stadium is now fully enclosed and an all-seater venue to rival the best in the world. The stadium also continues to be the centre of South African rugby.

The old South African Rugby Board was housed there from its formation in 1889, as is the present post-Apartheid South African Rugby Football Union. That pre-eminence stems from the dominance of Western Province, winners of the Currie Cup a record 29 times.

Parc des Princes

Paris, France

Capacity:
  50,000
Opened:
  1906
Hosted:
  1991 World Cup quarter-final

One of the most intimidating arenas in world sport, the Parc des Princes in the west of Paris was built in 1897 and first used as the home of French rugby in 1906, when a young French side were thrashed 38–8 by Dave Gallaher's New Zealand "Originals".

Although all matches against the Home Unions continued to be played there until 1920, it was then the French Federation's policy to stage half of the major internationals against touring sides in the south of the country, where rugby is infinitely more popular than in the more soccer-friendly north of France. This policy continues today, and in recent seasons internationals have been held in Lyons, Toulouse and Nantes.

In 1920, however, the primitive facilities of the Parc des Princes were being overshadowed by Racing Club de France's Stade Colombes to the north west of the city, and the French Federation eventually switched grounds when a programme of redevelopment had begun at the already impressive Stade Colombes ahead of the 1924 Olympics (at which the French were beaten 17–3 by the USA in the final.

The writing had been on the wall for the Parc as early as 1914, when England had played their Five Nations match at Colombes, winning 39–13 in what was to be the last major international before the outbreak of the First World War.

As ever in France, it was the decision by the Parisian municipal authorities to pump in funds which led to Colombes being abandoned in favour of Parc des Princes once again. The decision to return to the Parc was taken in 1971, more than half a century after the last international game was played there, and owed much to the £10 million reconstruction which was taking place for the purpose of staging international soccer matches.

Indeed, rugby and soccer have been bed-mates ever since in France, with the Parc des Princes also playing host to top soccer outfit Paris Saint Germain, plus at least two other top Parisian sides at various stages.

Soccer has had yet another role to play in the history of the Parc des

Princes, and this time it is a terminal one. Demolition started on the Parc in the spring of 1997 and as of 1998, the home of French rugby moved across the city at the purpose built Stade de France stadium which housed the 1998 World Cup soccer tournament.

The new, futuristic stadium has also proved to be an intimidating venue, even though at 80,000 it has a much larger capacity and spectators are therefore much further away from the action.

The decision to demolish the Parc des Princes was taken largely because it was felt that the Parc des Princes, with its capacity of 50,000, was simply too small to cater for the huge following that Five Nations rugby now commands. Yet in many ways it was the size of the Parc which gave it a special intensity unrivalled in Test rugby venues.

The steep, towering sides of the concrete edifice, and the cauldron-like feel that comes from the tight bowl shape (the Parc is fully enclosed), make this a naturally gladiatorial amphitheatre.

Extra spice is also added by the presence of the Dax Brass Band, a four-piece which strikes up from the terraces every time France score. The end product is a ground at which France have proved phenomenally difficult to beat, and of the regular visitors, Ireland, Scotland and Wales all have dismal records at the Parc, with Scotland only winning once (in 1995) in the 25 years of rugby at the ground. That, however, may well be about to change at the Stade de France. In its inaugural year, England easily overwhelmed France there, while Scotland scored a record number of points against France as they beat them 36-22.

Twickenham

Surrey, England

Capacity:
75,000
Opened:
1909
Hosted:
1991 World Cup final

There is a temptation to think of Twickenham as a part of rugby's furniture, a stadium that has been standing since the game began. Yet it is not so. England had already been playing international rugby for 36 years when the late, great referee Billy Williams began looking for a site on which to build a monument to English rugby.

Up to that point, internationals had been played all over the country, initially using the London cricket venue of The Oval, but spreading the honour around so that Blackheath, Richmond, Manchester, Leeds, Dewsbury, Birkenhead, Bristol, Leicester and Crystal Palace had all hosted England internationals.

Even with a mandate from the Rugby Football Union committee, of which Williams was a prominent member, it took more than a year to find a suitable spot. But when Williams alighted upon a ten and a half acre site in Twickenham the search was over and in 1907 the RFU handed over the considerable sum of £5,572 12s 6d and work started immediately.

The purchase of what was then a cabbage patch was fairly controversial, for the ground is almost 15 miles from the centre of London. Yet so desperate were the RFU for a permanent home that the dissent soon died down, and by 1909 the ground was finished.

Although Harlequins were the first side to play on the pitch when they met Richmond on 10 October 1909, the first Test match played on the sumptuous turf of "HQ" was in January 1910 against Wales.

Crowds grew steadily from the 17,000 that watched that international and by 1932, when the North Stand and West Stands had been built, and a second tier added to the East Stand, the ground could hold 72,500, of which almost half were seated (although 75,000 did crush in for the England vs. Wales match of 1950).

Until the new South Stand was built in 1981, Twickenham remained virtually lost in time, unchanged except for small touches such as the erection of the "Rowland Hill Memorial Gates", topped by a pair of famous golden lions, or the lavish refurbishment of the Royal Retiring Room, the cost of which was borne by

Shanghai RFC.

Yet when change started, it moved on apace. By 1995 the distinctively green West, East and North Stands had been rebuilt to form a distinctive horseshoe at a cost of £30 million. Within the next year, work will begin on rebuilding the South Stand so that the whole stadium forms a bowl.

This, plus the sliding roof which will cover the whole stadium, will cost a further £16 million, but will give Twickenham an all-seated capacity of 85,000 (from its present 75,000) making it one of the outstanding venues for sport in the world.

Although many players and supporters feel that the enlarged stadium has been de-personalised by the changes, the clamour to play at Twickenham and to watch games there has never been greater.

In the 1970s spectators could arrive on the day and buy a ticket, yet today despite rapidly escalating ticket prices virtually every match is sold out many times over, with black market tickets changing hands for ten times face value. The only way for many fans to see matches is to use the burgeoning corporate hospitality sector.

While this ensures the pennies keep rolling in to the RFU's account, it has left many fans unhappy at the increasingly difficult procedure for obtaining tickets for International matches.

Rugby Statistics

Up until a few years ago, the only competition of any note in international rugby was the Five Nations. But now there are a host of high-class tournaments, from the World Cup to the Tri-Nations to the Pacific Rim. Then there are also the club competitions from around the world, such as the Currie Cup, NPC and SWALEC Cup. Want to know all the winners? Read on...

World Cup 1987

Pool 1

Australia	19	England	6
USA	21	Japan	18
England	60	Japan	7
Australia	47	USA	12
England	34	USA	6
Australia	42	Japan	23

	P	W	D	L	F	A	Pts
Australia	3	3	0	0	108	41	6
England	3	2	0	1	100	32	4
USA	3	1	0	2	39	99	2
Japan	3	0	0	3	48	123	0

Pool 2

Canada	37	Tonga	4
Wales	13	Ireland	6
Wales	29	Tonga	16
Ireland	46	Canada	19
Wales	40	Canada	9
Ireland	32	Tonga	9

	P	W	D	L	F	A	Pts
Wales	3	3	0	0	82	31	6
Ireland	3	2	0	1	84	41	4
Canada	3	1	0	2	65	90	2
Tonga	3	0	0	3	29	98	0

Pool 3

New Zealand	70	Italy	6
Fiji	28	Argentina	9
New Zealand	74	Fiji	13
Argentina	25	Italy	16
Italy	18	Fiji	15
New Zealand	46	Argentina	15

	P	W	D	L	F	A	Pts
NZ	3	3	0	0	190	34	6
Fiji	3	1	0	2	56	101	2
Argentina	3	1	0	2	49	90	2
Italy	3	1	0	2	40	110	2

Pool 4

Romania	21	Zimbabwe	20
France	20	Scotland	20
France	55	Romania	12
Scotland	60	Zimbabwe	21
France	70	Zimbabwe	12
Scotland	55	Romania	28

	P	W	D	L	F	A	Pts
France	3	2	1	0	145	44	5
Scotland	3	2	1	0	135	69	5
Romania	3	1	0	2	61	130	2
Zimbabwe	3	0	0	3	53	151	0

Quarter-finals

New Zealand	30	Scotland	3
France	31	Fiji	16
Australia	33	Ireland	15
Wales	16	England	3

Semi-finals

France	30	Australia	24
New Zealand	49	Wales	6

Third place match

Wales	22	Australia	21

Final

Eden Park, Auckland, June 20, 1987

New Zealand 29
Tries : Jones, Kirk, Kirwan
Conversion : Fox
Penalties : Fox 4
Dropped Goal : Fox
France 9
Try : Berbizier
Conversion : Camberabero
Penalty : Camberabero

New Zealand : Gallagher; Kirwan, Stanley, Taylor, Green; Fox, Kirk (Capt); Mcdowell, Fitzpatrick, Drake; Pierce, G.Whetton; A.Whetton, Jones, Shelford.

France : Blanco; Camberabero, Sella, Charvet, Lagisquet; Mesnel, Berbizier; Ondarts, Dubroca (Capt), Garuet; Lorieux, Condom; Champ, Erbani, Rodriguez.
Referee : K.V.J.Fitzgerald (Aus)
Attendance : 48,350

World Cup 1991

Pool 1

NZ	18	England	12
Italy	30	USA	9
NZ	46	USA	6
England	36	Italy	6
England	37	USA	9
NZ	31	Italy	21

	P	W	D	L	F	A	Pts
NZ	3	3	0	0	95	39	9
England	3	2	0	1	85	33	7
Italy	3	1	0	2	57	76	5
USA	3	0	0	3	24	113	3

Pool 2

Scotland	47	Japan	9
Ireland	55	Zimbabwe	11
Ireland	32	Japan	16
Scotland	51	Zimbabwe	12
Scotland	24	Ireland	15
Japan	52	Zimbabwe	8

	P	W	D	L	F	A	Pts
Scotland	3	3	0	0	122	36	9
Ireland	3	2	0	1	102	51	7
Japan	3	1	0	2	77	87	5
Zimbabwe	3	0	0	3	31	158	3

Pool 3

Australia	32	Argentina	19
W.Samoa	16	Wales	13
Australia	9	W.Samoa	3
Wales	16	Argentina	7
Australia	38	Wales	3
W.Samoa	35	Argentina	12

	P	W	D	L	F	A	Pts
Australia	3	3	0	0	79	25	9
W.Samoa	3	2	0	1	54	34	7
Wales	3	1	0	2	32	61	5
Argentina	3	0	0	3	38	83	3

Pool 4

France	30	Romania	3
Canada	13	Fiji	3
France	33	Fiji	9
Canada	19	Romania	11
Romania	17	Fiji	15
France	19	Canada	13

	P	W	D	L	F	A	Pts
France	3	3	0	0	82	25	9
Canada	3	2	0	1	45	33	7
Romania	3	1	0	2	31	64	5
Fiji	3	0	0	3	27	63	3

Quarter-Finals

England	19	France	10
Scotland	28	W.Samoa	6
Australia	19	Ireland	18
NZ	29	Canada	13

Semi-Finals

England	9	Scotland	6
Australia	16	NZ	6

Third Place Match

NZ	13	Scotland	6

Final

Twickenham, 2 November 1991

Australia 12
Try : Daly
Conversion : Lynagh
Penalties : Lynagh 2

England 6
Penalties : Webb 2

Australia : Roebuck; Campese, Little, Horan, Egerton; Lynagh, Farr-Jones (Capt); Daly, Kearns, Mckenzie; Mccall, Eales; Poidevin, Ofahengaue, Coker.

England : Webb; Halliday, Carling (Capt), Guscott, Underwood; Andrew, Hill; Leonard, Moore, Probyn; Ackford, Dooley; Skinner, Winterbottom, Teague.
Referee : W.D.Bevan (Wales)
Attendance : 60,000

World Cup 1995

Pool A

South Africa	27	Australia	18
Canada	34	Romania	3
South Africa	21	Romania	8
Australia	27	Canada	11
Australia	42	Romania	3
South Africa	20	Canada	0

	P	W	D	L	F	A	Pts
South Africa	3	3	0	0	68	26	9
Australia	3	2	0	1	87	41	7
Canada	3	1	0	2	45	50	5
Romania	3	0	0	3	14	97	3

Pool B

W.Samoa	42	Italy	18
England	24	Argentina	18
W.Samoa	32	Argentina	26
England	27	Italy	20
Italy	31	Argentina	25
England	44	W.Samoa	22

	P	W	D	L	F	A	Pts
England	3	3	0	0	95	60	9
W.Samoa	3	2	0	1	96	88	7
Italy	3	1	0	2	69	94	5
Argentina	3	0	0	3	69	87	3

Pool C

Wales	57	Japan	10
NZ	43	Ireland	19
Ireland	50	Japan	28
NZ	34	Wales	9
NZ	145	Japan	17
Ireland	24	Wales	23

	P	W	D	L	F	A	Pts
NZ	3	3	0	0	222	45	9
Ireland	3	2	0	1	93	94	7
Wales	3	1	0	2	89	68	5
Japan	3	0	0	3	55	252	3

Pool D

Scotland	89	Ivory Coast	0
France	38	Tonga	10
France	54	Ivory Coast	18
Scotland	41	Tonga	5
Tonga	29	Ivory Coast	11
France	22	Scotland	19

	P	W	D	L	F	A	Pts
France	3	3	0	0	114	47	9
Scotland	3	2	0	1	149	27	7
Tonga	3	1	0	2	44	90	5
Ivory Coast	3	0	0	3	29	172	3

Quarter-Finals

France	36	Ireland	12
South Africa	42	W.Samoa	14
England	25	Australia	22
NZ	48	Scotland	30

Semi-Finals

| South Africa | 19 | France | 15 |
| NZ | 45 | England | 29 |

Third Place Match

| France | 19 | England | 9 |

Final

Ellis Park, Johannesburg, 24 June 1995

South Africa 15 *
Penalties : Stransky 3
Dropped Goals : Stransky 2

New Zealand 12
Penalties : Mehrtens 3
Dropped Goal : Mehrtens

South Africa : Joubert; Small (Venter 97'), Mulder, H.Le Roux, Williams; Stransky, Van Der Westhuizen; Du Randt, Rossouw, Swart (Pagel 68'); Wiese, Strydom; Pienaar (Capt), Kruger, Andrews (Straeuli 90').

New Zealand : Osborne; Wilson (Ellis 55'), Bunce, Little, Lomu; Mehrtens, Bachop (Strachan 66'-71'); Dowd (Loe 83'), Fitzpatrick (Capt), Brown; I.Jones, R.Brooke; Brewer (Joseph 40'), Kronfeld, Z.Brooke.

Referee : E.F.Morrison (England)
Attendance : 63,000
* After Extra Time
9-9 After Normal Time

The Five Nations Championship

1883 England
1884 England
1885 No comp
1886 Eng & Scotland
1887 Scotland
1888 No comp
1889 No comp
1890 Eng & Scotland
1891 Scotland
1892 England
1893 Wales
1894 Ireland
1895 Scotland
1896 Ireland
1897 No comp
1898 No comp
1899 Ireland
1900 Wales
1901 Scotland
1902 Wales
1903 Scotland
1904 Scotland
1905 Wales
1906 Ire & Wales
1907 Scotland
1908 Wales
1909 Wales
1910 England
1911 Wales
1912 Eng & Ireland
1913 England
1914 England
1915 No comp
1916 No comp
1917 No comp
1918 No comp
1919 No comp
1920 Eng & Scot & Wales
1921 England
1922 Wales
1923 England
1924 England
1925 Scotland
1926 Scot & Ire

1927 Scot & Ire
1928 England
1929 Scotland
1930 England
1931 Wales
1932 Eng & Wales & Ire
1933 Scotland
1934 England
1935 Ireland
1936 Wales
1937 England
1938 Scotland
1939 Eng & Wales & Ire
1940 No comp
1941 No comp
1942 No comp
1943 No comp
1944 No comp
1945 No comp
1946 No comp
1947 Wales & Eng
1948 Ireland
1949 Ireland
1950 Wales
1951 Ireland
1952 Wales
1953 England
1954 Eng & Fr & Wales
1955 Fr & Wales
1956 Wales
1957 England
1958 England
1959 France
1960 Fr & Eng
1961 France
1962 France
1963 England
1964 Scot & Wales
1965 Wales
1966 Wales
1967 France
1968 France
1969 Wales
1970 Fr & Wales
1971 Wales
1972 No comp
1973 Quituple tie

1974 Ireland
1975 Wales
1976 Wales
1977 France
1978 Wales
1979 Wales
1980 England
1981 France
1982 Ireland
1983 Fr & Ireland
1984 Scotland
1985 Ireland
1986 Fr & Scotland
1987 France
1988 Wales & France
1989 France
1990 Scotland
1991 England
1992 England
1993 France
1994 Wales
1995 England
1996 England
1997 France
1998 France
1999 Scotland

* No competition

The Bledisloe Cup

						NZ	16	Aus	6
					1978	NZ	13	Aus	12
1931	NZ	20	Aus	13		NZ	22	Aus	6
1932	Aus	22	NZ	17		Aus	30	NZ	16
	NZ	21	Aus	3	1979	Aus	12	NZ	6
	NZ	21	Aus	13	1980	Aus	13	NZ	9
1934	Aus	25	NZ	11		NZ	12	Aus	9
	Aus	3	NZ	3		Aus	26	NZ	10
1936	NZ	11	Aus	6	1982	NZ	23	Aus	16
	NZ	38	Aus	13		Aus	19	NZ	16
1938	NZ	24	Aus	9		NZ	33	Aus	18
	NZ	20	Aus	14	1983	NZ	18	Aus	8
	NZ	14	Aus	6	1984	Aus	16	NZ	9
1946	NZ	31	Aus	8		NZ	19	Aus	15
	NZ	14	Aus	10		NZ	25	Aus	24
1947	NZ	13	Aus	5	1985	NZ	10	Aus	9
	NZ	27	Aus	14	1986	Aus	13	NZ	12
1949	Aus	11	NZ	6		NZ	13	Aus	12
	Aus	16	NZ	9		Aus	22	NZ	9
1951	NZ	8	Aus	0	1987	NZ	30	Aus	16
	NZ	17	Aus	11	1988	NZ	32	Aus	7
	NZ	16	Aus	6		Aus	19	NZ	19
1952	Aus	14	NZ	9		NZ	30	Aus	9
	NZ	15	Aus	8	1989	NZ	24	Aus	12
1955	NZ	16	Aus	8	1990	NZ	21	Aus	6
	NZ	8	Aus	0		NZ	27	Aus	17
	Aus	8	NZ	3		Aus	21	NZ	9
1957	NZ	25	Aus	11	1991	Aus	21	NZ	12
	NZ	22	Aus	9		NZ	6	Aus	3
1958	NZ	25	Aus	3	1991**	Aus	16	NZ	6
	Aus	6	NZ	3	1992	Aus	16	NZ	15
	NZ	17	Aus	8		Aus	19	NZ	17
1962*	NZ	20	Aus	6		NZ	26	Aus	23
	NZ	14	Aus	5	1993	NZ	25	Aus	10
1962*	NZ	9	Aus	9	1994	Aus	20	NZ	16
	NZ	3	Aus	0	1995	NZ	28	Aus	16
	NZ	16	Aus	8		NZ	34	Aus	23
1964	NZ	14	Aus	9	1996	NZ	43	Aus	6
	NZ	18	Aus	3		NZ	32	Aus	25
	Aus	20	NZ	5	1997	NZ	31	Aus	13
1967	NZ	29	Aus	9	1998	Aus	24	NZ	16
1968	NZ	27	Aus	11	1998	Aus	27	NZ	23
	NZ	19	Aus	18	1998	Aus	19	NZ	14
1972	NZ	29	Aus	6					
	NZ	30	Aus	17					
	NZ	38	Aus	3					
1974	NZ	11	Aus	6					
	Aus	16	NZ	16					

* Indicates Two Separate Series Played During The Same Season

** Indicates World Cup Semi-Final Match

Hong Kong Sevens Winners

1976	Cantabrians
1977	Fiji
1978	Fiji
1979	Australia
1980	Fiji
1981	Barbarians
1982	Australia
1983	Australia
1984	Fiji
1985	Australia
1986	New Zealand
1987	New Zealand
1988	Australia
1989	New Zealand
1990	Fiji
1991	Fiji
1992	Fiji
1993	W.Samoa
1994	New Zealand
1995	New Zealand
1996	New Zealand
1997	Fiji*
1998	Fiji
1999	Fiji

* Indicates Tournament Doubled as World Cup Sevens

World Cup Sevens Winners
1993 at Murrayfield

Final   England   21   Australia 17

Plate Winners: Argentina

1997 at Hong Kong

1997   Fiji   24   South Africa 21

Plate Winners: Tonga

Middlesex Sevens Winners

1926	Harlequins	1963	London Scots
1927	Harlequins	1964	Loughborough
1928	Harlequins	1965	London Scots
1929	Harlequins	1966	Loughborough
1930	London Welsh	1967	Harlequins
1931	London Welsh	1968	London Welsh
1932	Blackheath	1969	St Luke's
1933	Harlequins	1970	Loughborough
1934	Barbarians	1971	London Welsh
1935	Harlequins	1972	London Welsh
1936	Sale	1973	London Welsh
1937	London Scots	1974	Richmond
1938	Met Police	1975	Richmond
1939	Cardiff	1976	Loughborough
1940	St Mary's Hos	1977	Richmond
1941	Cambridge Uni	1978	Harlequins
1942	St Mary's Hos	1979	Richmond
1943	St Mary's Hos	1980	Richmond
1944	St Mary's Hos	1981	Rosslyn Park
1945	Notts	1982	Stewart's-Melville F.P.
1946	St Mary's Hos		
1947	Rosslyn Park	1983	Richmond
1948	Wasps	1984	London Welsh
1949	Heriot's F.P.	1985	Wasps
1950	Rosslyn Park	1986	Harlequins
1951	Richmond II	1987	Harlequins
1952	Wasps	1988	Harlequins
1953	Richmond	1989	Harlequins
1954	Rosslyn Park	1990	Harlequins
1955	Richmond	1991	London Scots
1956	London Welsh	1992	W. Samoa
1957	St Luke's	1993	Wasps
1958	Blackheath	1994	Bath
1959	Loughborough	1995	Leicester
1960	London Scots	1996	Wigan RLFC
1961	London Scots	1997	Fiji
1962	London Scots	1998	Barbarians

British Lions Full Test Record

Year	Country	P	W	D	L	F	A
1891	South Africa	3	3	0	0	11	0
1896	South Africa	4	3	0	1	34	16
1899	Australia	4	3	0	1	38	23
1903	South Africa	3	0	2	1	10	18
1904	Australia &	3	3	0	0	50	3
	New Zealand	1	0	0	1	3	9
1908	Australia &						
	New Zealand	3	0	1	2	8	64
1910	South Africa	3	1	0	2	23	38
1924	South Africa	4	0	1	3	15	43
1930	New Zealand &	4	1	0	3	34	53
	Australia	1	0	0	1	5	6
1938	South Africa	3	1	0	2	36	61
1950	New Zealand &	4	0	1	3	20	34
	Australia	2	2	0	0	43	9
1955	South Africa	4	2	0	2	49	75
1959	Australia &	2	2	0	0	41	9
	New Zealand	4	1	0	3	42	57
1962	South Africa	4	0	1	3	20	48
1966	Australia &	2	2	0	0	42	8
	New Zealand	4	0	0	4	32	79
1968	South Africa	4	0	1	3	38	61
1971	Australia &						
	New Zealand	4	2	1	1	48	42
1974	South Africa	4	3	1	0	79	34
1977	New Zealand	4	1	0	3	41	54
1980	South Africa	4	1	0	3	68	77
1983	New Zealand	4	0	0	4	26	78
1989	Australia	3	2	0	1	50	60
1993	New Zealand	3	1	0	2	51	57
1997	South Africa	3	2	0	1	60	66

Sydney Premiership

1900	Glebe
1901	Glebe & Sydney Uni (Shared)
1902	Western Suburbs
1903	Eastern Suburbs
1904	Sydney University
1905	South Sydney
1906	Glebe
1907	Glebe
1908	Newtown
1909	Glebe
1910	Newtown
1911	Newtown
1912	Glebe
1913	Eastern Suburbs
1914	Glebe
1915	No competition
1916	No competition
1917	No competition
1918	No competition
1919	Sydney University
1920	Sydney University
1921	Manly
1922	Manly
1923	Sydney University
1924	Sydney University
1925	Glebe-Balmain
1926	Sydney University
1927	Sydney University
1928	Sydney University
1929	Western Suburbs
1930	Randwick
1931	Eastern Suburbs
1932	Manly
1933	Northern Suburbs
1934	Randwick
1935	Northern Suburbs
1936	Drummoyne
1937	Sydney University
1938	Randwick
1939	Sydney University
1940	Randwick
1941	Eastern Suburbs
1942	Manly
1943	Manly
1944	Eastern Suburbs
1945	Sydney University
1946	Eastern Suburbs
1947	Eastern Suburbs
1948	Randwick
1949	Gordon
1950	Manly
1951	Sydney University
1952	Gordon
1953	Sydney University
1954	Sydney University
1955	Sydney University
1956	Gordon
1957	St George
1958	Gordon
1959	Randwick
1960	Northern Suburbs
1961	Sydney University
1962	Sydney University
1963	Northern Suburbs
1964	Northern Suburbs
1965	Randwick
1966	Randwick
1967	Randwick
1968	Sydney University
1969	Eastern Suburbs
1970	Sydney University
1971	Randwick
1972	Sydney University
1973	Randwick
1974	Randwick
1975	Northern Suburbs
1976	Gordon
1977	Parramatta
1978	Randwick
1979	Randwick
1980	Randwick
1981	Randwick
1982	Randwick
1983	Manly
1984	Randwick
1985	Parramatta
1986	Parramatta
1987	Randwick
1988	Randwick
1989	Randwick
1990	Randwick
1991	Randwick
1992	Randwick
1993	Gordon
1994	Randwick
1995	Gordon
1996	Randwick
1997	Manly
1998	Gordon

English League Winners

1987–88	Leicester
1988–89	Bath
1989–90	Wasps
1990–91	Bath
1991–92	Bath
1992–93	Bath
1993–94	Bath
1994–95	Leicester
1995–96	Bath
1996–97	Wasps
1997-8	Newcastle
1998-9	Leicester

The English Cup

1972	Gloucester	17	Moseley	6
1973	Coventry	27	Bristol	15
1974	Coventry	26	London Scottish	6
1975	Bedford	28	Rosslyn Park	12
1976	Gosforth	23	Rosslyn Park	14
1977	Gosforth	27	Waterloo	11
1978	Gloucester	6	Leicester	3
1979	Leicester	15	Moseley	12
1980	Leicester	21	London Irish	9
1981	Leicester	22	Gosforth	15
1982	Gloucester	12	Moseley	12*
1983	Bristol	28	Leicester	22
1984	Bath	10	Bristol	9
1985	Bath	24	London Welsh	15
1986	Bath	25	Wasps	17
1987	Bath	19	Wasps	12
1988	Harlequins	28	Bristol	22
1989	Bath	10	Leicester	6
1990	Bath	48	Gloucester	6
1991	Harlequins	25	Northampton	13
1992	Bath	15	Harlequins	12
1993	Leicester	23	Harlequins	16
1994	Bath	21	Leicester	9
1995	Bath	36	Wasps	16
1996	Bath	16	Leicester	15
1997	Leicester	9	Sale	3
1998	Saracens	48	Wasps	18
1999	Wasps	29	Newcastle	19

Title Shared

French League Winners

1892	Racing Club
1893	Stade Français
1894	Stade Français
1895	Stade Français
1896	Olympique
1897	Stade Français
1898	Stade Français
1899	Stade Bordelais
1900	Racing Club
1901	Stade Bordelais
1902	Racing Club
1903	Stade Français
1904	Stade Bordelais
1905	Stade Bordelais
1906	Stade Bordelais
1907	Stade Bordelais
1908	Stade Français
1909	Stade Bordelais
1910	F.C.Lyon
1911	Stade Bordelais
1912	Stade Toulousain
1913	Aviron Bayonnais
1914	A.S.Perpignanaise
1915	No comp
1916	Stade Toulousain
1917	Stade Nantais
1918	Racing Club
1919	Stadoceste Tarbais
1920	Stadoceste Tarbais
1921	U.S.Perpignanaise
1922	Stade Toulousain
1923	Stade Toulousain
1924	Stade Toulousain
1925	U.S.Perpignanaise
1926	Stade Toulousain
1927	Stade Toulousain
1928	Section Paloise
1929	U.S.Quillanaise
1930	S.U.Agenais
1931	R.C.Toulonnais
1932	F.C. Lyon
1933	F.C. Lyon
1934	Aviron Bayonnais
1935	Biarritz Olympique
1936	R.C.Narbonnais
1937	C.S.Vienne
1938	U.S.Perpignanaise
1939	Biarritz Olympique
1940	No comp
1941	No comp
1942	No comp
1943	Aviron Bayonnais
1944	U.S. Perpignanaise
1945	S.U.Agenais
1946	Section Paloise
1947	Stade Toulousain
1948	F.C.Lourdais
1949	Castres Olympique
1950	Castres Olympique
1951	U.S.Carmausine
1952	F.C.Lourdais
1953	F.C.Lourdais
1954	F.C.Grenaoble
1955	U.S.Perpignanaise
1956	F.C.Lourdais
1957	F.C.Lourdais
1958	F.C.Lourdais
1959	Racing Club
1960	F.C.Lourdais
1961	A.S.Biterroise
1962	S.U.Agenais
1963	Stade Montois
1964	Section Paloise
1965	S.U.Agenais
1966	S.U.Agenais
1967	U.S.Montalbanaise
1968	F.C.Lourdais
1969	C.A.Beglais
1970	La Voulte Sportif
1971	A.S.Biterroise
1972	A.S.Biterroise
1973	Stadoceste Tarbais
1974	A.S.Biterroise
1975	A.S.Biterroise
1976	S.U.Agenais
1977	A.S.Biterroise
1978	A.S.Biterroise
1979	R.C.Narbonnais
1980	A.S.Biterroise
1981	A.S.Biterroise
1982	S.U.Agenais
1983	A.S.Biterroise
1984	A.S.Biterroise
1985	Stade Toulousain
1986	Stade Toulousain
1986	R.C.Toulonnais
1987	R.C.Toulonnais
1988	S.U.Agenais
1989	Stade Toulousain
1990	Racing Club
1991	C.A.Beglais
1992	R.C.Toulonnais
1993	Castres Olympique
1993	Stade Toulousain
1994	Stade Toulousain
1995	Stade Toulousain
1996	Stade Toulousain
1997	Stade Toulousain
1998	Stade Francais

Irish League Winners

1991	Cork Cons
1992	Garryowen
1993	Young Munster
1994	Garryowen
1995	Shannon
1996	Shannon
1997	Shannon
1998	Shannon
1999	Cork Cons

Irish Interprovincial Championship

1947	Ulster
1948	Munster
1949	Leinster
1950	Leinster
1951	Ulster
1952	Ulster
1953	Ulster & Munster
1954	Ulster
1955	Munster & Leins
1956	Ulster & Connacht
1957	Ulster & Leinster & Connacht
1958	Munster
1959	Leinster
1960	Munster
1961	Leinster
1962	Leinster
1963	Munster
1964	Leinster
1965	Leinster
1966	Munster
1967	Ulster & Munster
1968	Ulster
1969	Munster
1970	Ulster
1971	Ulster
1972	Leinster
1973	Leinster & Ulster & Munster
1974	Munster
1975	Ulster
1976	Leinster & Ulster & Munster
1977	Ulster
1978	Leinster & Ulster & Munster
1979	Munster
1980	Leinster
1981	Leinster
1982	Leinster
1983	Leinster & Ulster & Munster
1984	Leinster
1985	Ulster
1986	Ulster
1987	Ulster
1988	Ulster
1989	Ulster
1990	Ulster
1991	Ulster
1992	Ulster
1993	Ulster
1994	Leinster & Ulster & Munster
1995	Munster
1996	Leinster
1997	Munster
1998	Leinster

National Provincial Championship

1976	Bay Of Plenty
1977	Canterbury
1978	Wellington
1979	Counties
1980	Manawatu
1981	Wellington
1982	Auckland
1983	Canterbury
1984	Auckland
1985	Auckland
1986	Wellington
1987	Auckland
1988	Auckland
1989	Auckland
1990	Auckland
1991	Otago
1992	Waikato
1993	Auckland
1994	Auckland
1995	Auckland
1996	Auckland
1997	Waikato
1998	Otago

Scottish League Winners

1974	Hawick
1975	Hawick
1976	Hawick
1977	Hawick
1978	Hawick
1979	Heriot's FP
1980	Gala
1981	Gala
1982	Hawick
1983	Gala
1984	Hawick
1985	Hawick
1986	Hawick
1987	Hawick
1988	Kelso
1989	Kelso
1990	Melrose
1991	Boroughmuir
1992	Melrose
1993	Melrose
1994	Melrose
1995	Stirling County
1996	Melrose
1997	Melrose
1998	Watsonians
1999	Heriot's FP

Scottish Cup Winners

1996 Hawick 17 Watsonians 15
1997 Melrose 31 Boro'muir 23
1998 G Hawks 36 Kelso 14
1999 Gala 8 Kelso 3

The Currie Cup

1889	Western Province
1892	Western Province
1893	No competition
1894	Western Province
1895	Western Province
1896	No competition
1897	Western Province
1898	Western Province
1899	Griqualand West
1900	No competition
1901	No competition
1902	No competition
1903	No competition
1904	Western Province
1905	No competition
1906	Western Province
1907	No competition
1908	Western Province
1909	No competition
1910	No competition
1911	Griqualand West
1912	No competition
1913	No competition
1914	Western Province
1915	No competition
1916	No competition
1917	No competition
1918	No competition
1919	No competition
1920	Western Province
1921	No competition
1922	Transvaal
1923	No competition
1924	No competition
1925	Western Province
1926	No competition
1927	Western Province
1928	No competition
1929	Western Province
1930	No competition
1931	No competition
1932	Western Province & Border (Shared)
1933	No competition
1934	Western Province & Border (Shared)
1935	No competition
1936	Western Province
1937	No competition
1938	No competition
1939	Transvaal
1940	No competition
1941	No competition
1942	No competition
1943	No competition
1944	No competition
1945	No competition
1946	Northern Transvaal
1947	Western Province
1948	No competition
1949	No competition
1950	Transvaal
1951	No competition
1952	Transvaal
1953	No competition
1954	Western Province
1955	No competition
1956	Northern Transvaal
1957	No competition
1958	No competition
1959	Western Province
1960	No competition
1961	No competition
1962	No competition
1963	No competition
1964	Western Province
1965	No competition
1966	Western Province
1967	No competition
1968	Northern Transvaal
1969	Northern Transvaal
1970	Griqualand West
1971	Northern Transvaal & Transvaal (Shared)
1972	Transvaal
1973	Northern Transvaal
1974	Northern Transvaal
1975	Northern Transvaal
1976	Free State
1977	Northern Transvaal
1978	Northern Transvaal
1979	Northern Transvaal & Western Province (Shared)
1980	Northern Transvaal
1981	Northern Transvaal
1982	Western Province
1983	Western Province
1984	Western Province
1985	Western Province
1986	Western Province
1987	Northern Transvaal
1988	Northern Transvaal
1989	Northern Transvaal & Western Province (Shared)
1990	Natal
1991	Northern Transvaal
1992	Natal
1993	Transvaal
1994	Transvaal
1995	Natal
1996	Natal
1997	Western Province
1998	Northern Transvaal (Blue Bulls)

SWALEC Cup Results

1972	Neath	15	Llanelli	9
1973	Llanelli	30	Cardiff	7
1974	Llanelli	12	Aberavon	10
1975	Llanelli	15	Aberavon	6
1976	Llanelli	16	Swasnea	4
1977	Newport	16	Cardiff	15
1978	Swansea	13	Newport	9
1979	Bridgend	18	Pontypridd	12
1980	Bridgend	15	Swansea	9
1981	Cardiff	14	Bridgend	6
1982	Cardiff	12*	Bridgend	12
1983	Pontypool	18	Swansea	6
1984	Cardiff	24	Neath	19
1985	Llanelli	15	Cardiff	14
1986	Cardiff	28	Newport	21
1987	Cardiff	16	Swansea	15
1988	Llanelli	28	Neath	13
1989	Neath	14	Llanelli	13
1990	Neath	16	Bridgend	10
1991	Llanelli	24	Pontypool	9
1992	Llanelli	16	Swansea	7
1993	Llanelli	21	Neath	18
1994	Cardiff	15	Llanelli	8
1995	Swansea	17	Pontypridd	12
1996	Pontypridd	29	Neath	22
1997	Cardiff	33	Swansea	26
1998	Llanelli	19	Ebbw Vale	12
1999	Swansea	37	Llanelli	10

Cardiff won on "most tries" rule

Welsh League Winners

1991	Neath
1992	Swansea
1993	Llanelli
1994	Swansea
1995	Cardiff
1996	Neath
1997	Pontypridd
1998	Swansea
1999	Llanelli

Chronology

1175 First record of the "famous game of ball" being played in London

1314– Nine European monarchs make it a
1527 specific offence to play "foote balle", ordering their subjects to pursue archery instead. Punishments range from fines to imprisonment.

1618 James I issues Declaration of Sports, which encourages sport on Sabbath leading to increased participation

1823 William Webb Ellis catches the ball and runs with it at Rugby School. The practice did not catch on immediately

1839 Old Rugbeain Arthur Pell sets up first rugby club at Cambridge

1843 Rugby club formed at Guy's Hospital in London

1845 Laws of the game codified in simple terms. It was the act of committing these to paper which almost certainly accounted for the Rugby School code's ascendancy over the unwritten codes from other schools

1850 Rev Rowland Williams introduces rugby into Wales via St David's College, Lampeter

1854 Old Rugbeian RH Scott starts Ireland's first rugby club at Trinity College, Dublin

1858 The world's first independent rugby club founded at Blackheath

1858 Merchiston School first play Edinburgh Academicals in world's oldest surviving fixture

1863 Rugby Football and Association Football split when Blackheath and Richmond refuse to agree to ban on running with the ball

1863 Blackheath play Richmond in oldest surviving top-class fixture

1864 First game played in Australia at the Sydney University club

1870 First ever representative fixture takes place when Yorkshire meet Lancashire, thus also initiating the County Championship

1870 Charles John Munro introduces rugby to New Zealand, and schools such as Christ's College, Christchurch, which were already playing football, accept the rugby code

1871 The Rugby Football Union is formed after 20 clubs meet at the Pall Mall Restaurant on January 26th at the behest of Richmond's Edwin Hash

1871 England accept Edinburgh Academical FJMoncrieff's challenge to meet Scotland at Raeburn Place in Edinburgh and are beaten by a goal and a try to one try. After 1879 the fixture was played for the Calcutta Cup.

1872 The first Varsity Match takes place at Oxford, with the home side winning by a goal and a try to nil

1872 Rugby introduced to France by British wine merchants in Le Havre

1874 American University Harvard take on Canada's McGill University in first match in North America

1875 Size of teams begins to be dropped from 20 to 15 at behest of Varsity Match pioneers Oxford. This becomes standard practice a year later, and is adopted at international level in 1877

when England take on Ireland

1875 Hospitals Cup commences in England

1875 Hamilton RFC, South Africa's first open and independent club, is formed

1875 Ireland play their first international, losing to England by a goal, a try and a drop goal to nil at The Oval

1877 Scotland's HHJohnstone is the first to play as a single full-back

1878 Broughton v Swinton is the first flood-lit match

1878 Swansea win the first South Wales Cup, beating Newport by a goal to nil

1879 First Unions formed in New Zealand in Canterbury and Wellington

1881 Eleven Welsh clubs form Welsh Rugby Union at Castle Hotel Neath on March 12

1882 New South Wales tour New Zealand for the first overseas tour, winning four games but losing to Otago and Auckland (twice)

1883 Melrose butcher Ned Haig invents sevens and stages first tournament

1883 England win the Triple Crown. They have won it 19 times since

1884 Cardiff take up the four three-quarters system first tried by Coventry in 1893. It is soon taken up by all Welsh clubs and the top West Country clubs

1886 Despite opposition from Home Unions, the RFU adopts points system in which try is worth one, and a conversion two. Matches still cannot be won unless a goal (i.e: a converted try) is scored

1886 International Board formed in Manchester, but RFU refuse to join so Home Unions suspend matches against England

1888 Embryonic Lions side tours Australia and New Zealand under captaincy of R.L. Seddon, who is drowned in Australia. 15 of party are from Northern clubs which later leave for League, but Hawick send three players, while Wales and the Isle of Man also have one representative

1889 A close season is established in Northern Hemisphere, running from May 1

until September 1

1889 New Zealand Natives tour New Zealand, Australia and Britain, playing 107 games in 14 months, of which they drew six and won 78. Victims include Ireland

1889 Touch judges introduced at international level to complement neutral referees first used in 1881

1889 South African Rugby Board is formed, including areas that are now Kenya, Zimbabwe and Namibia

1890 The Barbarians founded in January and play their first fixture in December, beating Hartlepool Rovers 9–4.

1890 England join the International Board, but take six of the 12 seats

1891 Scot Bill Maclagan leads English-dominated side to South Africa at invitation of Cecil Rhodes, and wins all 19 matches, scoring 223 points and conceding only one. The tourists award the Currie Cup, donated by the Castle Shipping Line, to their hardest opponents Griqualand West, and the Cup is then played for every year. When British return in 1896, side is half Irish and half English

1892 New Zealand Rugby Football Union is formed

1893 Northern clubs' motion in favour of broken time payments is defeated

1894 Try becomes worth three points and conversion two points

1895 22 clubs from Yorkshire and Lancashire break away to form the Northern Union in Huddersfield.

1897 Jerseys become numbered

1897 Scotland and Ireland refuse to play Wales because of allegations of professionalism

1899 The first British Isles side to contain representatives from all four Home Unions tours Australia, winning all but three games.

1903 The Ranfurly Shield is given to NZRFU and awarded to unbeaten Auckland. The first challenge is in 1904, when Wellington win 6–3

1903 New Zealand play Australia for the

first time, winning 22–3 in front of 30,000 crowd in Sydney.

1903 Mark Morrison's British team lose last Test against South Africa to be beaten in a series for the first time

1904 Scot Darkie Bedell-Sivright leads Welsh-dominated British side to Australia, winning all 14 matches but losing the Test in New Zealand

1905 Dave Gallaher's "Originals" tour Britain, starting off with a 55–4 win over Devon and winning all but one of their matches, a controversial 3–0 loss to Wales. Gallaher plays as wing forward or "rover", a role unknown in Britain which excites much controversy

1906 France play their first official international (they had earlier put a side into the 1900 Olympics), but lose 35–8 to England at the Parc des Princes

1907 Paul Roos' powerful Springboks tour Britain and France, winning 27 games out of 30. They beat Ireland, Wales and a French XV, but lose to Scotland and Cardiff and draw with England

1908 Wales are first side to win Grand Slam

1908 Berkeley, from California, beat France to win Olympic gold, sparking a riot

1908 Anglo-Welsh side fails to win a Test in New Zealand

1909 Australians beat England on their first tour of Britain, winning 25 of 31 games

1910 England play first game at Twickenham, beating Wales for the first time since 1898

1912 Springboks beat all 4 Home Countries

1914– Official internationals cease, although
18 unofficial military internationals continue in which League players are also allowed to participate. 111 internationals lose their lives, including All Blacks captain Dave Gallaher and Ronnie Poulton Palmer

1921 Springboks tour Australia and New Zealand for first time, winning all four matches in Australia and drawing three-match series in NZ. In all, the Boks lost only two matches on tour

1924–5 Cliff Porter's All Black "Invincibles" sweep through the British Isles and

France undefeated, but fail to notch a Grand Slam as Scotland refuse to play a team they consider professionalised. New Zealanders win all 30 matches, scoring 721 points and conceding 109

1926 Australia, South Africa and New Zealand join International Board

1929 Wallabies whitewash New Zealand in the Bledisloe Cup for the first time

1930 Lions lose series in New Zealand by 5–1

1931 France thrown out of the Five Nations for violence and professionalism. They were not allowed to rejoin until after 1945, and formed FIRA in 1934 to ensure international fixtures

1932 Danie Craven and the Springboks complete Grand Slam tour of Britain, a feat they repeated twenty years later, thrashing Scotland 44–0 at Murrayfield

1937 All Blacks are beaten 2–1 on home soil by South Africa, the New Zealanders' first series loss on home soil

1938 Sam Walker's British Lions lose series 2–1 in South Africa

1939–45 Series of wartime matches, in the first of which The Army beat an Empire XV 27–9 at Richmond. League players represent their countries (except Scotland) in Red Cross Internationals and Rugby League XV beat a Rugby Union XV 15–10 in Bradford

1949 Bill Allen's All Blacks whitewashed 4–0 in South Africa. Controversy over refereeing standards ensures heightened rivalry between the two countries

1949 Australian Rugby Union founded

1950 Karl Mullen's Lions fail to win a Test in New Zealand, but win in Australia

1951 France beat England at Twickenham for the first time

1953 All Blacks are beaten twice at Cardiff Arms Park – by Cardiff and Wales – within a month

1955 Springboks and Lions share series marked by brilliant open play

1956 New Zealand get revenge for the whitewash of Bill Allen's "49ers" when they beat South Africa 3–1

1958 France win series in South Africa at first attempt

1960 Scotland become the first Home Union to tour overseas when they leave for South Africa

1963 Wales tour for the first time, losing Test in South Africa

1965 Dawie de Villiers' Springboks tour Britain and fail to win a match, losing 5 and drawing 1. They lose series in Australia 2–0 before ending year with a 3–1 series loss to New Zealand

1966 Lions whitewashed 4–0 for the first time in a series in New Zealand

1968 Replacements allowed for injuries

1971 Inspired by Barry John, Lions win a series in New Zealand for first time

1972 "The Troubles" in Ulster are so intense that Scotland and Wales refuse to travel to Ireland. England travel and are beaten 16–12 in the year in which a try becomes worth four points

1972 England beaten by all top class provincial opposition, but stun the Springboks by winning 18–9 at Ellis Park

1973 Miserable in the run-up to the Test, touring England once again beggar belief by beating New Zealand 16–10 at Eden Park

1973 New Zealand end British tour with a rematch against 1971 Lions masquerading as Barbarians. In memorable running game, Barbarians win 23–11

1973 Wallabies lose 16–11 to Tonga in Brisbane in Australian rugby's lowest ebb

1974 Cantabrians from New Zealand win the first Hong Kong Sevens tournament

1974 Lions are denied 4–0 whitewash of South Africa when Fergus Slattery's last minute try in Fourth Test is controversially disallowed and game ends a draw

1977 A Lions party containing 18 Welshmen suffers an unhappy tour of New Zealand and loses the series 3–1

1978 All Blacks complete Grand Slam tour of Britain

1980 Lions salvage last Test win to avoid whitewash in South Africa

1981 All Blacks win third Test against South Africa in remarkable fashion to win series 2–1, but the tour is disrupted by anti-Apartheid demonstrations and divides New Zealand opinion. Nicknamed the "Barbed Wire Tour".

1983 Lions whitewashed in New Zealand

1984 The Ella brothers star for the Wallabies on their Grand Slam tour of Britain

1986 Denied the chance to tour South Africa as All Blacks, New Zealand's top players tour the Republic as the Cavaliers, but are comprehensively beaten three of the four Tests. Argentina, disguised as the South American Jaguars, also tour South Africa three times between 1980–84, while a World XV attends the SARB Centenary Celebrations in 1989 in defiance of sporting sanctions

1987 The inaugural World Cup is held, and New Zealand are convincing winners. France and Australia stage one of the best ever games in the semi-final

1989 Lions come back from First Test defeat to physically overwhelm the Wallabies and take the series 2–1

1990 Unbeaten underdogs Scotland beat in-form England at Murrayfield in a Grand Slam showdown. England then go on to win back-to-back Grand Slams for the first time since 1923–4

1991 Fresh from inflicting a record defeat on the Welsh, beating England 40–15 and sharing the Bledisloe Cup with New Zealand, Australia are the class act of a World Cup held in the Five Nations, beating hosts England 12–6 in the final

1991 The USA win the inaugural Women's World Cup, beating England 19–6 at Cardiff ARms Park

1992 Post-Apartheid South Africa re-commence international competition, but are comfortably beaten by New Zealand, Australia and England. Series defeats follow in 1993 against New Zealand, Australia and France, the last on home soil

1993 Lions are crushed by the All Blacks, who come back from a 10–0 half-time deficit, to win the decisive last Test 30–13

1993 England upset the form book by winning the inaugural World Cup Sevens at Murrayfield, beating Australia 21–17 in the final

1994 Queensland win inaugural Super 10 Championship, beating Natal 21–10

1994 England lose 2–1 in South Africa, but France are the first national side since the 1937 Springboks to win a series in New Zealand.

1995 England captain Will Carling is sacked for calling the RFU committee "57 old farts", only to be reinstated

1995 South Africa beat favourites New Zealand 15–12 in extra-time to win the World Cup on their own soil. Jonah Lomu emerges as the most high profile superstar ever in the game

1995 The onset of professionalism cannot be halted, and with Rugby League's Super League threatening to engulf Australasian Union, the three Southern Hemisphere giants sell a 10-year package to Rupert Murdoch's News Corporation for £340 million. The formation of the Super 12 provincial competition and the Tri-Nations tournament is professional rugby union.

1995 The International Board rubber stamps the de facto professionalism of the game and declares it "open"

1995 Jonathan Davies becomes the first man to be transferred back across the "free gangway" between League and Union when he signs for Cardiff from Warrington for £90,000. He is later followed by players such as Scott Gibbs and Allan Bateman

1995 Famous English club Newcastle Gosforth is sold to local entrepreneur Sir John Hall for £2 million, sparking a series of takeovers of top English clubs that make English rugby the richest in the world. The process culminates in Newcastle paying £1 million to buy former All Black wing Tuigamala out of his League contract

1996 RFU sign exclusive deal which gives TV rights to their Five Nations games to sattelite TV and are thrown out of the competition by the other Home Unions. The RFU recant and then face a challenge from the top clubs.

1996 Rugby is in the law courts. Gloucester forward Simon Devereux is jailed for nine months for a punch that shatters a London Irish opponent's jaw and a referee is held liable for a Colt's injury after a collapsed scrum.

1996 New Zealand win the inaugural Tri-Nations series remaining unbeaten in their four matches against South Africa and Australia. The All Blacks then travel to South Africa and become the first New Zealand side to beat the Springboks in a Test series on their home turf.

1997 South African coach Andre Markgraaf is forced to resign after tape recordings of his racist tirade are leaked

1997 Fiji win the second World Cup Sevens, held in Hong Kong

1997 The first professional British Lions tour party proves the cynics wrong by winning a hard-fought series in South Africa by 2-1.

1997-8 Continual battle between clubs and RFU almost brings English rugby to standstill. Mayfair Agreement in May 1998 brings some stability.

1998 Bath prop Kevin Yates banned for the game for six months for allegedly biting off the ear lobe of London Scottish flanker Simon Fenn.

1998 England send weakened squad to Australia, New Zealand and South Africa and are humiliated. Beaten by New Zealand Academy, England are routed 76-0 by Australia but saved against South Africa by a downpour.

1998 Italy are invited to join Five Nations Championship in season 1999–2000.

1999 Gary Teichman's exhausted Springboks cruise through a tour of Britain looking for a Grand Slam, but fall at the last when they are beaten at Twickenham. That match stops the South Africans setting a record for the most consecutive number of Tests won, which they equalled at 17.

1999 Enterprising Scotland win last ever Five Nations Championship.